THE WAY TO HELL

THE WAY TO HELL

Machiavelli for Catastrophic Times

NATHAN CRICK

THE UNIVERSITY OF ALABAMA PRESS

Tuscaloosa

The University of Alabama Press
Tuscaloosa, Alabama 35487-0380
uapress.ua.edu

Typeface: Baskerville

Cover design: Lori Lynch

Cataloging-in-Publication data is available from the Library of Congress.
ISBN: 978-0-8173-2210-6 (cloth)
ISBN: 978-0-8173-6158-7 (paper)
E-ISBN: 978-0-8173-9528-5

To the Last Generations

Contents

Acknowledgments

THE WRITING OF THIS BOOK HAS BEEN MADE POSSIBLE BY THE workings of fortune and the virtue of others. Fortune first appeared in the form of an invitation by Kevin Barge in spring 2013 to join the faculty at Texas A&M University. It intervened a second time when Randy Kluver graciously invited me to participate in a study abroad program called "COMM to Italy" soon after I started my job. At the time, the Department of Communication and Journalism brought four faculty members every spring to teach twenty-five Texas A&M students at the Santa Chiara Study Center in Castiglion Fiorentino, Italy. When I accepted Randy's invitation, I knew nothing of the Italian Renaissance or of Machiavelli. But I chose to teach these topics anyway, impetuously believing that I could learn them with a year of preparation. This necessity to fill the gaps in my knowledge led to a third fortunate encounter, namely with the work of Lisa Kaborycha, whose eloquent textbook, *A Short History of Renaissance Italy*, became my early foundation for the course I would ultimately teach. After I met Lisa for lunch in Santo Spirito, she helped me reach out to the friendly and talented staff at the ACCENT Center in Florence (Michelangelo, Francesco, Daniela, Lisa, Lillia, and Eleonora, thank you!), who assisted me in developing my own study abroad program, which I have run almost continuously for six years. A course that began as a general introduction to the Renaissance soon became a focused course on Machiavelli, featuring a lunch and wine tasting at Machiavelli's villa, L'Albergaccio. Florence has become my de facto winter home, and a good portion of this manuscript has been written and revised in my favorite rental apartment on Via dei Banchi, just down the street from the Duomo.

I also have relied considerably on the virtue of others. First, I must acknowledge the incredible scholarship written on Machiavelli in the last few decades. Erica Benner's many books on Machiavelli have offered bold reinterpretations that have challenged traditional readings and reintroduced his work to popular readers. Maurizio Viroli brings a passion and beauty to his writing that is a pleasure to read. Yves Winter's highly innovative and philosophical interpretation of violence as an instrument of politics has played a central role in my analysis of power in Machiavelli's work. The political readings of John McCormick, Catherine Zuckert, Filippo del Lucchese, David Levy, and Diego von Vacano have illuminated the relevance of Machiavelli's work to present problems. I have savored the translations and interpretations by Harvey Mansfield throughout my writing. And I must also recognize the foundational work by Leo Strauss, whose writing I always enjoy even when I frequently draw the opposite conclusions. Although I came to Machiavelli late in my career, I have been fortunate to be writing at a time when I can rely on such scholarship in order to participate in this lively conversation.

Lastly, this book as it presently stands would not have been possible without the generous, critical, and creative feedback from Robert Hariman and Ned O'Gorman, two incredible scholars, committed teachers, and virtuous souls. After several false starts and dead ends on my part, they suggested framing the book as the act of reading Machiavelli in catastrophic times. As soon as I adopted their recommendation, all the pieces fell into place. Robert and Ned helped me find my "voice" through trial and error. One thing I have learned is that writing about Machiavelli is like walking through a minefield. I managed to survive many poorly placed steps. But at the moment, I am still standing, thanks to these guides.

We do nothing solely on our own. I would have it no other way.

THE WAY TO HELL

CHAPTER 1

Why We Cannot Quit Machiavelli

I was sitting on the toilet when your messenger arrived, and just at that moment I was mulling over the absurdities of this world; I was completely absorbed in imagining my style of preacher for Florence: he should be just what would please me, because I'm going to be as pigheaded about this idea as I am about my other ideas. And because never did I disappoint that republic whenever I was able to help her out—if not with deeds, then with words; if not with words, then with signs—I have no intention of disappointing her now. In truth, I know that I am at variance with the ideas of her citizens, as I am in many other matters. They would like a preacher who would teach them the way to Paradise, and I should like one who would teach them the way to go to the Devil. Furthermore, they would like their man to be prudent, honest, and genuine, and I should like to find one who would be madder than Ponzo, wilier than Fra. Girolamo, and more hypocritical than Frate Alberto, because I think it would be a fine thing—something worthy of the goodness of these times—should everything we have experienced in many friars be experienced in one of them. For I believe that the following would be the true way to go to Paradise: learn the way to Hell in order to steer clear of it.[1]

—Niccolò Machiavelli to Francesco
Guicciardini, May 17, 1521

When Niccolò Machiavelli wrote these lines to his friend Francesco Guicciardini, he was living in political exile at his villa in Sant'Andrea in Percussina and was eager for work. The Florentine Wool Guild had agreed to pay him to use his rhetorical skills to convince a famous preacher from Carpi to travel to Florence to deliver the Lenten sermons. Typical of Florentine attitudes, the guild members wanted a preacher who would genuflect to conventional pieties and reassure them of their chance at salvation. In contrast, Machiavelli, inspired by a combination of pigheadedness and patriotism, felt that Florence would be better off with a friar who actually reflected the spirit of the times—that is, one who was a mad, wily hypocrite "who would teach them the way to go to the Devil."[2] But there was an important (if unstated) qualification to this plan; the lies of this preacher would have to be identified and exposed. Machiavelli therefore wanted a friar who would, through self-conscious performance, expose the techniques of the Devil in order to inoculate the people to manipulations of the genuine article. For this reason he concluded that "the following would be the true way to go to Paradise: learn the way to Hell in order to steer clear of it."[3] Whatever the Devil's faults, Machiavelli reasoned, the Devil was a pragmatic empiricist and a student of human nature. To learn how the Devil manipulated people was to learn something about ourselves and our weaknesses.

Today, we might need the Devil's help, too. After all, catastrophe increasingly seems upon us. For instance, in August 2022 an article in *Earth* magazine reported that a group of University of Cambridge researchers had called for study into what they "call the 'four horsemen' of the climate endgame: famine and malnutrition, extreme weather, conflict, and vector-borne diseases" (their updated version of the traditional quartet of Famine, Plague, War, and Death).[4] The atmosphere of catastrophe appears so transparently obvious that even ordinary language has captured the neurosis of our age with a new word, *doomscrolling*, which *Los Angeles Times* reporter Mark Z. Barabak defined in 2020 as "an excessive amount of screen time devoted to the absorption of dystopian news."[5] To provide just one example, the *Washington Post* featured this headline for its June 29, 2020 edition: "The World's Climate Catastrophe Worsens amid the Pandemic." In that article, Ishaan Tharoor writes this sentence: "The giant plumes of Saharan dust that wafted over the Atlantic and choked a whole swath of the southern United States—where authorities are, as it is, struggling to cope with a surge of infections of a deadly respiratory disease—was a generational event, which some scientists link to deepening, climate change-induced droughts in North Africa."[6] Later in the article, Tharoor describes how swarms of locusts devastated crops in India, how many nations are now at risk of starvation, how the Arctic is literally on fire (which "some scientists branded 'zombie' blazes," he notes), and how the "lungs of the world" in the Amazon are being deforested into oblivion.[7] For those who hoped for political leadership in times of crisis from the United States, Tharoor reports, "The Trump administration, of course, is the climate villain of the moment—rejecting international pacts, gutting national environmental protections and regulations, and sidelining and censoring its own climate researchers and scientists."[8] If the twenty-first-century horseman of Conflict felt neglected, he had only to wait around for the Russian invasion of Ukraine, which began a few months before what would become at that point the hottest summer on record.

Machiavelli, were he still living, would probably lament that we hadn't listened to him. Despite his warnings, he would say, human beings seem to be taking the way to Hell. Then again, there would be good reason to distrust him. Perhaps we have listened to him too well. When reading Machiavelli, after all, it is notoriously difficult to distinguish a recommendation from a warning. In his attempt to master and teach us the ways of the Devil, he may have been too good a student and an even better teacher. The private Machiavelli, in letters to his friends, might have composed witty verses on the toilet in a way that made him appear playfully ironic, disarmingly humane, and tactically prudent. Yet the public Machiavelli that history has encountered in *The Prince* will, despite scholarly reinterpretations, never quite escape the reputation of being a counselor to tyrants, who recommended with a straight face the murder of opponents, the betrayal of faith, and the ruthless expansion of power. It remains a matter of debate whether we are approaching the world Machiavelli created or are heading toward the future he feared. But what is perfectly clear is that we have reached a point in history in which the way to Paradise appears to us a circuitous, dangerous, and daunting ascent up a mountain, while the way to Hell lies before us as being straight downhill from here.[9]

In any case, here we are. Whether humanity turns toward salvation or barrels onward toward damnation, one thing is certain: Machiavelli will be there with us in spirit. And that is because we cannot seem to escape him. Especially in an age of doomscrolling, Machiavelli haunts the headlines. He sometimes provides a face of evil by which we can know evil. The *Washington Post* says, "Donald Trump Is the American Machiavelli."[10] *Europe Now* explores "Putin and Political Theory: A Machiavellian and Pan-Slav Mindset."[11] Other times he seems simply a man of experience. The RAND Corporation is interested in "Applying Machiavellian Discourses to the Wars in

Afghanistan and Iraq."[12] Vox wants to show "What Machiavelli Can Teach Us about Trump and the Decline of Liberal Democracy."[13] *Foreign Policy* serves up "Machiavelli's Lessons for America's Jan. 6 Tumult."[14] The *New Statesman* wants to tell us "What Machiavelli Knew about Pandemics."[15] And then there are moments when Machiavelli appears as a genuine guide. *Open Democracy* explains "Why Putin Still Has a Lot to Learn from Machiavelli."[16] The *Washington Post* is curious about "What Machiavelli Would Do about Climate Change."[17] And the *American Interest* suggests, "Let's Dance the Machiavelli."[18]

In short, catastrophe never fails to resurrect the ghost of the Florentine Second Chancellor. Like one of Dante's spirits called forth to give counsel to the living, Machiavelli dispenses wit and wisdom before descending back into his infernal grave. Put simply, we cannot quit Machiavelli because there is something irrepressibly intriguing and stimulating about his writing. Louis Althusser, for instance, calls Machiavelli's worldview *gripping, elusive*, and *strange* and describes the totality of his writings as representing "discovery, an untrodden path, unknown lands and seas: new because unknown, unprecedented."[19] Machiavelli is, in a word, exciting. Patrick Boucheron describes the reason for the enduring popularity of Machiavelli's writings this way: "There are books you hang on to as though they were life buoys. When everything around you is pitching, when capsize seems inevitable, they stay afloat, they emit a signal, they save you from shipwreck. Machiavelli's books are of that kind. Throughout history, they have been the faithful allies of those who sought to understand the drift of politics."[20] There are good reasons why his works possess that quality. Like those generations living through the first decades of the twenty-first century, Machiavelli understood what it meant to confront the real possibility of the End of Things. His life spanned the years 1469 to 1527, including fourteen years (1498 to 1512) as a dedicated civil servant of the Florentine Republic, in which he served as the second chancellor; his job "consisted primarily of writing letters, both for the government of the city and for important citizens. His day-to-day concern is with the production of clear and persuasive prose, with practical rhetoric."[21] But in his later life he saw the power and independence of his beloved city-state of Florence destroyed by waves of foreign invasion while the Italian peninsula, once the center of European Renaissance, began its decline into a mere Mediterranean backwater. *The Prince* was Machiavelli's attempt to save Italy itself from the "barbarians" of Spanish, French, and German troops. Machiavelli saw a zero-sum competition between the rising nation-states of

Europe and hoped for an aspiring "prince" of a not-yet-formed Italian state to invent new modes and orders that would forestall catastrophe. The only thing that he believed could prevent total ruin was power. In *The Prince*, Machiavelli used all of his rhetorical skill and political knowledge to craft a guide to avoid ruin. The extraordinary modes he advocated in this text must be understood in this context.

It is worth noting the way Machiavelli would interpret the use of the term "extraordinary" here. Machiavelli famously called for implementing "new modes and orders" that would be necessary to meet the challenges of his time. By orders (*ordini*), Machiavelli meant stabilized practices that have become formalized and sanctioned by ruling authorities and that establish the rules and pathways people use to exert power through the state; for him, the word *order* denotes the rules, institutions, or ways of organizing behavior. Modes (*modi*), meanwhile, are specific practices that function as a means to attain specific ends that have become habitual and characteristic for an individual or group. Modes are habitual ways of adapting to circumstances and attaining ends. A mode is therefore "ordinary" (*ordinario*) when it conforms to and supports a stable order of things and established modes. In contradistinction, that which is "extraordinary" (*estraordinario*) stands outside of and overreaches the boundaries of the established order. To pursue an extraordinary mode is therefore to seek one that stands above or in violation of some law or norm, usually to meet some unprecedented and immediate threat. In this way, catastrophe brings out the "extraordinary" in people when they must radically innovate in order to survive. Consequently, Machiavelli's work always takes on a newfound relevance whenever crisis makes extraordinary action seem necessary.

But Machiavelli is more than just a crisis counselor; he is also a human being whom it is difficult to dislike at some level. Despite his reputation as a consummate villain, his personal writings reveal a complex and charming individual. Niccolò Machiavelli was a lifelong Florentine civil servant, a frequently unfaithful husband, a moderately loving father of five children, and (for the last fifteen years of his life) a writer in exile who, after having been expelled by the Medici for his republican sympathies, lived on his family's small farm within sight of his native city. In a letter to his friend Francesco Vettori, we catch a comic glimpse of his daily life in exile. He writes, "Having eaten, I return to the inn; there is the host, ordinarily a butcher, a miller, two bakers. With them I become a rascal for the whole day, playing at cricca and tric-trac, from which arise a thousand quarrels and countless abuses with insulting words, and most times we are fighting over a penny and yet we can be heard shouting from San Casciano."[22] But even in this environment, Machiavelli's political consciousness could not stop its incessant strategizing. As he confessed to Francesco Vettori in another letter, "If I could talk to you, I could not help but fill your head with castles in air, because Fortune has seen to it that since I do not know how to talk about either the silk or the wool trade, or profits or losses, I have to talk about politics."[23] Driven by a personal compulsion to "talk about politics," Machiavelli spent the last years of his life in exile pouring his soul into treatises that few people outside of his close friends would read during his lifetime. Taken together, his letters and works still, today, communicate Machiavelli's irrepressible character. He is, I have found, an enjoyable companion.

Still, one must admit that if we take much of his counsel at face value, there seems more reason to silence Machiavelli than to allow him to keep talking. For instance, some of his teachings include never trusting the people, cruelly eliminating your enemies as soon as possible (and en masse), only following the law when it serves your immediate interest, and always being ready to use violence as an instrument of political power. For Leo Strauss, whatever virtues Machiavelli might possess are outweighed by his vices. Strauss thus denies him any hint of lofty "tragic" character that could redeem his flaws. Strauss's Machiavelli possesses no expectation of nobility, no sense of a higher ideal that motivates heroes to great sacrifices: "In Machiavelli we find comedies, parodies, and satires but nothing reminding of tragedy. One half of humanity remains outside of his thought. There is no tragedy in Machiavelli because he has no sense of the sacredness of 'the common.'"[24] This "common" for Strauss represents an underlying morality that reveals itself in ordinary life to perceptive thinkers, a law that applies to everyone and sets the standards for nobility. Comparing Machiavelli and Thucydides, for instance, Strauss finds a key difference. Both authors, it is true, share "the same 'realism,' i.e., the same denial of the power of the gods or of justice and the same sensitivity to harsh necessity and elusive chance."[25] Yet Thucydides maintains his tragic nobility throughout. For Strauss, "Thucydides never calls in question the intrinsic superiority of nobility to baseness, a superiority that shines forth particularly when the noble is destroyed by the base. Therefore Thucydides' History arouses in the reader a sadness which is never aroused by Machiavelli's books."[26] In Strauss's reading, Machiavelli's characters may make tragic choices but they lack tragic sensibility; their only goal is to maintain power at all costs. They aspire not to greatness but to endurance; they are guided not by the highest honor but by the basest prudence. Insofar as we understand evil as a morally wrong action that brings harm and suffering to others in the service of one's own selfish interests, Strauss declared Machiavelli to be a "teacher of evil."[27]

Yet Machiavelli has, especially more recently, had his defenders. Perhaps the most vocal has been Erica Benner, who completely rejects Strauss's reading and finds Machiavelli a vastly misunderstood figure by contemporary historians and political theorists. In her reinterpretation of *The Prince*, Benner adopts two ways of approaching Machiavelli that allow him to speak more directly to modern readers. First, she argues that Machiavelli used coded language to argue that brutal tyrants, while successful in the short term, are actually terrible models for those who seek to establish long-term foundations. Benner stresses that one of Machiavelli's "favourite techniques of ironic praise is to lavish good words on a subject while describing his actions in ways that jar with the praise."[28] Although Benner finds Machiavelli's writing full of contradictions and sudden reversals of tone, she also has identified a consistent pattern in which he frequently follows his most shocking statements with important qualifications and even at times complete rebuttals. Consequently, one can find equal and opposite rules to counter the Devil if one reads him carefully. These rules include that the people are the most reliable allies, that cruelty provokes hatred and revolution, that lasting power grows out of an uncorrupted legal order, and that violence is a counterproductive means of maintaining power. Second, she argues that Machiavelli, far from being an amoralist, in fact adhered to essentially Socratic notions of justice. Benner's scholarship thus seeks to renew "a very old tradition of Machiavelli readership: one that sees him as a moral philosopher whose political theory is based on the rule of law, and whose 'manner' and 'matter' of writing are heavily indebted to ancient Greek ethics."[29] Rather than *The Prince* being the founding text of political realism, Benner finds that "at the [book's] core is a biting critique of both ruthless *realpolitik* and amoral pragmatism, not a revolutionary new defense of these positions."[30] In Machiavelli, she argues, contemporary political theorists find a fellow traveler.

I quite happily find myself between both positions, learning from both but siding with neither. I cannot deny that Strauss and his followers are justified in claiming that Machiavelli taught "evil" when he praised acts of deception, assassination, betrayal, and conquest that served only the self-interest of a cruel individual. But I believe the majority of his writing does not reflect this quality. In fact, Machiavelli constantly stressed how any real choice involved competing evils and competing goods, and he took great pains to document the pros and cons of any judgment. This type of analysis is not "evil" but realistic. I am also convinced by Benner's arguments that Machiavelli's works are polyvocal texts that often seem designed to intentionally generate cognitive dissonance in the reader. At the same time, Benner's Socratic reinterpretation of Machiavelli's most notorious statements as coded condemnations demands too much subtlety and gives back too little reward. If we remove the sharp edges from Machiavelli and interpret every distasteful suggestion as a coded warning, he no longer serves to shock and challenge us. I also want a Machiavelli with whom I can disagree. Thus, I prefer a "middle" reading that encounters Machiavelli as a brilliantly flawed human being containing the same levels of cruelty and charity as most people. I neither wish to save nor condemn Machiavelli. I want to interpret his work in a way that stimulates the dialectical consciousness and the political imagination, in which the former enables us to see two sides of every issue while the latter empowers us to envision future possibilities. Rather than determining what the "real" Machiavelli thought, I prefer to side with Walt Whitman and accept that if Machiavelli contradicts himself, he contradicts himself.[31] Like the rest of us, Machiavelli contains multitudes.

One of those sharp edges that I hope to retain in Machiavelli is the one commonly called his "political realism." I was drawn to Machiavelli's work precisely because I hoped that studying it would help me evaluate the degree to which his political realism might be useful as a tool in confronting catastrophe. This decision did not necessarily come easily. Because I spent much of my career writing in the tradition of democratic humanism embodied in the work of John Dewey, political realism has always represented the very opposite of my philosophical worldview. Furthermore, I remain committed to the ethics of democratic humanism in which (to quote myself) "power is the creative capacity for individuals to recognize, cultivate, and actualize human potentialities within a pluralistic communicative environment that balances difference with cooperation."[32] My personal commitments to fostering democratic humanism through the arts of communication have not changed. Yet having spent so much of my professional life constructing a vision of democratic humanism centered on the work of John Dewey, I am keenly aware of the limits of

pragmatic critique. To defend Dewey's presuppositions of the primacy of communication to human experience and the possibility of democratic community
is to evoke, in political realist circles, an immediate eye roll and the accusation
of "idealism." Machiavelli's name, by contrast, is virtually synonymous with
modern political realism. As John Bew notes, "Machiavelli is commonly understood to be the father of *Realpolitik.*"[33] I wanted to discover what could be
gained by approaching a common problem from the opposite end of the spectrum in the hope, through my "middle" reading of Machiavelli, to also find
a middle ground. Machiavelli, in short, would force me to inhabit a different
vocabulary of politics by which to confront the greatest challenge of our age.

That challenge, to repeat, is the threat of global catastrophe. As Robert
Hariman has argued, "catastrophe is emerging as a representative rhetorical
figure for twenty-first-century social thought."[34] Anyone familiar with doomscrolling can understand why: "As bubbles burst, states fail, humanitarian interventions assist regimes of domination, modernization projects doom traditional communities, global markets escalate income inequality both within
and between societies, and the environmental costs of affluence rise omi-
nously, more and more people are coping with the paradoxical condition
of normal system operation becoming indistinguishable from system breakdown."[35] By "catastrophe," then, Hariman and Cintron mean an event or
sequence of events that arises from outside of human intention, is driven by
the force of overwhelming necessity, and "features overturning or destructive
transformation, but with no fixed intention or end."[36] Catastrophes can be
sudden or cumulative, occurring in an instant or over decades, but the outcome is the same. Catastrophes rupture the established order, undermine old
authorities, overturn hierarchies, disable common sense practices, and thwart
predictable outcomes. As opposed to the more progressive figure of *revolution,*
whereby human agents collectively remake society through autonomous political action and violence, *catastrophe* better captures the disorientation that
comes from being forced from behind into the unknown. As Hariman explains, "whatever the inflection, catastrophe pitches everyone into a condition
of rupture where society's basic capacity to function is called into question; in
that condition, no new social order is provided to replace the ancien régime,
inaction does not restore the status quo ante, action is both unusually difficult
and absolutely required, and the outcome is not known."[37] Catastrophe (or
those forces of fortune that threatens us with what Machiavelli preferred to
call "ruin") is therefore our shared condition.

What makes Machiavelli both stand out from his contemporaries and speak to our own time is how he responded to catastrophe. Rather than find comfort in denial or release through elegy, Machiavelli crafted what today has been called the "rhetoric of catastrophe." According to Diana Goncalves, "a rhetoric of catastrophe is a compilation of discursive strategies that help manipulate and shape a specific event in order to integrate it into cultural memory."[38] In her study of the 9/11 terror attacks, for instance, Goncalves identifies the typical forms such a rhetoric might take, include characterizing catastrophe as a "fall" from order, as an exceptional event, as an exposure of vulnerability, as a memorial to the fallen, or as an opportunity for reconstruction that "consists in seizing the destruction to job and execute comprehensive plans to (re) build and create a new order, a new *topos*, and thus start anew."[39] In Machiavelli's case, these past events were the various invasions of Italy by foreign powers that had laid waste to the countryside and thrown political orders into turmoil. *The Prince* represented a call for renewal to meet these challenges and avoid an even greater catastrophe to come. Whatever the form it takes, however, a rhetoric of catastrophe activates human agency after a period of dislocation and disorientation, using symbolic and discursive resources to impose meaning upon a series of events that makes them accessible to human understanding.

Like Machiavelli's own writing, however, the rhetoric of catastrophe contains a fundamental ambiguity. On the one hand, Murdoch Stephens shows through his study of environmental communication that a reconstructive rhetoric of catastrophe "is that in which a terrible future is foretold, but human emancipation from its catastrophic potential is also imagined through the political struggles of the present."[40] Here, the rhetoric of catastrophe supports the progressive hope of revolution. On the other hand, the urgency and force of this type of rhetoric can also be seen as exploiting catastrophe to impose a new kind of tyranny in the name of necessity. According to Antonio Y. Vázquez-Arroyo, "the rhetoric of catastrophe, its menacing shadows, is deployed to depoliticize populations, as well as to legitimize catastrophic situations that are already under way."[41] Similarly, Garnet Kindervater argues that the rhetoric of catastrophe often is employed as a "force aimed to threaten populations and necessitate the authorization of unusual uses of power."[42] In both cases, the rhetoric of catastrophe promises salvation, but in one it unites people in a common goal of mobilization and reconstruction, while in the other it subordinates people to authoritarian rule in the name of security and order.

Because Machiavelli's writing employs both types of rhetoric, his work provides an ideal text through which to investigate the types of conditions that empower one or the other discourse in the face of catastrophe. Indeed, Allison McQueen argues that his unique brand of political realism is best understood as a way of conceptualizing the nature of politics under threat of catastrophe. In McQueen's account, political realism in general sees politics as an autonomous sphere of action in which moral imperatives do not apply, emphasizes that conflict, disagreement, and the pursuit of self-interest are ever-present constraints on political action, and seeks to "prioritize the requirements of order and stability over the demands of justice."[43] But in her view, political realism should be understood more as a genre of rhetoric than as a genre of philosophy, at least insofar as we understand rhetoric to be a way of confronting exigencies through the medium of persuasion. McQueen reads Machiavelli's work alongside that of Hobbes and Morgenthau as being composed as a practical response to "apocalyptic contexts."[44] For her, an apocalypse threatens "an imminent and cataclysmic end to the known world, along with its attendant 'evils.' It is a rupture in the apparent temporal continuity of history, a revelatory moment around which the past is given meaning and a radically new future is announced."[45] Apocalypses thus stimulate radical experiments in political realism as a mode of thinking and writing at the edge. As she sees it, "tracing these thinkers' responses to hopes and fears about the end of the world prompts us to consider the rhetorical and normative challenges of responding to catastrophes today."[46] In the case of Machiavelli, for instance, "the final chapter of Machiavelli's *Prince* begins to look less like a strategic ploy to curry favor with the Medici and more like an apocalyptic exhortation of despair and redemption."[47] Political realism was thus Machiavelli's rhetorical instrument for imagining and instigating radical changes he believed to be necessary in confronting extraordinary times.

But political realism is more than an ideology. It is also a matter of style. In his masterful reading of Machiavelli's texts, Hariman identifies what he calls a "realist style, which places reality outside of the grasp of political texts and promotes strategic thinking as the pure form of political intelligence."[48] For Hariman, the problem with the realist style, no matter its content, is that it positions the reader outside the communicative complexities of the human condition, flattening the world into a topographical map in which pieces move and can be moved according to a fixed and predictable logic. It is this style, Hariman argues, that is the real achievement of *The Prince*. Much of the content of Machiavelli's writings, he posits, differs little from the type of humanistic counsel that was prevalent in the political culture at the time. But Machiavelli's style is altogether different. Paradoxically, Machiavelli manages, through his realist style, to use rhetoric as a means of downgrading rhetoric. The kind of republican discourse and debate so characteristic of Ciceronian republicanism thus becomes relegated as "extrinsic to reality, so power becomes objectified, something existing independently of language, texts, and textual authority."[49] In short, Machiavelli moves "political power away from an association with textual authority and toward an association with material force."[50] Per Hariman, this type of attitude that reduces human action to relations of forces is the inevitable product of Machiavelli's deceptively simple form of flattery. By addressing readers as if they possessed some secret code to unlock the doors to power, Machiavelli's style creates the very conditions for the cult of realpolitik that holds political rhetoric in contempt (dismissing it simply as "idealistic") while using appeal to "reality" as a means of masking even the most vacuous intelligence with the verbose posturing of enlightened cynicism and self-interested calculation.

All of this is true. Yet I believe that if we can read past the spectacle of his realist style, there is genuine substance to his work. Specifically, Machiavelli narrated, described, and composed rhetorics of catastrophe in a way that captured and dramatized the repertoire of persuasive tools available to political actors in times of crisis. Although he liked to present himself as harboring dark secrets, Machiavelli was not a prophetic genius who revealed the hidden underbelly of human nature and overturned millennia of ethical and political thinking. He was just a keen observer of human nature who had a fondness for universalizing rules for the sake of a clever antithesis or moral reversal, which makes him supremely quotable. What makes him such an engaging writer is less the radical novelty of his political philosophy and more the dramatic honesty of his political imagination. David Levy describes Machiavelli's writings as a "mode of education" because "his apparent hesitations and contradictions seem intended to puzzle the reader and force him to think."[51] Regardless of whether he inhabited the role of princely villain, republican patriot, or popular champion, Machiavelli possessed that rare ability to put himself in the position of others and play out every available means of persuasion and action to its ultimate end. His narratives draw from history and his own experience to vividly dramatize what he believed were the live possibilities of tactical and strategic action in any given case. Machiavelli was thus fascinated by catastrophe because it allowed him to exercise his rhetorical consciousness at peak performance, testing out different lines of attack until he arrived at what he believed to be the perfect argument for a given set of interests under pressure from necessity. In short, Machiavelli is strongest when he shows us how different actors think and act in the face of catastrophe as a means of displaying what he called *virtú*, or skill in overcoming obstacles.

That said, reading Machiavelli can nonetheless be an exasperating experience. One obstacle for contemporary readers is that neither *The Prince* nor *The Discourses on Livy* (Machiavelli's major political treatises) lead a reader through any continuous political history in which to visualize the subtleties of his analysis. Machiavelli throws at his reader a dizzying array of disjoined vignettes, mostly from Ancient Rome, that he employs to illuminate this or that maxim. Because these events are often only superficially sketched, anyone unfamiliar with Roman history finds that any complexity is quickly lost and the lesson is reduced to a simplistic tactical rule to be taken out of context as a catchy political aphorism. As a result, Machiavelli's insights become condensed to a series of commandments and repackaged to meet the needs of social climbers. (See, for instance, the 2017 *Times Higher Education* article titled "A Machiavellian Guide to Getting Ahead in Academia," which tells us, "To succeed, you will need stamina, determination—and just a little ruthlessness.")[52] A genuinely Machiavellian "guide," however, should not come in the form of a bullet point list; it should more deeply immerse the reader in Machiavelli's way of thinking through a problem. In order for Machiavelli's writing to productively stimulate serious thinking, his ideas must be played out on a clear and continuous stage of action with which he was intimately familiar and that engages our own imaginations. We need to be able to first see how his ideas can be understood as fitting responses to catastrophic situations before we can evaluate their ethical and political value for our time.

That stage, I believe, is Renaissance Florence as portrayed through Machiavelli's *Florentine Histories*. As seen in his letter to Guicciardini, Machiavelli was a lifelong Florentine citizen and patriot who aspired (at least in his own image of himself) never to disappoint it. Although his commitment to republicanism remains a matter of debate, his love of his native city has never been questioned. Machiavelli lived and breathed Florentine politics until he died, and he spent the bulk of his later years writing his *Florentine Histories* under the patronage of Pope Clement VII (Guilio de' Medici). In that work, Machiavelli retells the history of his city from the birth of Dante Alighieri in 1265 to the death of Lorenzo de' Medici in 1492. But typical of Machiavelli's writing, this was no dry recounting of history. As Anna Maria Cabrini writes, "The fundamental interpretive framework of the *Histories* is its analysis of the kinds of frequency of civil conflicts, closely connected to the problem of the absence or defective nature of Florence's *ordini*."[53] In Cabrini's reading, two motives drove the writing of the *Histories*: "on the one hand, an intimate connection with political theory; on the other, as a field of action and critical, polemical persuasion."[54] In other words, Machiavelli wished to exercise his political theory on a grand scale while at the same time providing a grounded critique of Florentine politics. The *Histories*, as his last great work, thus put all of his maxims and conjectures to the test.

In many ways, the *Florentine Histories* is therefore Machiavelli's most rhetorical work. Machiavelli narrates the history of Florence as a series of catastrophes to which the Florentines had to rhetorically respond. Unlike in *The Prince*, in which rhetoric is largely subordinated to force, Machiavelli in the *Histories* characterizes rhetoric as the primary mode of orchestrating political power. The *Histories* showcases dozens of speeches of Machiavelli's own creation in order to reveal the unique political logics in contention. These speeches were not simply transcriptions from actual records; they were products of Machiavelli's rhetorical imagination. In this practice, he followed the model of the Greek historian Thucydides, who reconstructed speeches, according to Werner Jaeger, "based on his conviction that every standpoint in such a conflict had its own inevitable logic, and that a man who watched the conflict from above could develop that logic adequately."[55] For Machiavelli, the history of Florence could only accurately be told through a rhetorical history that was recounted, in part, by reconstructing plausible (but ultimately fictional) speeches by the real actors in actual events. His goal was not to create ventriloquist puppets to spout his own opinions but rather to construct representations of human motives based on how a reasonable actor with specific interests might respond to the necessities of a rhetorical situation.

I believe what we discover in these orations is a far more nuanced application of Machiavellian principles adapted to confronting very specific necessities than is usually understood. The result is a more grounded, realistic interpretation of his maxims. Although Machiavelli believed these speeches reflected the perspectives of the actors he narrated, he could not avoid making his orators uniquely adopt his own forms of reasoning and style. Consequently, we learn much about Machiavelli's method of thinking by analyzing how the speakers he portrayed sized up their rhetorical situations. While one should be cautious in identifying any of these orations as reflecting what Machiavelli "really" thought, a textual reading can easily find resonances between their logics and his own. Often, the rhetorical deliberations he presents are seen as crucial tools for avoiding ruin. Other times, his speakers' rhetoric is the necessary prelude to the accrual of arms and the direction of force. In all cases, the speeches occur at moments of decision that ultimately determine the course of the city's history.

Once we begin to see parallels between his time and our own, Machiavelli's work becomes an important resource for what Kenneth Burke called "equipment for living." For Burke, the sociological and rhetorical value of proverbs, literature, histories, and philosophies grows out of our assumption that not every situation in human history is a singularity. Our names for types of situations, including those we call catastrophic, identify what Burke calls "typical, recurrent situations" that recur "so frequently that they must 'have a word for it.'"[56] Without these names, we would confront every event as if it was a novelty, thus exposing us utterly to the vicissitudes of fortune. Similarly, proverbs attain their value because they provide ways of responding to these recurrent situations. According to Burke, then, "proverbs are *strategies* for dealing with *situations*."[57] Proverbs define an individual situation as belonging to a recognizable type and then provide rules of behavior. Even whole works of literature can function this way, thereby allowing us to treat them as "*equipments for living*, that size up situations in various ways and in keeping with correspondingly various attitudes."[58] In a description particularly fitting for readings of Machiavelli's work, Burke suggests that reading works of art gives us "strategies for selecting enemies and allies, for socializing losses, for warding off evil eye, for purification, propitiation, and desanctification, consolation and vengeance, admonition and exhortation, implicit commands or instructions of one sort or another."[59] Works of literature accomplish these things symbolically. Machiavelli's work performs them explicitly. But if we consider his writing as equipment, we need not follow his commands. For our equipment also includes our ability to identify and anticipate the strategies we find destructive and wish to resist or to avoid.

I believe that Machiavelli's equipment is designed to help us stimulate the historical, political, and rhetorical imagination necessary to make judgments in catastrophic situations. Like the thinking of a modern-day script writer for blockbuster movies, Machiavelli's was drawn to those situations in which necessity forced actors to consider extraordinary modes of action to achieve their desired outcomes. It is his flair for the dramatic that makes his writing so engaging. The difference is that Machiavelli's stories were intended not only to be understood as accurate representations of political reality but also to be taken, more often than not, as models for imitation. The perennial scandal that is *The Prince* arises not from what he describes but from what he counsels, namely, to imitate the actions of villains if we ever find ourselves driven into similar corners. But that scandalous character of his work is precisely its value. We are only able to confront catastrophic situations intelligently and ethically when we are aware of the choices we must make and have inoculated ourselves ahead of time from the temptation to take the path to Hell. Machiavelli's *Histories*, in particular, are showcases of rhetorical manipulation, self-aggrandizement, distortion, and pandering that are characteristic responses, in both his time and in ours, by those who would seek to exploit catastrophes for their own short-term gain and every else's long-term ruin. But they are also sympathetic studies of ordinary people caught up in extraordinary times. And Machiavelli's basic humanity, his ability to put himself into the position of others, is perhaps what is most unsettling of all. We learn about ourselves by identifying with villains. But this exposure also teaches us the way to avoid becoming one.

Today, the threat of global catastrophe requires us to confront hard choices with policies that undoubtedly will require a combination of sacrifice, persistence, and vision. The Hell that awaits us is not simply one of war but of drought, heat, starvation, pandemic, overpopulation, and ecosystem collapse. And making things worse is the fact that one of the most appealing responses to this catastrophe will be, political speaking, to choose the quickest route to this apocalyptic outcome. Justified by so-called Machiavellian political realism, a new crop of "princely" leaders will seek to dominate diminishing resources by dividing populations against one another, closing borders against imagined enemies, and implementing authoritarian forms of rule upon their own people in the name of making their nations great again. Particularly in the current age of fascist resurgence in the face of coming calamity, Machiavelli can be used to rationalize undermining democratic institutions and consolidating princely dominance for the sake of recapturing some idol of greatness. We can, of course, condemn these movements from the outside, drawing on traditional religious, moral, and ideological discourses. But this strategy is to speak only to oneself and one's circle. I believe a more effective way of resisting Machiavellian forms of politics is to use Machiavelli to not only to identify but also to disable them. Regardless of his intentions, there are principles in Machiavelli's political realism that demonstrate quite clearly that the only way to achieve order, justice, and power over the longer term is through a rhetoric of catastrophe that preserves and expands republican freedoms while refusing to sacrifice the future for the present. There is a lesson in Machiavellian virtù still to be learned in our contemporary world. As Ned O'Gorman writes:

> For Machiavelli, virtù is the political skill of navigating winds of change so as to create new, relatively stable political orders. This will be a major political challenge in the coming years of the twenty-first century. The crises that confront us now—climate change; massive wealth and income inequalities; debt crises; the capture of communication networks by powerful interests; the automation of industry and thus the displacement of workers; refugee crises; nuclear and chemical weapons; growing surveillance powers—these will not magically dissolve. There are not simple market solutions available, no technological fixes, and no automatic historical destiny on which to rely. There is only you, me, and a bunch of other people, and our capacity for judgment, rhetoric, imagination, and action. We need to renew our commitment to our own political power and do something new.[60]

I couldn't agree more. Therefore, to facilitate this project and help us avoid taking the way to Hell, this book reads Machiavelli's works in catastrophic times as a way of meeting today's challenges and renewing our commitment to virtuous politics. But to accomplish this task, I also read Machiavelli's writings in the context of Florentine political history, specifically during the centuries beginning with the origin of the republic in the time of Dante to its demise soon after the death of Machiavelli. After a chapter introducing Machiavelli and providing a guide to interpreting his work, I then draw heavily from Machiavelli's own historical writing in the *Florentine Histories* (supplemented by other contemporaneous authors) to illuminate the meaning of some of the core rhetorical principles of Machiavelli's political theories documented in *The Prince* and the *Discourses on Livy*. This approach provides a continuous political microcosm by which to investigate the modes of political action within a republican context that was close to Machiavelli's heart. But the goal here is not to imitate the modes of political action popular in Renaissance Florence, which by contemporary standards was a highly restricted, patriarchal, and sectarian oligarchy even in its most egalitarian form. The goal is to abstract from the historical events the modes of rhetorical and political action available to us in the present day. Through this analysis, I hope to stimulate critical thinking via an imagined dramatization of the past. After all, we gain perspective on our own time only by seeing it from a distance. By detachment, we gain insight.

Like Virgil had done with Dante, Machiavelli becomes our guide through the political inferno of Florence to help save us from pursuing our own damnation. And here we might take advice from Dante. In *Purgatorio*, Dante encounters a fellow Lombard who offers the counsel that Machiavelli, too, would embrace over two centuries later. Against those who would deny the responsibility and the power to make choices, who throw up their hands to fate and claim that some other power had dictated their future—whether it be the stars, God, nature, technology, or history—the Lombard retorts:

> The stars may initiate your movements;
> I do not say all of them, but suppose I should say so,
> There is a light to tell good from evil
> And free will; which, if it makes an effort
> Throughout the first battles with the stars,
> Will be victorious, if it is well-nourished.
> Free as you are, you are subject to a greater law
> And a better nature; and that creates in you
> The mind the stars do not have in their charge.
> So, if the present world is going off course,
> The reason is in you, and should be sought there;
> And I will tell you truly how the land lies.[61]

Whoever or whatever gave human beings the power to reason, the fact remains that the capacity to reason remains within our power. And we have the free will to determine our own fate. If our world is going off course, we must consciously choose to chart another direction. To be able to confront the catastrophes before us, those generations today who fear they may be the *last* generations to experience our world before total societal collapse must believe the power is within them to change the future. For only through the self-conscious cultivation and embrace of democratic power can the peoples of the world find a way to save humans and nonhumans alike from taking the way to Hell.[62]

CHAPTER 2

How Catastrophe Forces Tragic Choices upon Us

M ACHIAVELLI MAY NOT HAVE BEEN A TRAGIC THINKER, BUT HE most certainly was a theorist of tragic choices. Unlike in the case of classical tragic writers, his political actors do not strive for higher justice and suffer for the greater good; they seek proximate goals through the most efficient means. But even if his heroes do not aspire to grand ideals, they are nonetheless constantly forced into tragic situations in which sacrificing some good and committing some evil is unavoidable. There are no easy decisions in a world rife with conflict. Machiavelli warns that no state should "ever believe that it can always adopt safe courses; on the contrary, it should think it has to take them all as doubtful. For in the order of things it is found that one never seeks to avoid one inconvenience without running into another; but prudence consists in knowing how to recognize the qualities of inconveniences, and in picking the less bad as good."[1] Few heroes are less tragic than ones who choose the "less bad" rather than striving ahead to gloriously suffer their fate, come what may. Yet they face tragic choices, nonetheless.

To be confronted with a tragic choice is to be placed in an impossible situation. Competing goods tempt us in different directions while their corresponding evils warn us away. As Cornel West puts it, "the tragic consists of moral choices that must be made in the face of irreconcilable values, and especially conflicting obligations."[2] And even where we would refuse a choice that necessitates evil, such refusal might invite even greater ruin. When a plague burns through a territory or a foreign army batters at the city walls, not to choose is itself a choice. Isaiah Berlin once wrote, "If, as I believe, the ends of men are many, and not all of them are in principle compatible with each other, then the possibility of conflict—and of tragedy—can never wholly be eliminated from human life, either personal or social. The necessity of choosing between absolute claims is then an inescapable characteristic of the human condition."[3] Machiavelli agrees, and his thinking thrives in such situations. That is why his writing is so dramatic. The events that capture his attention are those that force ordinary characters to make extraordinary choices that are unthinkable in times of peace and order.

The type of tragic choice that fascinated Machiavelli was analogous to what today might be found in contemporary disaster narratives in literature, documentary, and especially summer blockbuster films. According to Eva Horn, "disasters are situations with limited options, intense time pressures, and great danger," in which "people are forced to act and make grave decisions."[4] Disaster narratives inevitably take on a tragic character insofar as "tragic choices are faced when there is not enough for everyone yet when everyone has a legitimate claim on a particular resource."[5] And by being tragic, these narratives are very often political as well. Their political character derives from the fact that "they bring order into the complicated, tragic, or just obscure situations that social life has to confront. The fiction of an ongoing catastrophe enables the suspension of certain rules of justification and due process in favor of the swift and brutal decision solicited by states of emergency."[6] For example, Horn points to the popularity of "Lifeboat Earth" scenarios found in books like *The War of the Worlds* or movies like *The Day after Tomorrow*, in which a catastrophe "brings about a situation of scarcity that makes it necessary to kill or leave behind some of one's *own* people."[7] These choices stimulate rhetorical debate among the characters and force them to make extraordinary political decisions. These are the types of tragic choices that Machiavelli faced in his own time.

So let us grant the position of Machiavelli's critics. Because of its fixation on tragic choices, the Machiavellian universe represents a kind of political inferno that few of us should want to inhabit if given the choice. Any sane person would choose not to live in such a world. To individuals with the good fortune to live in peace, love their neighbors, trust their state, and have confidence in progress, Machiavelli's work can only be seen as a guide for criminals, tyrants, and terrorists. And for good reason. Machiavelli's writings outline a dispiriting view of human nature that necessitates adopting deceptive and often cruel modes of action for political survival. As Friedrich Meinecke writes, in Machiavelli we find a "picture of Man, stripped of all transcendent good qualities, left alone on the battlefield to face the daemonic forces of Nature, who now feels himself possessed too of a daemonic natural strength and returns blow for blow."[8] For those who are fortunate enough never to have experienced such existential trauma and who have trust in the power of goodness, Machiavelli's world can appear nothing but demonic. Like a good action film, we like to watch it from a distance but wouldn't want to live there.

Certainly, for instance, nobody would actually wish to associate with or live during the time of Cesare Borgia (1475–1507), the dashing, charismatic, and arguably psychopathic son of Pope Alexander VI, Rodrigo Borgia (1431–1503). Yet in any description of Machiavelli's political thinking, Cesare almost always emerges as the exemplar of the ideal prince despite being responsible for numerous assassinations and thousands of deaths. In Machiavelli's skilled hands, Cesare becomes the prototype for every Hollywood villain (and a popular television and video game character in his own right), a master of manipulation and betrayal, a brilliant political strategist, and a skilled military tactician willing to use any means necessary to expand his family's dynasty. During Machiavelli's time as second chancellor of Florence, Cesare played a leading role in late Italian Renaissance drama when he resigned his cardinal's hat to lead the papal armies (assisted initially by French arms) in an effort to achieve his father's ambition of Vatican control of central and northern Italy. For Machiavelli, the daring modes he employed to spectacular success in pacifying and uniting the central Italian region of the Romagna made him a model to follow for any aspiring leader of the peninsula. As he wrote in *The Prince*, "Whoever judges it necessary in his new principality to secure himself against enemies, to gain friends to himself, to conquer either by force or fraud, to make himself loved and feared by the people, and followed and revered by the soldiers, to eliminate those who can or might offend you, to renew old orders through new modes, to be severe and pleasant, magnanimous and liberal, to eliminate an unfaithful military, to create a new ones, to maintain friendships with kings and princes so that they must either benefit you with favor or be hesitant to offend you—can find no fresher examples than the actions of that man."[9] A few notable examples stood out for Machiavelli as worthy of imitation. First, although he started out relying on the arms of others (namely of the French and of the Orsini and Vitelli families of Rome), Cesare eventually acquired his own arms by first gaining the loyalty of Orsini's own military leaders through allowances, affection, and government posts. Second, to eliminate potential enemies and acquire remaining arms, he invited both the Vitelli and Orsini leaders to dine with him at Sinigaglia, where he promptly had them all assassinated. Third, to pacify the Romagna, which was at the time "commanded by impotent lords who had been readier to despoil their subjects than to correct them," he hired Remirro de Orca, "a cruel and ready man," to bring the lords to heel through a civil court set in the middle of the province.[10] Fourth, knowing Remirro may have generated hatred, Cesare made him a scapegoat in spectacular fashion by having "him placed one morning in the piazza as Cesena in two pieces, with a piece of wood and a bloody knife beside him. The ferocity of this spectacle left the people at once satisfied and stupefied."[11] With the people he had conquered now solidly behind him, Cesare stood on the verge of taking the rest of northern Italy, as Pisa, Lucca, Siena, and Florence seemed ready to topple in quick succession. Only the sudden death of his father and his own sickness (possibly both from poisoning) thwarted his ambition, leaving him to live out the remaining few years of his life syphilitic and friendless. But the pathetic end of his life did not diminish, for Machiavelli, the greatness of Cesare's achievements when he was on the verge of being master of northern Italy.

I begin with the case of Cesare because it is the most shocking and problematic example in all of Machiavelli's writing. After all, if we take his praise of Cesare as representative of the entirety of his thought, Machiavelli seems to have little to offer any serious student of politics. Except in novels, film, and television, gone are the days when a swashbuckling man on a horse with a band of mercenaries and a loyal assassin can coerce, poison, and seduce his way into power. But even when updated for modern technological reality, the only people who might take literally Machiavelli's recommendations on these points are aspiring neofascist militias, organized crime syndicates, and terrorist groups with territorial aims. Given this fact, it is difficult to hold Machiavelli in high regard when he upholds men like Cesare as ideals. David Hendrickson, for instance, admires that Machiavelli "made a heroic attempt to see the political world as it really was," but he nonetheless condemns his doctrines as "offensive to basic propositions of morality and justice."[12] Hendrickson thus ultimately sides with Strauss in asserting that "we are obliged to condemn him as a teacher of evil."[13] For Hendrickson, no amount of inquiry into historical context or subtle interpretations of Machiavelli's texts can excuse his recommendation of Cesare as worthy of imitation. No matter what other wisdom can be found in Machiavelli's writing, the example of Cesare will always undermine his reputation.

I prefer to approach Cesare as a challenge. On the one hand, I reject the judgment of Machiavelli as a teacher of evil. On the other hand, I refuse the temptation to reinterpret his praise of Cesare as an ironic condemnation. If we are to learn the ways of the Devil, we must use different equipment than crude labels of "good" and "evil" that do little but label an action so that we might more effectively ignore it. A better way to use this example is as an opportunity to develop strategies for reading Machiavelli. Learning how to interpret his complex and contradictory texts therefore is not a straightforward affair; it requires combining or contrasting different interpretive perspectives. Specifically, there are at least six different perspectives a reader might take on any particular passage in his writings. I call these the *literal, epistolary, biographical, cultural, textual,* and *rhetorical* perspectives. Each of these readings emphasizes different possible meanings by viewing the text against different contexts. But this polyvocality, once again, is a virtue of his writings. Because they invite multiple interpretations, many of them contradicting one another, passages in Machiavelli can become sources of inquiry, debate, and experimentation. Adopting one perspective and then the other, a reader learns to master the art of thinking and criticism. Combining them allows us to acknowledge competing motives at stake in Machiavelli's writing in order to avoid simplistic judgments. This chapter will thus explore ways of reading Machiavelli in order to better interpret his work through the *Florentine Histories* in subsequent chapters.

To highlight some of Machiavelli's core ideas that led to his praise of Cesare, I begin by exploring these different types of reading by focusing on one of the most controversial and, quite frankly, offensive passages in Machiavelli's corpus. In the penultimate chapter of *The Prince*, Machiavelli contrasts what he sees as the two essential forces of human history, that of Fortune (*fortuna*), which directs events that happen beyond human control, and that of Skill (*virtú*), which channels the individual initiative that humans possess to direct their own fate. But the style in which he sets the two forces in opposition certainly does not win him many contemporary fans. In this passage, the voice of Italian machismo seems to overwhelm his critical faculties. I cannot help imagining Machiavelli in a tavern, inflated by ale, resentment, and testosterone, pointing a sweaty finger in the reader's face and speaking with a drunken slur: "I judge this indeed, that it is better to be impetuous than cautious, because fortune is a woman; and it is necessary, if one wants to hold her down, to beat her and strike her down. And one sees that she lets herself be won more by the impetuous than by those who proceed coldly. And so always, like a woman, she is the friend of the young, because they are less cautious, more ferocious, and command her with more audacity."[14] Yes, there it is. Machiavelli uses the image of domestic violence to inspire his future prince. And so we begin with our first reading strategy.

When encountering this passage, any contemporary reader cannot help but react to the *literal reading* of the words. Taken at face value, Machiavelli seems to be saying that men caught up in a political crisis can quite literally dominate the female personification of fortuna by adopting the attitude of a rapist. When paired with his praise of Borgia, this passage gives significant warrant for Strauss's understanding of Machiavelli as a teacher of evil. In this voice we hear that fundamental, irrational drive for dominance that propels men to rash, abusive, violent action. Encouraged by a crude misogyny and bolstered by puffed-up machismo, men who heed this voice hope through some impetuous beating to recover their "lost" virility. The literal meaning wastes no time with context or subtlety. It leaps straight to judgment, which is its obvious limitation. However, it is the reaction that provokes our interest and gains our attention. One of the reasons Machiavelli is such a pleasure to read is that he shocks, angers, and surprises. And sometimes the literal meaning may, in fact, be the correct one. In any case, we must always begin with the literal reading because it is the most immediate.

The challenge, however, is to stay with a passage for longer in order to approach it from different directions. For instance, many of the statements that we might assume to be reflections of Machiavelli's actual beliefs can be readily discounted through an *epistolary reading*, which views his work as a kind of letter written to address a specific target audience and persuade them to act in a specific way, usually related to the writer's personal interests. In this case, Machiavelli wrote, dedicated, and delivered *The Prince* to the young Lorenzo di Piero de' Medici (the foppish and unimpressive grandson of Lorenzo the Magnificent and son of Piero the Unfortunate) who had been installed as the de facto prince of Florence after the Medici's return to power. In his letter to Vettori, Machiavelli explicitly mentions writing a book called *De principatibus* that he will deliver to the Medici in the hope to "win them over" in the "desire that the Medici princes begin putting me to use, even if at first only to roll a stone."[15] Under an epistolary reading, therefore, the very adolescent bluster Machiavelli used to characterize his ideal prince could be seen as a persuasive tactic to flatter the young Lorenzo into accepting Machiavelli into his patronage (even if just to perform Sisyphean labor). In this case, Machiavelli included this boast about striking down fortuna to get into the good graces of a potential future employer. An epistolary reading helps fill out the reception history of his publication by making the audience of the book as important as the author. The danger, however, is that it risks turning every provocative claim into just a clever publicity trick designed to elicit a positive reaction.

Another approach decenters Machiavelli even further. A *cultural reading* places an author in historical and cultural context. From this perspective, Machiavelli is placed within a long tradition of humanistic scholarship and writing going back to Ancient Rome. For instance, one can see his pairing of fortuna and virtú as simply carrying forward a Roman tradition. According to Felix Gilbert, "in the ancient world man's *virtus* was placed in relation to *Fortuna*; *virtus* was an innate quality opposed to external circumstances or chance."[16] In the Renaissance, however, "*virtú* was not one of the various virtues which Christianity required of good men, nor was *virtú* an epitome of all Christian virtues; rather it designated the strength and vigor from which all human action arose."[17] Machiavelli's "vision of *virtú* as action, prowess, reason, and cunning" was thus consistent with the usage of his times.[18] And dramatizing virtú through Italian machismo was a typical trope not only of the tavern but also the palace. What strikes us as uniquely Machiavellian in a literal reading becomes just a repetition of a cultural commonplace.

A *biographical reading*, for its part, looks at an author's writing in relationship to other personal writings and his or her relationships with others. In this case, such a reading casts doubt on whether Machiavelli actually believed what he said. From evidence of his actual relationships with women (including his wife), Machiavelli emerges as a highly flawed but sentimental courtier who often fell in love and treated the objects of his infatuation with kindness and affection. Certainly, no evidence exists that Machiavelli was ever physically abusive toward women. Furthermore, his recommendation to Lorenzo to be bold and impetuous can be read as highly disingenuous, given that in another letter to Vettori in 1513, he had ridiculed the whole idea of an Italian military confederation: "As for the rest of the Italians uniting, you make me laugh; first, there will never be any union in Italy that will do any good; even if all leaders were united, that would be inadequate because the armies here are not worth a red cent."[19] These biographical details do not negate the literal reading of these lines from *The Prince*, but they complicate any attempt to interpret that passage as a reflection of Machiavelli's sincere beliefs.

Furthermore, a *textual reading* interprets this passage against the total corpus of an author's thought, looking for resonances, contradictions, exceptions, and continuities in wordings, reasonings, examples, and tendencies. In this case, it becomes readily apparent that Machiavelli, while often favoring bold and impetuous action, clearly did not believe fortuna could be so manhandled by an impudent young prince. As Catherine Zuckert notes, this statement cannot be taken "seriously or literally in this context."[20] For in the same chapter, Machiavelli quite clearly states that fortuna should be considered like those violent rivers to which everyone must yield "without being able to hinder them in any regard."[21] So much for Italian machismo. Within this metaphor, fortuna can only be opposed only through prudent foresight and long-term preparation. Machiavelli even confessed in a letter to a friend that such control of fortuna was impossible: "In the first place, men are shortsighted; in the second place, they are unable to master their own natures; thus it follows that Fortune is fickle, controlling men and keeping them under her yoke."[22] For Machiavelli, fortuna may not dictate all of our fate, but it takes extraordinary virtú to be able to bend the arc of history toward the destination we desire.

Lastly, a *rhetorical reading* interprets a work created as a pragmatic response to a situated exigence of the author's own time, meant to read and acted by an audience with the power to leverage control over a crisis. If we place *The Prince* within the context of the Italian Wars of the late fifteenth and early sixteenth centuries, for instance, Machiavelli's exaggerated praise of boldness and impetuosity might be interpreted as what he saw as a necessary response to actual conditions. The final chapter of *The Prince* is titled "Exhortation to Seize Italy and to Free Her from the Barbarians." By "Barbarians," Machiavelli meant the foreign forces that occupied different parts of Italy and were fighting for supremacy on the peninsula. Looking at the miserable state of his native land, Machiavelli could not help yearn for a rebirth of the classical spirit in which men would live, in the words of Guiddo Ruggiero, "in the best of possible worlds, with true *virtú* assuring that not only would men seem to be good but—in a good state, with good laws and with good rulers—they actually would be good again, as they had been in the glorious days of the ancient Roman Republic."[23] Although he certainly had doubts about the capability of Italian arms, the forcefulness of his appeal, and the consistency by which he referred to it in letters and writings, indicates that he genuinely hoped that some strong leader might arise to lead a bold and impetuous campaign to unite the cities of Italy in order to repel the barbarians and establish the peninsula's independence. That is why Machiavelli closes his text with these nationalistic verses from the fourteenth-century poet Francesco Petrarch: "Virtue will take up arms against fury, and make the battle short, because the ancient valor in Italian hearts is not yet dead."[24]

Just how one ultimately interprets this passage depends on the weight one places on different readings. And this is a highly personal choice. For my part, I tend to settle on the following interpretation, which explains both his praise of Cesare and his distorted picture of fortuna. Machiavelli ultimately wished to use Cesare as a model of imitation for a leader who might quickly unify the Italian peninsula. His urgent and exaggerated prose was an explicit rhetorical technique meant to inspire his reader to bold action while also flattering him enough to earn Machiavelli further patronage from the Medici family, who were then in control of both Florence and the papacy. With respect to the political pragmatics of praising Cesare, it is quite clear that Machiavelli does not present him as the ideal leader to be imitated by everyone in all situations. Consistent with the redemptive vision of *The Prince*, Machiavelli holds Cesare up as a model of imitation specifically for the future leader of a unified Italy who must rise "to empire through fortune and by the arms of others."[25] That is to say, Cesare shows how a political leader can begin with the good fortune to be the son of the pope with access to foreign arms but then, through his own skill (virtú), can lay the foundations of an autonomous state in possession of its own military. Everything Machiavelli praises about Cesare therefore comes back to a single lesson—that despite having to rely on French and mercenary armies at the beginning of his campaigns, "he was never so much esteemed as when everyone saw that he was the total owner of his arms."[26] If Italy was to attain its liberty and independence, the acquisition of one's own arms was a precondition. Machiavelli therefore did not consider Cesare an "ideal prince" for all seasons; he simply recognized the necessity for adopting Cesare's modes of action when a powerless party must find a way, through force or fraud if necessary, to acquire its own arms to throw off foreign domination and overturn domestic corruption. In short, he crafted his own rhetoric of catastrophe that called for youthful impetuosity as the only way to avoid ruin.

Machiavelli's controversial passage about fortuna, therefore, displays qualities that are both admirable and despicable in the rhetoric of catastrophe. On the one hand, there is something noble in Machiavelli's call for resilience, boldness, and courage in the face of overwhelming odds. He stresses how the act of confronting overwhelming necessity with great character is an ennobling condition. The pressure to make tragic choices can force actors to embrace extraordinary modes of speech and action they never thought possible. For instance, in the *Discourses* he marvels at "how useful is necessity to human action and to what glory they have been led by."[27] For "the hands and the tongue of man—two very noble instruments for ennobling him—would not have worked perfectly nor led human works to the height they are seen to be led to had they not been driven by necessity."[28] For Machiavelli, when peace reigns, greatness sleeps. When Machiavelli looks back through history and compares it with his own experience in the Florentine Republic, he sees that "it has always been, and will always be, that great and rare men are neglected in a republic in peaceful times. For through the envy that the reputation their virtue has given them has brought with it, one finds very many citizens in such times who wish to be not their equals as their superiors."[29] Yet when great necessities arise, heroes are born: "Fortune does this well, since when it wishes to bring about great things it elects a man of so much spirit and so much virtue that he recognizes the opportunities it proffers him."[30] Even if ruin may follow in the wake of these great things, history will remember the works of the tongue and the hands of those who achieved glory through necessity. I cannot deny that there is something rousing in this call to action. The image of meeting great threats with great deeds is at the heart of every inspirational speech and disaster narrative for a reason.

On the other hand, I cannot help but find contemptible the fact that Machiavelli felt he had to appeal to the baser motives of resentment, misogyny, and arrogance that have always been used by men to justify impetuous cruelty and shameless brutality when they feel their pride to be threatened. Strauss, for instance, finds that the lesson Machiavelli teaches here is to purge oneself of any remnant of human goodness by bolstering machismo in preparation to commit atrocity: "Just as a man who is timorous by training or nature cannot acquire courage, which is the mean between cowardice and foolhardiness, unless he drags himself in the direction of foolhardiness, so Machiavelli's pupils must go through a process of brutalization in order to be freed from effeminacy."[31] Similarly, Machiavelli's language reflects what Stephen J. Hartnett calls the trope of "manly consciousness" common to fascist movements, like that led by Italian dictator Benito Mussolini, who believed such an attitude was necessary to overcome the threat of catastrophe and carnage. According to Hartnett, this trope "promises to right the ship of state by responding to this betrayal-driven state of carnage by institutionalizing authoritarian masculinity."[32] As seen in the "fetishism for uniforms and flags, salutes and marches, and guns and weapons," this kind of manly consciousness typically shuts down intelligent debate in favor of military bravado.[33] Consequently, the public sphere as a place to engage in meaningful dialogue becomes redefined as a "public space for demonstrations of male heroism."[34] And this pattern, too, reflects traditional disaster narratives insofar as there often comes a time when a typically male hero must silence discussion and call for taking impetuous and violent action. I find none of this useful as a model for imitation.

But one's distaste for certain attitudes or expressions of Machiavelli requires neither a wholesale dismissal of his work nor a heroic effort to redeem him. I prefer Machiavelli as a complicated and imperfect guide. After all, the demand that we should seek counsel only from those who precisely reflect our own ideas and values ultimately ends in narcissistic mirror-gazing. We gain wisdom from figures from the past only to the degree that our charity allows us to hear their wisdom. To be sure, guides must possess more than just shock value, something often forgotten in today's media environment in which offensive bluster is passed off as truth-telling. If Machiavelli had only written in praise of men like Cesare Borgia in the style of a drunken sailor, he would rightly have been forgotten. Fortunately, he did not. Most of his writing represents a careful and objective assessment of the choices available to those who find themselves confronting tragic situations. Furthermore, although the exaggerated style with which he praises Cesare and rallies his "prince" to impetuous action invites easy condemnation from the casual reader, the motive that inspired those words was formed within a tragic context. Machiavelli wrote all of his major political works with a desire to investigate the modes and orders he believed were necessary to save Italy from catastrophe. And I believe that once we are able to forgive Machiavelli his trespasses, we can use him as a guide to avoid our own.

At this point, I wish to return to the notion of catastrophe in order to better contextualize Machiavelli's work and explore its relevance to our own time. For catastrophe is a complex term. In its immediate reference, catastrophe denotes disruption and collapse. According to Vazquez-Arroyo, "the concept of 'catastrophe' suggests a radical break from 'what is,' a diremption in the perceived order of things that brings with it destruction and loss, an irreversible transformation of the present, a turning point, and a sense of irremediable defeat for those who are on the receiving end of it."[35] For instance,

Kindervater explains that "devastating earthquakes, tsunamis, and hurricanes; large-scale terrorist attacks and other surprising, unconventional uses of force; epidemics and pandemics; extinction events; and often enough, economic crises, are all bundled within the language of catastrophe."[36] But catastrophe also connotes the possibility of a renewal that follows on the heels of ruin. Thus, we can follow Kindervater in thinking of catastrophe as having a dialectical character and being both a source of destruction and a source of creation. For him, "catastrophe means a radical break from the past but it also calls forth new futures, new possibilities. Though catastrophe may decimate, it also may till new ground."[37] When a catastrophe approaches, the present appears threatened, the past haunts us with what might have been, and the future looms as "a species of uncertainty and of indetermination," namely as either an apocalypse to avoid at all costs or a utopia that might emerge from the wreckage.[38] It is therefore because catastrophe both creates a crisis and generates opportunities that Machiavelli found it appropriate to call on his ideal "prince" to imitate Cesare and use any means necessary to redeem Italy.

But catastrophe is also not simply a "given," a thing that exists objectively out in nature. Machiavelli in *The Prince* did not refer to an external event with a single interpretation that called forth a specific type of response; he created his own version of that catastrophe through his rhetoric. We should therefore think of catastrophe both as an event and as a category of the intersubjective mind that is created and brought into being through discourse. In order to stress what she calls this "psychological" character of catastrophe, Adi Ophir introduces the notion of discursive catastrophization, focusing attention on the process whereby language, in particular through the act of naming, constitutes the "objects to be observed, described, measured and analyzed, predicted, and interfered with by and through a certain discourse."[39] Discursive catastrophization does not simply point to an already defined event to call attention to it; through rhetorical intervention, it constitutes one as a stable object of meaning. Extending Ophir's insight, Kindervater captures the nature of the process this way: "Discursive catastrophization does not hail subjects separate from the catastrophic event. It orients subjects to the definitions of what is catastrophic. It defines what matters, what is adequate to the terms of harm and injury. It positions subjects by emplacing them as political inhabitants of a clearly defined set of questions about survival itself. It animates a mode of catastrophic thought by avowing, mobilizing, and delimiting what is a tolerable life and what is unendurable."[40] In the title for the closing chapter of *The Prince*, for instance, Machiavelli names the most pressing catastrophe as the suffering of Italy as a whole under "barbarian" occupation. His readers thus become placed as political inhabitants of a single political whole (that of "Italy") that did not in fact exist yet as a political entity. Furthermore, Machiavelli establishes what is desired (national freedom), what must be endured (sacrificing regional autonomy), and what must be done (being seized by a single prince). The catastrophe of political subjection by the regional powers thus becomes an opportunity for national unity once resources are mobilized and directed. Machiavelli rhetorically constructs both a crisis and an opportunity.

The rhetoric of catastrophe therefore explores discursive catastrophization as an art of persuasion that is self-consciously deployed to constitute an audience as a particular agent of change. This conception of rhetoric is continuous with the definition originally proposed by Lloyd Bitzer, for whom "rhetoric is a mode of altering reality, not by the direct application of energy to objects, but by the creation of discourse which changes reality through the mediation of thought and action."[41] For Bitzer, rhetoric neither originates in the mind of the speaker nor finds justification by the arguments in the text alone. Rhetoric "comes into existence for the sake of something beyond itself; it functions ultimately to produce action or change in the world; it performs some task."[42] Specifically, that task is to use language, adapted to the *constraints* of a situation, as a pragmatic tool to influence an *audience* to action in the face of a shared *exigence*. In the rhetoric of catastrophe, the threat of catastrophe itself is the exigence. According to Bitzer, an exigence is "an imperfection marked by urgency; it is a defect, an obstacle, something waiting to be done, a thing which is other than it should be."[43] And a rhetorical exigence is one that requires the intervention of an audience to resolve, specifically an audience whom the speaker feels would not otherwise act prudently if not persuaded to do so. In the case of Machiavelli, for instance, he composed *The Prince* as a rhetorical response to the exigence of the loss of Italian independence, and he appealed to a member of the powerful Medici clan who he believed could unite the competing states of the peninsula to cast out the "barbarians."

The emphasis Bitzer places on "constraints" in rhetorical situations also echoes Machiavelli's constant stress on the need to adapt to what he called necessity (*necessitá*). Machiavelli almost exclusively employs a rhetorical understanding of necessity as what Benner calls "strongly constraining causality."[44] This necessity comes in five different forms. First, *supernatural necessity* are those constraints "imposed by fortune, fate, or the will of the gods."[45] Second, *natural necessity* includes "the physical attributes of the sites at one's disposal and, in some cases, natural disasters such as floods that force people to change the location and build new cities from scratch."[46] Third, *social necessity* "encompasses historical, economic, or political pressures that motivate people to build new cities, including external wars that drive them from their homelands."[47] Fourth, *human necessity* includes "certain desires, humors, and drives exhibited by human beings in all times and places."[48] Lastly, *legal necessity* is identical with law (*leggi*), which for Machiavelli refers to "man-made constraints that acquire authorities through the assent of those who live through them," particularly when "the 'necessitating' force of laws is backed by physical force."[49] Necessity thus appears in Machiavelli sometimes as a force of stability (as in the ordering effect of law) but more often than not as "as extreme and hostile pressures that must be dominated."[50] In these cases, it functions as a rhetorical constraint that stimulates actors to great speeches that call on people to meet these challenges head-on.

As Ophir and Kindervater have stressed, however, the rhetoric of catastrophe does not assume, as both Bitzer and Machiavelli sometimes imply, that a rhetorical situation exists as an objective phenomenon apart from the discourse that describes it. In previous work, I have used John Dewey's pragmatism to modify Bitzer's original conception to better account for the constitutive power of language on experience. From a pragmatic perspective, situations do not precede language but are products of it. Certainly, our experience with the world relates to real qualities and events that occur in time and place. But the moment we describe parts of our experience with language, through what Dewey calls the act of "designation," we impose order, stability, and meaning upon the flux of experience. From his perspective, "to designate is thus to abstract from events certain things with specific properties to which we can give a name and thereby grant the status of 'existence,' an activity that over time creates a stable realm of meanings called 'facts' that can endure through the course of events."[51] For instance, Machiavelli designates most non-Italian troops in Italy as "barbarians," thus establishing a fact of foreign occupation that evokes a reaction of repugnance. A rhetorical situation is simply a broader and more complex construction, uniting established facts with new designations, responding to timely events, and threading these "objects, agents, and events into a contextual whole in which an audience is not only affected but somehow implicated."[52] From a rhetorical perspective, "people often do not encounter situations first and then afterward determine how they will act, they first define who they wish to be and then interpret the situation according to the dramatic needs of their chosen role."[53] In this sense, Machiavelli's *Prince* constructed a situation in which he could act as prophet to his imagined Italian redeemer.

The case of Cesare, however, also exemplifies one of the political dangers inherent in the rhetoric of catastrophe. When people are faced with the prospect of imminent ruin, they often are attracted to leaders who show contempt for democratic processes and boast of their willingness to break any rule and commit any act to ward off a threat. According to Vasquz-Arroyo, "the threat of catastrophe is a powerful narrative and rhetorical device to invoke and authorize otherwise unpalatable political practices and policies."[54] In the case of Cesare, Machiavelli uses the threat of barbarian invasion and occupation of the Italian peninsula to encourage populations to passively accept the overthrow of their native rulers in the name of consolidating power under a single prince. In Machiavelli's logic, facing political catastrophe requires consolidation of one's "own arms" under a single leader, thus requiring the implementation of authoritarian rule and the mass recruitment of soldiers under his leadership. Thus, as Kindervater explains, "rhetorical narrative, threat, and political agency become linked. From the idea of actually existing catastrophes results a political manipulation in the effort to disenfranchise populations by urgent political threat in which the failure to capitulate might well result in catastrophe."[55] In short, in authoritarian "narratives about catastrophe, rhetorical strategies meet subjects as soft recipients: either meet fate with power or succumb to catastrophic costs."[56] The result is a depoliticization of populations. Persuaded that the only alternative to submission is destruction, they give up their right and freedom to autonomous or collective action to become mere resources to be used.

But rhetoric never has only a single tendency. The very nature of a rhetorical situation is uncertainty and possibility. To only conceive of the rhetoric of catastrophe as a mode of authoritarianism is to reinforce the type of conspiracy thinking that both denies actual catastrophes and renders populations powerless to develop any capacity for cooperative intelligence. In order to allow for constructive and democratic responses, Kindervater stresses that the political "subject of catastrophization is no mere recipient object, but alert, aware" and is "cognizant of the presence of catastrophic possibility and cost, danger and vulnerability."[57] Certainly, fear can be used as a means to frighten populations into submission, making them feel desperate enough to abandon their freedoms in the name of survival. But Kindervater also recognizes that fear can be motivational. Fear breaks people out of their habits and forces them to consider alternatives. Fear of catastrophe can thus manifest itself as a political force and "truly bring people to action."[58] The rhetorical challenge is to define catastrophe in a way that is actionable by being neither too vague, too distant, nor too overwhelming. Thus, "a problem faces those who wish for survival in an age that might be understood as barreling headlong towards catastrophe precisely because catastrophe is so difficult to imagine."[59] To properly identify an audience as an agent of change, the rhetoric of catastrophe must define the problem as significant enough to warrant a response but manageable enough that the audience feels empowered to act.

In Machiavelli, we find an example of this more constructive genre of the rhetoric of catastrophe in his treatment of Lucius Junius Brutus, the founder of the Roman Republic. This is not the Brutus who assassinated Julius Caesar but the man who led a mass revolt against the oppressive monarchy of Tarquin the Proud. Machiavelli narrates the events as follows. In 509 BCE, Tarquin's son Sextus set in motion a revolution against his father's monarchical rule by raping Lucretia, the wife of an aristocrat, resulting in her suicide. News of her assault and death caused a general uprising against Tarquin rule, the rape of Lucretia being the last straw after decades of tyrannical rule based on extortion, coercion, cruelty, and humiliation. After expelling the Tarquins, Brutus sought to implement a political system that would eliminate the monarchy altogether. In its place, he instituted a three-hundred-seat senate and created the position of consul, a joint position of shared leadership in which two consuls would be elected by an assembly to serve one-year terms, to which he and Lucretia's husband were immediately appointed. Had all gone to plan, this narrative would have resulted in a happy ending.

But Machiavelli is not interested in happy endings. Machiavelli tells the story to demonstrate the tragic choices one must make to preserve newly acquired freedom. Despite Brutus's initial victory, he soon was faced with a terrible decision. Tarquin was still alive, after all, working to ferment counterrevolution among those who felt nostalgic for the old monarchy and were not convinced of the benefits of the new republic. Furthermore, as an innovator, Brutus found himself surrounded by potential enemies and unreliable allies, "for the introducer has all those who benefit from the old orders as enemies, and he has lukewarm defenders and all those who might benefit from the new orders."[60] Unfortunately for Brutus, the ranks of his opponents soon came to include Brutus's own wife and two sons. The price of ridding Rome of the evil of kings, he soon found out, was to earn the hatred of everyone who believed they could benefit from being connected with a monarch, however tyrannical. His wife and sons, facing the loss of their privilege, "were induced to conspire with other young Romans against the fatherland because of nothing other than that they could not take advantage extraordinarily under the consuls as under the king, so that the freedom of that people appeared to have become their servitude."[61] But the conspiracy was uncovered and the sons of Brutus arrested. The tragic choice Brutus faced is summarized by Raymond Belliotti: "Brutus had to choose between the rule of law and his family. He chose the rule of law."[62] Brutus condemned his sons and all the conspirators to death. He even witnessed the executions.

Core elements of tragedy are embedded in this story. If this were performed on a Greek stage, Brutus would have played the role of tragic hero so committed to an ideal of republican justice that he was willing to sacrifice those he loved. As Machiavelli remarks, "it is an example rare in all memories of things to see the father sit on the tribunals and not only condemn his sons to death but be present at their death."[63] His darkly tragic character is captured by the Roman historian Plutarch, who castigated Brutus for his inflexibility: "That ancient Brutus was of a severe and inflexible nature, like steel of too hard a temper, and having never had his character softened by study and thought, he let himself be so far transported with his rage and hatred against tyrants, that, for conspiring with them, he proceeded to the execution even of his own sons."[64] The Roman poet Virgil, by contrast, finds a higher nobility in his action. In *The Aeneid*, a seer of the underworld foretells to Aeneas that Brutus will be forced to decide whether to call "for the death penalty in freedom's name," but "Love of the fatherland swayed him—and unmeasured lust for fame."[65] Machiavelli sides with Virgil, but without the poet's tragic sentiment. In Machiavelli's untragic account of Brutus's tragic choice, the core takeaway for Machiavelli is a simple rule of political prudence: "Whoever takes up a tyranny and does not kill Brutus, and whoever makes a free state and does not kill the sons of Brutus, maintains himself for little time."[66] In short, "there is no remedy more powerful, no more valid, more secure, and more necessary, than to kill the sons of Brutus."[67] In Machiavelli's view, had Brutus shown leniency toward his children, he would have undermined the republic at its origin while emboldening his enemies to topple the fledgling state. The virtú of

Brutus thus included not only his courage in defeating Tarquin but his honor in killing his sons.

The case of Lucius Junius Brutus offers a more complex and modern example of a disaster narrative than that of Cesare Borgia. Whereas Machiavelli praises Cesare for his ability to acquire his own arms through murder, deception, and spectacle, he praises Brutus for having defended a newly free state from the threat of tyranny. The newly installed republican leaders faced imminent catastrophe in the forms of assassination, rebellion, and the installation of a reactionary dictatorship worse than the one that had been deposed. For Machiavelli, should leaders in analogous situations choose the mode of forgiveness and leniency out of deference to goodness, they provide time and resources to the forces of reaction to organize and mount a counteroffensive. If they impose emergency rule in the form of an authoritarian state, they abandon the republican principles that inspired their revolt. But if they implement the law with equity and severity, they are forced to kill former friends, allies, and family to prove their commitment to republican justice. For Machiavelli, the choice is obvious. Republicans who strive to preserve an uncorrupted order must embrace a rhetoric of catastrophe that includes a warrant for killing the sons of Brutus as a way of preserving political freedom.

Yet even if Machiavelli's utilitarian logic sounds reasonable, his rather crass dismissal of moral objections cannot help but offend. To eliminate pieces on a game board is one thing; to actually execute one's own children is quite another. Even in the context of an arguably noble aim, as we find in Brutus, it is easy to see how one might associate the pursuit of Machiavellian *virtú* with an embrace of evil. Machiavelli often contrasts virtue (virtú) with goodness (*bontá*), associating the former with princes and the latter with the people. Although he never offers a clear definition of goodness, typically he means commonly shared commitment to the "Christian" virtues like mercy, loyalty, honesty, generosity, and love that are usually sufficient to govern our everyday interpersonal relations. But Machiavelli consistently stresses that princes often face extraordinary circumstances that demand a different prudential calculus. Mansfield points out that "from the standpoint of the virtue of Machiavelli's princes, virtue is distinct from goodness because it is willing, or eager, to do evil."[68] As Machiavelli writes with characteristic rhetorical flourish in the *Discourses*, "goodness is not enough" (*la bontá non basta*).[69] In this context, "evil" simply means those actions condemned by the standards of goodness, such as cruelty, disloyalty, dishonesty, ambition, and hatred. Thus even when one seeks a noble end, as with Brutus, the choice of evil means cannot escape the moral judgment of goodness.

But this is precisely Machiavelli's challenge to his reader—to reevaluate our standards of good and evil. In one of his most infamous passages, Machiavelli warns his reader that he departs from others by not seeking only to flatter his reader with attractive illusions. He writes, "Since my intent is to write something useful to whoever understands it, it has appeared to me more fitting to go directly to the effectual truth [*veritá effectuale*] of the thing than to the imagination of it. And many have imagined republics and principalities that have never been seen or known to exist in truth; for it is so far from how one lives to how one should live that he who lets go of what is done for what should be done learns his ruin rather than his preservation."[70] The measure Machiavelli promises to employ in his work is the effectual truth. The adjective *effetuale* is a word of his own invention, a neologism that joins the meaning of three words together, "fact" [*factus*], the "effect" [*effectus*], and the verb "to do" or "to make" [*facere*].[71] According to Yves Winter, "the adjective *effectuale* refers both to a truth that produces certain effects in the world, and to a truth that is efficacious in its operations."[72] Effectual truth is thus public, consequentialist, and pragmatic rather than private, intangible, and transcendent; effectual truth evaluates the worth of thoughts, words, and deeds by the facts they bring forth, the measurable effects they produce, and the tangible appearances they communicate. Under Machiavelli's formula, even if goodness might save souls, the effectual truth saves lives. In his transvaluation of values, effectual truth becomes the new measure by which we determine ethical action within the sphere of political realism.

The reason we need this transvaluation is entirely pragmatic. Catastrophe, quite simply, forces us to make tragic choices that exceed the ability of goodness to handle. In fact, for Machiavelli, adhering to the standards of goodness in catastrophic situations often leads directly to ruin, thus producing the very evils that goodness seeks to avoid. For him, catastrophic situations require us to consider evil and good not just as means, but as outcomes. Evil in this case would be something suffered, such as being pillaged, raped, and murdered, while the good would be that which we protect or preserve, such as our property, bodies, and lives. Although executing one's own sons might be reprehensible by the moral standards of goodness, by a utilitarian calculus those executions secured the good of the state and the freedom of its citizens.

Catastrophes therefore force us to reevaluate our standards of goodness by the measure of effectual truth. But this does not mean abandoning our desire for the good. It means, rather, that we must learn how to think at the edge of an abyss, adapting our principles the best that we can to the demands of the times. To borrow the words of Isabelle Stengers, we might use catastrophe to enact "the transformation of a problematic situation into a cause for collective thinking."[73] For the abyss is what we all feel we are approaching at ever increasing speed. Bruno Latour, for instance, find evidence of this anxiety even in the basic political positions embraced by the next generations: "When young people baptise their movement 'Extinction Rebellion,' you don't have to be a rocket scientist to see this as a symptom of agonizing doubt about the flow-on of generations . . . It's as if people were saying: 'There's no longer anything beyond this limit: *no future.*'"[74] Today, this fear of having no future, of belonging to the last generations of human beings to experience modern civilization before it collapses, will inevitably bring out both the worst and the best in humanity. The aspiring Cesare Borgias will embrace the means of brutality to consolidate nationalist power within the context of diminishing resources, while others may adhere to the republican ideal and call for a higher loyalty and shared sacrifice as a way of establishing order and protecting civil liberty. Either way, to be able to recognize recurrent patterns of thought and action between Machiavelli's world and ours is to become better equipped to deal with catastrophic situations to ensure our future through more innovative and humane ways of overcoming disaster.

Whether or not we wish for innovation, catastrophe forces innovation upon us. Our tragic choices derive from the fact that when we face catastrophic situations, not choosing is itself to choose, to choose is to sacrifice, and to sacrifice is to change. Events themselves conspire against staying the same. In his canonical rhetorical treatise, *Permanence and Chance*, for instance, Kenneth Burke distinguishes between two types of decisions: "Some decisions merely apply ways of thinking with which the deliberator was already quite at home. Other decisions, made at times of 'Crisis' (which is but the Greek word for 'judgment') characteristically involve an unsettling, an attempt (or temptation?) to think in ways to which the deliberator was not accustomed."[75] Machiavelli clearly sees crises as opportunities. That is why his conception of virtú, according to J. G. A. Pocock, was defined in innovative terms as "the creative power of action to shape events."[76] In Burke's terminology, virtú would thus be a necessary, if not sufficient, component of any effort to rhetorically construct a new order of permanence to stabilize the flux of change, which is to say to build a new piety atop the wreckage and collapse of the old. It also recalls Burke's imperative to never forget that "men build their cultures by huddling together, nervously loquacious, at the edge of an abyss."[77] We cannot avoid the crises before us. But we can either face that looming abyss honestly, collectively, and intelligently or flee from reality in order to embrace illusion, isolation, and brutality. I believe that reading Machiavelli in catastrophic times can help us choose the first alternative, not by telling us what to do but by showing us how to think. But ultimately it is up to us to determine our fate.

CHAPTER 3

On the Vices of Humans and the Virtues of the Beasts

THE HUMAN SPECIES NEVER TIRES OF PROJECTING ITS VICES ON others. We attribute to beasts our own vices in order to find something to blame for corrupting our supposedly divine essence. Cicero, for instance, contrasted the purity of human virtue with the corruption of the animals, writing, "There are two ways in which injustice may be done, either through force or through deceit; and deceit seems to belong to a little fox, force to a lion. Both of them seem alien to a human being; but deceit deserves a greater hatred. And out of all injustice, nothing deserves punishment more than a man who, just at the time when they are most betraying trust, acts in such a way that they might appear to be good."[1] One can certainly sympathize with Cicero's hatred of deceit and betrayal. But it hardly makes sense to symbolize these human vices through the behavior of the "little fox." What are we to learn from such a comparison? The fox deceives in order to escape being hunted, whereas Cicero's deceiver betrays the trust of a friend to satisfy his own ambition and greed. Only if we assume the fox is somehow *wrong* to resist being killed and skinned by a human pursuer can this analogy hold true. But in that case, Cicero would imply that it is the moral duty for foxes to sacrifice themselves for human pleasures.

If Cicero blamed beastly attitudes for corrupting the natural order of a republic, Strauss condemns them for turning our eyes from Heaven. Strauss explicitly chastises Machiavelli for having praised the character of Chiron the centaur, the learned half-horse teacher of Achilles, for Chiron's beastly virtues. By Strauss's reasoning, Machiavelli "replaces the imitation of the

God-Man Christ by the imitation of the Beast-Man Chiron."[2] In Strauss's reading, since Machiavelli's prince "is the being that must try to transcend humanity, he must transcend humanity in the direction of the subhuman if he does not transcend it in the direction of the superhuman."[3] Strauss assumes, in other words, that to be truly human is to seek also to imitate God in all things; anything less is to descend into the realm of the subhuman, the "Beast-Man." Like Cicero, then, Strauss uses animal imagery to condemn human action, in this case a comparison that speaks more to the bias against the savagery associated with lions. For both of them, the wars and atrocities that make up the bulk of our history can be attributed not to human passions and desires but to the evil influence of foxes, lions, and horses. Chiron at his worst could not have matched such cruelty and deception.

Of course, today the virtues of the beasts seem to need no defense. The careful study of the animal world has shown them to possess considerable intelligence, sophisticated emotions, and an admirable will to sacrifice their lives for their offspring. Our literature and entertainment revel in the celebration of animal powers, whether they be in the form of magic, mutants, or mascots. To acquire exaggerated animal senses and instincts is to be gifted with the means to defend oneself, one's school, one's family, and (in science fiction at least) even one's home planet. When force and cunning must be harnessed against a common threat, we inevitably find kinship with our beastly brethren. Moreover, human beings share a great deal with animals. Our impulses, desires, hates, and fears arise from our physical response to our environment no differently than how animals respond to the stresses, the dangers, and the opportunities of their habitats. The difference is that our rational minds are more complex than those of animals. We can imagine great expanses of time and space and coordinate our activities at a breadth unimaginable to even the most intelligent of beasts, and more importantly we can put ourselves in the perspective of others and empathize with their suffering. This capacity at times approximates the divine but just as often makes us even more brutal.

In any case, Machiavelli rejects the type of anthropocentric bigotry we see reflected in Cicero and Strauss. As Machiavelli taught his aspiring prince, "You must know that there are two kinds of combat: one with laws (*leggi*), and the other with force (*forze*). The first is proper to man, the second to beasts; but because the first is often not enough, one must have recourse to the second. Therefore it is necessary for a prince to know well how to use the beast and the man."[4] Here we find expressed the spirit of what Timothy Lukes calls

Machiavelli's "princely animalism."[5] None of this means that Machiavelli denies the importance of our rational capacities. Reason remains in Machiavelli an important tool for politics; as Cicero rightly argued, reason generates law and establishes the order of states. Yet reason (like goodness) is not enough. In a political environment populated with wolves, the true teachers of princes must themselves be half animal, just as the teacher of Achilles was Chiron the centaur. For "to have as teacher half-beast, half-man means nothing other than that a prince needs to know how to use both natures; and the one without the other is not lasting."[6] On the one hand, even the most rational constitution is just empty words without the resources of the beasts to ward off the enemies of reason. On the other hand, a prince might come to power using force and fraud, but without reason that prince will soon find a state descending into chaos.

Important to understanding Machiavelli's reinterpretation of Cicero, however, is that he rejects his predecessor's identification of lions with aggressive force and foxes with manipulative fraud. Ironically, this accusation actually imposes distinctly human vices upon our animal brethren. Machiavelli's beastly mentors have quite simple lessons to teach. He suggests that "since a prince is compelled of necessity to know well how to use the beast, he should pick the fox and the lion, because the lion does not defend itself from snares and the fox does not defend itself from wolves. So one needs to be a fox to recognize snares and a lion to frighten the wolves."[7] Nothing in this passage suggests that a lion should vindictively tear its opponents to pieces or that a fox is capable of setting traps that lead its victims to ruin—suggestions that would be completely counterfactual to animal behavior. In fact, the description focuses purely on their skills in avoiding conflict and suffering. As Benner points out, Machiavelli's description "points not to the strengths of foxes and lions that princes should imitate, but to their weaknesses: lions do not defend themselves against snares, while foxes are vulnerable to wolves."[8] The obvious parallel, therefore, is that "human beings often display the same weaknesses. The first thing to learn from these beasts, then, is the means of *self-defense*, including defensive modes of *combattere*."[9]

Although Machiavelli does not consistently hold to this strictly defensive interpretation, these are the applications of the beasts that shall be the focus of this chapter. The Machiavellian lion will be seen as the embodiment of military force (*forza*). According to Yves Winter, force "stands for forms of actions associated with arms; it is synonymous with 'armed force' or simply 'arms' and connotes a technical quality grounded in physical or military strength."[10] Force can be used well or badly. It can liberate a city and maintain the peace; it can overthrow a republic and institute tyranny. But throughout his work, argues Winter, Machiavelli always "emphasizes its constitutive nature."[11] Force is used to accomplish some aim. Specific to the lion, therefore, is to use the force of arms to ward off assaults from predatory states or domestic tyrants. As we shall see in a subsequent chapter, this kind of force is not equivalent to cruelty but to armed resistance and defense. Cruelty is not a mode of the lion but of the human.

The Machiavellian fox, by contrast, is less the master of cunning deception than of clever escape. As Benner stresses, the writers of folklore who treat foxes as creatures of fraud are simply mistaken: "Fraud aimed at taking advantage of others is a distinctively human talent. Real foxes, the ones with fur and tail, have nothing to teach men about lying or cheating, even to trap their small prey. Their talent, which so few humans have, is to recognize snares, and avoid being trapped."[12] Consequently, the fox represents "a very different kind of vulpine guile: the kind that sees through ruses, decent words or sacred oaths."[13] To escape a trap, a fox may employ one of two methods of fraud. *Simulation* means to pretend to have that which one does not, as one might lay down a false trail or pretend to have more arms than one does. *Dissimulation* pretends not to have what one does, such as hiding one's wealth or making a promise one does not intend to keep. Francis Bacon, for instance, describes three degrees of hiding or veiling oneself. The first is to stay reserved and secret, "the second, dissimulation, in the negative; when a man lets fall signs and arguments, that he is not, that he is. And the third, simulation, in the affirmative; when a man industriously and expressly feigns and pretends to be that he is not."[14] In politics, therefore, to employ the mode of the fox is to employ any means of concealment to avoid being exposed, cornered, and captured.

In what context is the use of force justified in self-defense? And when should one lie or break promises for the greater good? Today, these are questions that are being asked with greater frequency with the resurgence of autocratic styles of rule even in many modern democracies. For just as Florence had to constantly chase off predators who wished to devour its republican freedom, many nations today face a threat from aspiring autocrats within their own political system. In their book *How Democracies Die*, for instance, Stephen Levitsky and Daniel Ziblatt sound the alarm that democracies usually die not from outside invasion but from the internal corruption and weakening of democratic institutions by authoritarian leaders. Symptoms of potential death include "when a politician 1) rejects, in words or action, the democratic rules of the game, 2) denies the legitimacy of political opponents, 3) tolerates or encourages violence, or 4) indicates a willingness to curtail civil liberties of opponents, including the media."[15] Cases in which this has occurred, they argue, include Italy under Benito Mussolini, Germany under Adolf Hitler, and Venezuela under Hugo Chavez. Today, one might also point to political trends in Russia, Turkey, India, Brazil, France, Italy, and not least the United States.

But Levitsky and Ziblatt also suggest their own strategies of action to resist these threats, finding them, historically speaking, in places such as Belgium, Finland, and Austria. When political leaders act with mutual toleration and institutional forbearance, political leaders have the ability to "heed the warning signs and take steps to ensure that authoritarians remain on the fringes, far from the centers of power. When faced with the rise of extremists or demagogues, they make a concerted effort to isolate and defeat them."[16] Specifically, they suggest that resisting authoritarianism requires doubling down on the Ciceronian ideal of republican statesmanship before democracy collapses beyond repair. For instance, mutual toleration requires a commitment to "collective willingness to agree to disagree," while institutional forbearance requires rejecting "dirty tricks or hardball tactics in the name of civility and fair play."[17] Once these two bulwarks against the tide of authoritarianism give way under pressure, then democracy will die one way or another. Yet despite the temptation to listen to Machiavelli, Levitsky and Ziblatt nonetheless resist calling for the fox and the lion to defend against these threats. Instead, they hope that responsible politicians and parties will hold the line and make such modes unnecessary.

I find such an approach incomplete. Ultimately, Levitsky and Ziblatt fail to confront the tragic nature of politics. Instead, they envision good on one side and evil on the other, with (to borrow their fitting metaphor) guardrails in between them. Their answer to the corruption and decay of the political system is to Just Say No and Hold on Tight. This strategy may, in fact, work when the stress to the system is kept to a minimum and can be managed by institutional flexibility or simply the dissipation of energy over time. But Machiavelli would say that these tensions would then be nothing more than "ordinary" politics that require ordinary modes. But what happens when politics does, in fact, go off of the guardrails? Levitsky and Ziblatt provide no answer that is not fatalistic. In their view, democracy dies. But is that outcome inevitable? Machiavelli certainly would not accept such an answer. He would seek alternatives. The fox and the lion represent such alternatives. But to investigate these modes, one must bear the weight of tragic choices. We must ask ourselves when it is necessary violate the guardrails—that is, to act in an extraordinary mode—if we wish to rebuild them. That is to say, sometimes we must learn to do battle as beasts if we are to try to live like humans.

Part of developing our historical imagination is to look back to the past so that we might see our own situations in a new light. Levitsky and Ziblatt help stimulate the historical imagination in their own work. But I believe they can be supplemented by Machiavelli's narrative of Florentine history in the thirteenth century. This period provides an ideal starting place because it shows Florentine reaction to an aspiring tyrant after he had, indeed, broken the guardrails. During the latter part of the thirteenth century, Florence had risen in economic and political power and had achieved success in laying the foundations for a republican civic order. But factional strife within the city had opened the door for an aspiring tyrant, Charles of Valois, who had taken power in the name of establishing peace but ended up fostering strife to advance his own ambitions. Machiavelli and the early Florentine chronicler Dino Compagni clearly demonstrates that Charles was able to quickly consolidate his rule precisely because the Florentine political elite were committed to the very strategies recommended by Levitsky and Ziblatt. In a political context fraught with distrust and threatened by violence, the republican leaders found that their tools of faith and reason not only failed to defend them but actually enabled Charles's assault on the city's freedoms. In other words, while the actions of Charles, among other corrupt leaders, followed precisely the authoritarian playbook outlined by Levitsky and Ziblatt, their rapid success even in the face of mutual toleration and institutional forbearance leads us consider the virtues of Machiavelli's princely animalism. Florentine history thus presents us with a clear question of political ethics: Are there times when we must act more beastly in order to become more human? This is often the most wrenching decision we must make when responding to catastrophe. Machiavelli provides a stage on which to exercise our judgement.

To properly understand what was at stake during these years, we must first immerse ourselves in the complexities of Florentine politics in the lifetime of Dante (1265–1321). In these decades, Florence had begun its traumatic transition from a late-medieval commune dominated by the old feudal nobility (the *magnati*) to an early Renaissance republic dominated by the rising urban merchant class and guild artisans (the *popolo*). Within this latter class was a division between the *popolo minuto* (the "small people" of small proprietors, petty merchants, and skilled laborers denied representation in civic life) and the *popolo grasso* (the "fat people" of wealthy middle class of merchants belonging to the major guilds who dominated the political life of the Italian communes). These classes had concentrated in Florence as the center of a new economic order based on manufacturing, banking, and trade. Unlike the relatively static medieval towns and villages built upon hills, Florence with its geographical position along a river gave it "an economy characterized by risk and speculation, sharp fluctuations of wealth and income, a high degree of social mobility."[18] Dante, for instance, was himself a member of the popolo (his father having been a notary), but he disliked their obsession with material gain. As Brucker explains, "Dante, the aristocratic conservative, perceived and deplored the trend in Florence toward a regime with a broader social base, in which 'new men' challenged the old ruling class and obtained a greater share of offices and power."[19] These new hierarchies began ranking people by wealth rather than honor, a shift in social values that Dante found distasteful. But the wealth they produced beautified the city and made it a center of growth, industry, and learning, a circumstance Dante exploited by becoming a poet.

Another cause of the city's prosperity was that Florence had established an early republican form of government as a way of resolving the conflict between the Guelf and Ghibelline factions that had caused so much violence throughout Italy. Since the resurgence of Italian power in Europe, Italian cities had been divided between loose confederations of noble families who saw benefit in aligning either with the power of the Vatican in Rome and its affiliation with the rising merchant elites (the Guelfs) or with the authority of the landed feudal lords aligned with the Holy Roman Emperor located in Germany (the Ghibellines). Under the old feudal systems of governance, these two parties constantly fought each other for control of Florence until a brief peace was established after the death of Emperor Frederick in 1250. Machiavelli writes that at that point they realized that "it might be better to reunite the city than to ruin it by keeping it divided," and so they lay the foundation for communal governance by diving the city into six parts and electing two citizens from each part to govern it.[20]

A major step in establishing the republic was to create new forms of arms that recruited the citizen population, thus making them active participants in the state. Rather than rely on the mounted cavalry of feudal lords to dispense crude justice, "they provided for two foreign judges, one called 'Captain of the People' and the other 'Podestá,' who were to judge cases, civil as well as criminal, arising from the citizens."[21] The captain of the people was a uniquely republican innovation. It created, in effect, a civic militia independent of the forces of individual nobility. Using a bell and a great wagon, the captain would rally forces from among the men of the republic, drawn from neighborhood militias from city and countryside, each organized under its own banner. For Machiavelli, it was "on these military and civil orders that the Florentines founded their freedom. Nor could one conceive how much authority and force Florence had acquired in a short time: it became not only head of Tuscany but was counted among the first cities of Italy."[22] For Machiavelli, then, the republic was an order that deserved praise not only for its civil ideals but also for the way its modes increased the power of the city.

Dante was a beneficiary of this prosperity. By 1282 Florence had grown in population, forcing it to extend its walls as its economy continued to expand, while the city became a center of wool textile manufacturing and banking. With the rising power of the guilds, the capacity to exert power in civic office became dependent on guild membership. A new body called the General Council of about three hundred citizens had been established that widened participation in the government, followed by the creation of a new magistracy called the Signoria made out of eight priors drawn from the major guilds and housed in the new Palazzo della Signoria (today the Palazzo Vecchio). But the Guelf and Ghibelline tensions remained; nobles continued to fight factional battles in contempt of the laws of the city. Machiavelli laments that "every day someone of the people was injured, and neither the laws nor the magistrates were sufficient to avenge him because every noble, with his relatives and friends, would defend himself against the forces of the Priors and the Captain."[23] To remedy this situation, in 1293 the Signoria created the position of gonfalonier, or the "Standard-bearer of Justice," who effectively controlled an even more empowered citizen militia. They also passed the so-called Ordinances of Justice, which banned the magnati (and therefore most of the Ghibellines) from holding public office. And they made guild membership a requirement to hold office, thereby assuring the power of the popolo. In Machiavelli's words, "never was our city in a greater and more prosperous state than in those times, when it was replete with men, riches, and reputation."[24]

When Dante, then a member of the Guelfs, ascended to the position of prior in 1300, he was the inheritor of decades of steady reform.

But another crisis was unfolding behind the scenes of this triumphant drama that would culminate in catastrophe. The strife began simply enough—with the braying of an ass. The *Chronicle* of Dino Compagni written at about this time records that in the year 1299 "the city was ruled with little justice, and fell into fresh danger because the citizens became divided by competition for offices, each one hating his rival."[25] This was just a few years after the institution of the Ordinances of Justice. During this period, two families began competing for influence in the city. The Cerchi family were typical representatives of the "new men" Dante so despised. They were "men of low estate, but good merchants and very rich; they dressed well, kept many servants and horses, and made a brave show."[26] In 1280 they had bought a house next to the more ancient Donati noble family, led by Corso Donati, a knight and leader of the Guelf party. As the years passed, "the Donati, seeing the Cerchi rising—they had walled the palace and increased its height, and lived in high style—began to nurse a great hatred of them."[27] By the end of the 1290s Corso began lobbing crude insults at Vieri de' Cerchi, "calling him the ass of Porta San Piero, because he was a very good-looking man, but not very astute or articulate. And so he often used to say: 'Has the ass of Porta San Piero brayed yet today?' He disparaged him greatly and called him Guido a blockhead."[28] Henceforth began a concerted propaganda campaign on the part of the Donati: "All the jesters repeated this, especially one named Scampolino who exaggerated things when he repeated them, so that the Cerchi would be provoked to brawl with the Donati."[29] The Cerchi refused to take the bait, but the abuse would set in motion a cascade of effects that would result, strangely enough, in Dante's banishment. In his *Chronicle*, Compagni provides his reader with a mocking call to arms that graphically represents what for him was the nature of the catastrophe that would soon unfold: "Arise, wicked citizens full of discord: grab sword and torch with your own hands and spread your wicked deeds. Unveil your iniquitous desires and your worst intentions. Why delay any longer? Go and reduce to ruins the beauties of your city. Spill the blood of your brothers, strip yourself of faith and love, deny one another aid and support. Sow your lies, which will fill the granaries of your children . . . Do not delay, wretches: more is consumed in one day of war than is gained in many years of peace, and a small spark can destroy a great realm."[30]

The small spark was the conflict between the Cerchi and the Donati family; it would soon erupt into a violent civil war between the so-called White and Black factions in Florence (of which Dante, as a White, was the most famous victim). Machiavelli relates the story of how the spark was lit. In the city of Pistoia, about twenty-five miles from Florence, there lived many members of the Cancellieri family, "very powerful in wealth, nobility, and men." One day, it happened that two young men of different branches of that clan, Geri and Lore, were playing and "they came to words and Geri was slightly wounded by Lore." Lore's father, "thinking that with humanity he could take away the scandal," ordered his son to visit the house of Geri's father and ask for his pardon; but no pardon was to be had. Geri's father "had his servant seize Lore and cut off his hand, and for greater insults, on a manger, while saying to him: 'Go back to your father and tell him that wounds are treated with steel and not with words.'"[31] The cruelty of the act aroused a desire for vengeance in Lore's father. Soon the whole city of Pistoia was divided into competing factions. Any sense of shared civil responsibility to the common good was quickly replaced by allegiance to family and ally.

Anticipating the twentieth-century fascist fetish for colored shirts and uniforms, the competing factions of the Pistoia families wanted a visible (if meaningless) icon around which to rally their forces. They found a simple contrast of color to be convenient: "Because the Cancellieri were descended from Messer Cancelliere, who had had two wives, one of whom was named Bianca, one of the parties who were her descendants named itself 'White' and the other party, so as to take a contrary name, was named 'Black.'"[32] But this reduction of politics to differences in color had widespread impacts. Being abstract, color meant both nothing and everything. Consequently, the colors allowed identification with a side to expand beyond the boundaries of Pistoia. As the fighting increased in ferocity and scale, each side sought allies from among the citizens of the larger city of Florence. The logic of the balance of power took over. The Blacks, being related to the Donati, allied with Corso, while the Whites tied themselves to the Cerchi "so as to have powerful support to sustain them against the Donati."[33] This escalation in tensions made the Cerchi fearful of an all-out war, and so they began making alliances with the Pisans, Aretines, and Ghibelline exiles. Finally, around the year 1300, "the Donati were frightened and said that the Cerchi had made league with the Ghibellines of Tuscany. And they defamed them so much that it came to the ears of the pope."[34] And thus it came to pass that name-calling between revival Florentine patriarchs combined with a scuffle between two boys in a nearby town resulted in a catastrophe that almost ended republican rule in Florence.

The modes of the fox and the lion enter the story at this point. What we find in the events that followed are three distinct rhetorics of catastrophe that responded to the rise in civic strife. First, we find elements of what we might call *authoritarian* rhetoric, which seeks to use the presence of violence and discord as a justification to implement either one-party or one-man rule to suppress dissent and impose minority control over a population. This was the rhetoric of the wolves employed by Corso Donati and later by the Donatis' papal champion, Charles of Valois. Second, we find *republican* rhetoric, which takes the form of dialogue among political elites who rely on the good faith of promises and the integrity of institutional procedures to reduce political tensions and reinforce the legitimacy of the state. This was the type of rhetoric employed by the Whites and the republican leaders of Florence, including Compagni himself. Lastly, we find a *populist* rhetoric, in which the people take it upon themselves to enact their own form of justice in a way that exceeds legal and ethical boundaries to protect their own interests and liberties. This was the type of rhetoric that ultimately justified the modes of the fox and the lion as a way to reclaim the republic from the wolves that were tearing it apart.

Importantly, Machiavelli's narrative of these events clearly shows how the modes of the beast were used as defensive actions taken (or, in many cases, not taken) by the city in order to suppress the factional violence and preserve peace. The mode of the ferocious lion, for instance, was employed by the priors just after the institution of the Ordinances of Justice in 1295. At the time, the popolo had an early champion in the form of Giano della Bella, who had sought to vigorously enforce the ordinances against the insolence of the nobles. But then a faction led by Corso Donati successfully argued that Giano had overstepped his office and succeeded in having him expelled from the city. Without its lion, the city's ordinances were considerably weakened and the republic found itself exposed to attack. After Giano's departure, a group of nobles, orchestrated by Corso to portray itself as the victim of tyranny, rose up against the Signoria "in the hope of regaining its dignity."[35] After occupying several places in the city, representatives from the Signoria made an embassy to the leaders of the nobility in order to appeal for them to stand down, using the threat of the Florentine civil militia. Machiavelli recreates what he believed was probably said during this meeting: "They reminded the nobles that their pride and their bad government were the cause of the honors taken from them and the laws made against them, that their taking up arms now to regain by force [forza] what they had allowed to be taken from them on account of their own disunion and their evil ways was nothing other than to wish to ruin their fatherland and to worsen their own condition; and they should remember that the people were far superior to them in number, riches, and hatred, and that the nobility by which it appeared to them that they were superior to others would not fight and would not turn out to be, when it came to steel [ferro], an empty name that would not be enough to defend them against so many."[36] Particularly notable about this episode is how the priors explicitly used the threat of force (in this case of "steel," a favorite Machiavellian metonym) not to undermine civic order but to defend it. Through the mode of the lion, the wolves were chased back into their dens. According to the representatives of the republic, the nobles were deluded as to their own superiority. For once it came to force, their appeals to "nobility" would turn out to be empty because it was not backed by sufficient steel. Their bodies would bleed like any other bodies, and overwhelmed by the force of the people and their hatred, their corpses would inevitably lie in the streets or hang from tower windows. This threat of force effectively secured a few years of peace for Florence as it strove to reach the height of its power and prosperity through a revived republican order.

Yet the Florentine republic was slow to adopt the vulpine guile it needed to save it from the many traps being laid to ensure its capture and ruin. For soon there were too many wolves at the gate to be chased away. During the conflict between the Blacks and the Whites in the years that followed Giano's expulsion, Corso Donati had gained an ally in Pope Boniface (whom Dante would place in Hell). Now, under the pretense of moderating tensions between the two factions, the pope sent a new ruler to govern the city, Charles of Valois, brother to the king of France. In fact, Charles was to be the instrument by which the Whites would be suppressed. Machiavelli writes, "Thus Charles came, and although the Whites, who were then ruling, were suspicious of him, nonetheless, as he was the head of the Guelfs and had been sent by the pope, they did not dare to obstruct his coming; but, to make him a friend, they gave him authority enabling him to dispose of the city according to his own will."[37] In other words, instead of protecting themselves against the bad faith of this foreign ruler, they chose to put their own faith in the resilience of the republic and the promises of a man they did not trust. Their choice not to be like the fox thus very quickly led them straight into a trap, for "with his authority, Charles had all his friends and partisans armed."[38] Before long, the Whites (including Dante) were banished. Ironically, the force and fraud that Cicero had condemned were precisely the modes required to *protect* virtue by disarming and exposing the tyrants who ruined Dante and sent his great city into turmoil.

Unfortunately, Machiavelli's history leaves out many of the details of this period of Florentine history that could shed more light on the specific tactics employed both by Charles and by the people who resisted his rule. However, we find many of these details in the *Chronicle* of Dino Compagni, a source Machiavelli drew on heavily in his own account. Compagni provides us the firsthand narrative of these crucial events in Florentine history that show the necessity of using the virtues of the beasts to save the young republic from an early death. His account, of course, is not unbiased. Compagni became a prior during the year of Charles's arrival and was directly involved in defending the integrity of the republic against the encroaching tyranny of the Blacks and their new papal strongman. However, because Compagni directly influenced Machiavelli's retelling of history, we can use his account to better understand the lessons that Machiavelli drew from how Charles ascended to power. What we find is that Compagni clearly showed the limits of faith and reason to meet the challenge of catastrophic political crisis. Like Machiavelli, he aspired to the Ciceronian ideal of a republican order even as he recognized that the modes of the beast were necessary to protect it.

But as with all catastrophic situations, there were no easy answers. The threat the Whites faced was complicated. Charles arrived with papal support and all the appearances of being a mediator of justice and a man of peace. The reality ended up being quite different. Compagni writes that through the cleverness of Corso Donati, "the pope was persuaded to break the power of the Florentines, and so he promised to aid the Black Guelfs with the great power of Charles of Valois."[39] But characteristic of the rhetoric of authoritarianism, none of these intentions were made explicit. As a master of dissimulation, "the pope wrote that he wanted messer Charles to make peace in Tuscany, opposing those who had rebelled against the Church. This commission of peacemaker had a very good name, but its purpose was just the opposite, for the pope's aim was to bring down the Whites and to raise up the Blacks, and make the Whites enemies of the royal house of France and of the

Church."[40] The priors were being led into a trap; it seemed they could neither escape nor scare off the wolf at the door. The Signoria called a general council of the Guelf party and the craft guilds to have them declare each of their positions in writing as to whether Charles should come to Florence as peacemaker; all replied that "he should be allowed to come and should be honored like a lord of noble blood—all except the bakers, who said that he should be neither received nor honored, for he was coming to destroy the city."[41] They should have listened to the bakers.

Forgoing force or fraud, the priors adopted a republican rhetoric that sought to limit the actions of Charles through the modes of faith and reason. They requested of Charles "sealed letters promising that he would not exercise any jurisdiction over us, nor occupy any city office, whether by imperial title or any other means, nor tamper with the laws or customs of the city."[42] Charles delivered them. Invoking faith, Compagni assembled "many good citizens in the baptistry of San Giovanni" so that they would "swear a good and perfect peace among yourselves, so that the lord who is coming may find all the citizens united."[43] Standing under the newly completed golden mosaic images of Christ and the Last Judgment, Compagni delivered a speech that sought to appeal to the Florentines' highest ideals, arguing that "all alike received sacred baptism at this font, reason compels and binds you to love one another like dear brothers."[44] All those assembled complied. Compagni held out the Bible, and "while physically touching the book, they swore to uphold peace in good faith and to preserve the offices and governance of that city."[45] With these binding promises in place, on November 4, 1301, Charles arrived in Florence. The city honored him with races and jousting.

One of the clear lessons that Machiavelli learned well from Compagni's account is how futile it is to fight force and fraud with faith and reason. The moment Charles was enshrined in office with the apparent blessing of God and sanction of the state, he broke every oath he had made. The duplicity of Pope Boniface set the stage for the rapid dissolution of order: "The pope sent enticing words with one hand and with the other set this lord over us; once he saw that messer Charles had entered the city, he stopped his blandishments and used threats."[46] Specifically, the pope urged the Florentines to elect a new Signoria and allow those exiled under the ordinances to return to the city. The Black Guelfs, confident that they had the backing of the pope, prepared to take power, telling themselves that "'if' they accept it, let us seize our swords and take from them whatever we can.'"[47] Under pressure, the city agreed to the terms. As soon as the Blacks "heard that the magistrates would obey the pope they immediately armed themselves and began to attack the city with fire and sword, devastating and destroying it."[48] Meanwhile, Charles did nothing to suppress the violence. Instead, he "had his people armed and stationed them inside and outside the gates of the city."[49] Worse still, he tried to catch the priors in a snare by inviting them all to dinner. In this case, however, they finally took counsel from the fox. They courteously declined, knowing that Charles intended to "kill us outside the gate and assail the city for the Black Party."[50] The republic was technically still standing; but Compagni and the rest of the priors "were harried from all sides . . . and so they lived with trouble."[51]

Reflecting on these events, Compagni regretted that he had not acted more like the fox at the beginning. Despite his suspicions, he had placed his faith in the binding power of promises made in the eyes of God. But in the inferno of politics, there exists no divine Maker as in Dante's *Inferno* to expose the false and resist the ferocious. Consequently, "those wicked citizens, who there displayed tears of tenderness and kissed the book and showed the most ardent good will, proved to be the leaders in the destruction of the city."[52] Compagni accepts the blame for his own gullibility and lack of vulpine guile: "If there was any fraud in the words, I must suffer the penalty for it, although good intentions should not be rewarded with injury. I have shed many tears over this oath, thinking how because of it so many souls were damned for their malice."[53] Damned in the next world, perhaps, but they prospered in this one. And so Compagni captured in a phrase a proverb of political realism: "Decency is of no avail against great malice."[54] This was to be the maxim that Machiavelli would make the basis of his political theory.

The events that followed in Compagni's account demonstrate just how close the Florentine Republic had come to destruction because of its defenders' failure to embrace the virtues of the beasts to overcome the vices of humans. The priors and the embattled faction of the Whites were both slow to realize this truth. The priors, still aspiring to follow the "human" modes of republican rhetoric, placed their hopes in the power of moral and legal necessity to constrain civic violence. Compagni writes that, first, "in the councils we passed harsh and strong laws that gave the magistrates authority against whoever might start a brawl or tumult; we imposed penalties against persons and had the axe and block set up in the piazza to punish evildoers and lawbreakers."[55] Second, a holy man named Friar Benedetto suggested that the bishop stage a religious procession throughout the city: "We followed his advice, though many sneered at us, saying that it was better to sharpen the swords."[56] But the effect of these rules was to prevent the Whites themselves from adopting the mode of the lion to chase away Charles's wolves. Although they were aligned with the popolo grasso who dominated the Signoria, they were reluctant to violate the harsh laws passed by their own friends that threatened to punish anyone who assembled a private troop of armed men. As a result, they obeyed the law and did nothing, cowering in their homes, while the laws were then freely broken by their enemies, who feared no reprisal. Compagni, once again, chastised these actions as foolish and cowardly, writing that "friends should not have believed that their own friends would have put them to death for trying to save their city, despite the ordinance."[57] And Compagni regretted, too, that they had not pursued the wolves with more leonine ferocity: "The Priors strove hard to defend the city from the malice of their adversaries, but nothing worked because they used peaceful means when they should have been strong and violent."[58] In Compagni we thus hear the stirrings of a populist rhetoric that is frustrated and disillusioned by republican pieties and begins to place hopes in the organized resistance of the masses to confront authoritarian tyranny.

But even this populist rhetoric came too late. Soon the republican bulwark collapsed. The priors had delayed too long in their tragic choice and the citizens of Florence paid the price for their complicity and naivete. On November 8, 1301, new priors were elected, all *popolani* (that is, powerful leaders emerging out of the popolo and not the magnati) of "the worst sort, and powerful in their party."[59] Compagni names names—the Alberti, della Tosa, Spini, Slaterelli, Frescobaldi, and Scali—and laments their complicity with the coming terror: "Oh you, *popolani*, who craved office and sucked the honors and occupied the palaces of the magistrates, where was your defense? In lies, simulating and dissimulating, blaming your friends and praising your enemies, merely to save yourselves."[60] Suffering came in waves. An authoritarian political strategy took hold that consolidated power by setting one faction above another and allowing its members free reign to suppress the opposition. First, the priors of the new Signoria passed many ordinances that enabled virtually any citizen to be accused of conspiracy and be fined a thousand florins. Those who refused were fined nonetheless and their goods confiscated, but even "those who obeyed the summons, paid the fine; and then, accused of new crimes, they were expelled from Florence without the slightest compassion."[61] Second, as he perceived an opportunity to enrich himself, "the time had come for messer Charles of Valois, a lord given to lavish and uncontrolled spending, to reveal his wicked intentions, and so he began to try to extort money from the citizens."[62] For instance, Charles had even a good man like Rinuccio di Senno Rinucci, who had received Charles at his house, "arrested and demanded a ransom of four thousand florins, or else he would send him to Apulia as a prisoner."[63] Third, while Charles sought to plunder the citizens of their wealth, the Blacks and their allies gave full license to their desires and hatred: "One enemy attacked the other: houses were set afire, robberies were committed, and belongings fled from the homes of the powerless. The powerful Blacks extorted money from the Whites; they married young girls by force; they killed men."[64] Justice had truly fled from the city. Florence became an inverted image of Dante's *Inferno*. Compagni describes:

> Many who had formerly been unknown became great through wicked deeds. Ruling with cruelty, they exiled many citizens and made them into rebels and condemned them in their goods and their persons. They laid waste many great houses and punished many, as they had agreed in writing among themselves. No one escaped without being punished: kinship and friendship were worth nothing, nor could the predetermined penalties be reduced or changed. New marriages were worth nothing; every friend became an enemy. Brother abandoned brother, son abandoned father. Every affection, all humanity was extinguished. They sent many into exile sixty miles from the city. They laid on them many heavy burdens and taxes and took from them great sums; many fortunes were destroyed. No accord, pity, or mercy was to be found in anyone. The greatest man was he who cried loudest: "Death, death to traitors."[65]

In April 1302 Charles sprang his final trap; under the pretext of prosecuting a traitorous conspiracy, he summoned the heads of many of the dominant families belonging to the White Guelfs and banished them. As Machiavelli notes in his *Florentine Histories*, after the Black ascendency in 1302, all of the "followers in the White party, among whom was the poet Dante, were banished, their goods confiscated, and their homes destroyed," and "they scattered in many places, seeking new fortune with new trials."[66] Charles's authoritarian tactics had dominated the opposition by using political divisions as a pretext for taking power; then he had fanned further violence into a conflagration that took on the appearance of a catastrophe. Finally, he could point to this catastrophe as further warrant for asserting total domination of the city.

During all of this time, of course, Corso Donati had not been idle. He and his party had been the primary beneficiary of Charles's campaign of terror. And soon he, too, would have the opportunity to orchestrate his own campaign. For despite all of Charles's success, he did not wish to be a lifelong ruler. He was an adventurer. So once his victory was complete, Charles simply filled his pockets with money and left Tuscany to fight the Aragonese for possession of Sicily. He left the city under the rule of Corso Donati and the Blacks, who continued to torture and exploit the powerless who remained. But soon a populist rhetoric arose to resist Corso's faction, while even those within his own party began to be suspicious of his desires to install himself as the city's *signore* (that is, its tyrant and sole leader). As Machiavelli narrates the denouement of his life, Corso "thought he would make the indecency of his intent appear decent with a decent cause, and he slandered many citizens who had administered public money, saying that they had used it for private comforts and that it would be well to find them out and punish them."[67] New factions began to form between Corso and the magnati on one side and the Signoria and the popolo on the other.

Over the coming years, Corso would be exiled twice and then twice seek to return. Finally, on October 6, 1308, suffering gout that made it impossible to walk or to fight, "he let himself fall off his horse; and when he was on the ground, his throat was cut by one of the men leading him."[68] Machiavelli eulogized him this way: "Such was the end of Messer Corso, from whom his fatherland and the party of the Blacks realized many goods and many evils; and had he been of a quieter spirit, his memory would be more prosperous."[69] For eight years Corso had agitated to become a signore, leaving devastation and division in his wake. Compagni describes him as "full of malicious thoughts, cruel and astute" and who "lived dangerously and died reprehensibly."[70] We might be tempted to conclude that he allowed animalistic impulses to overwhelm his human reason, but this would falsify the truths of nature. Corso used his human faculty reason to rationalize his uniquely human greed, and his rule ended only after the foxes sniffed out his duplicity and the lions ripped out his throat.

Should one prefer to use inappropriate animal epithets, one might accuse men like Charles and Corso of being "beasts" rather than men, or perhaps half-men, half-beasts. But what type of lion ties the arms of its prey with a rope and hangs it from a winch until they confess before cutting off its head? And what type of fox makes oaths on the Bible and invites people to dinner so he can have them all assassinated? No, the matter stands quite the opposite. The lion protects its pride by rushing to frighten predators who would devour its children while the fox perceives and escapes the snares of those that would capture and kill it for its fur coat. Machiavelli learned from Compagni's account that there is no shame in adopting the modes of the beast if employed against opponents of great malice. Compagni regretted for the rest of his life that he had trusted in the modes of reason, law, and faith in a situation rife with spitefulness, corruption, and greed. Had he and the other priors of Florence roused the force of the lion, they would not have been trapped like mice cowering in their homes. Had they employed the fraud of the fox they would not have been led like lemmings to their own destruction by those whose oaths were duplicitous and hollow. By holding themselves to a false ideal of what it meant to be "human" they allowed themselves to be treated like swine.

In his reading of Florentine history, Machiavelli clearly despised Charles of Valois and saw Corso Donati as a source of corruption in the city, despite the fact that both men might conform to the stereotypical image of the kind of "prince" he is often said to celebrate. By contrast, Machiavelli's imagined oration portrayed the representatives of the early republic with respect and showed how their arguments dignified the state when they could be backed by the loyalty and military force of its citizens. The combined lesson of Compagni and Machiavelli is that a state secures its freedom only when it has the arms to defend itself, the cleverness to see beyond lies, and the prudence not to trust that decency alone can defeat great malignancy. None of this is to say that reason is irrelevant. Reason, as Machiavelli stresses, has a crucial place within a republican order. Indeed, he states quite clearly that reason is the mode most proper to human beings. But when wolves who care nothing for such promises threaten that order from outside, one needs the modes of the beast to make reason effective.

If we take this early episode in Florentine history as representative of the modes of the beast, we can see that the strategies of the fox and the lion are neither to manipulate the powerful through blackmail nor institute a violent rebellion. That would be simply to regress to the fraud and force condemned by Cicero. The point is more subtle. Machiavelli neither encourages the reckless use of lies and violence (which can only serve to destroy the power one possesses) nor discourages the use of reason (which in fact represents the ideal instrument of politics). As he writes when justifying his own arguments, "I do not judge nor shall I ever judge it to be a defect to defend any opinion with reasons, without wishing to use either authority or force for it."[71] What Machiavelli says about his own work thus also applies in the realm of civic life—although with qualification. Reason can only function as a medium of order among citizens who hold to a common good and are protected from the vices of malignant actors by the virtues of the beasts. But when it lacks both authority and force, reason is a largely useless weapon against evil. From Machiavelli's perspective, Compagni was not wrong for valuing faith and reason; he was wrong for believing they could, on their own, defeat ambition and greed. Reason, in short, must often be able to defend itself with something other than reason.

There is much in the narratives of Machiavelli and Compagni that resonates with the warnings of Levitsky and Ziblatt. Like the embattled priors of Florence under Charles, Levitsky and Ziblatt struggle to answer the questions of, first, whether or not an aspiring autocrat "will subvert democratic institutions or be constrained by them," and, second, how political leaders of established parties might "work to prevent them from gaining power in the first place."[72] What they fear the most is what they call a descent into a "politics without guardrails" in which autocrats translate every potential loss into "a full-blown catastrophe."[73] Many of the tactics of authoritarian rhetoric they identify were employed by Charles of Valois, including restricting basic civil and political rights, undermining the legitimacy of elections, describing rivals as subversive, prosecuting rivals as criminals, and encouraging mob attacks and paramilitary violence. Lastly, they echo the hope of the White Guelfs that through a republican rhetoric that seeks to bolster the legitimacy of pre-existing democratic orders, political leaders, and most importantly political parties, will "heed the warning signs and take steps to ensure that authoritarians remain on the fringes, far from the centers of power."[74] For once politics without guardrails takes hold, they argue, democracies and very quickly give way to popular fascist regimes that destroy freedom from within.

Yet Machiavelli departs from their analysis in distinct ways. Whereas Levitsky and Ziblatt double down on the necessity to stay firmly within democratic (or what Machiavelli would call republican) modes of action, Machiavelli openly embraces the use of deception and violence when one is driven into a corner. In fact, Machiavelli suggests there should be no restraints on action that threatens the liberty of a state. Speaking in the *Discourses* of the defense of the Roman Republic, Machiavelli says, "where one deliberates entirely on the safety of his fatherland, there ought not to enter any consideration of either just or unjust, merciful or cruel, praiseworthy or ignominious; indeed every other concern put aside, one ought to follow entirely the policy that saves its life and maintains its liberty."[75] In particular, Machiavelli stresses the need for the fox in cases where promises have been made through coercion. For him, "it is not shameful not to observe the promises that you have been made to promise by force; and when the force is lacking, forced promises that regard the public will always be broken and it will be without shame for whoever breaks them."[76] Levitsky and Ziblatt see these recommendations as simply abandoning democracy altogether; once those guardrails are broken, it is hard to get back on the straight and narrow path. But Machiavelli suggests it is better not to be run off the road in the first place.

When we turn to our present moment, the fox teaches us that we should be wary of keeping faith with the faithless and that we should not be bound by promises we have made to dishonest actors under coercion—whether those actors be con men, corporations, or autocrats. A fox not only learns to avoid traps but is also prepared to escape from them if caught. Today, it is the latter challenge that perhaps is most pressing. Although this chapter has focused on the immediate resistance to an aspiring authoritarian, the larger and more systematic problems we face are inherited. The past two centuries of modernity have resulted in the majority of global resources being dominated first by colonial powers and then by private corporations. Indigenous peoples, in particular, have had their land wrested from them by force only to then have the theft sanctioned by law, but the problem extends to any population unable to defend itself from industrial capital backed by force and sanctioned by authoritarian rule. Movements to reclaim expropriated land and to liberate populations oppressed by unjust laws speak to the need to reconsider the mode of the fox in terms of social justice and reparations. These issues are by no means simple. But these tragic choices must begin, from a Machiavellian standpoint at least, from the position that we might just as much perpetuate injustice by keeping faith with agreements as by violating them. Certainly, we cannot justify the wholesale pillage of fisheries, forests, and land resources in the name of protecting property rights. To do so would be akin to granting the descendants of Charles of Valois permanent private ownership over the city of Florence.

Assessing the mode of the lion is even more complicated. On the one hand, few would question the right of any people to self-defense in the face of naked aggression or tyrannical domination. We see the mode of the lion celebrated, for instance, in the story of Exodus, the revolt of Spartacus, the Boxer Rebellion, the Anglo-Zulu War, Tecumseh's leadership of Native American tribes, the Battle of Stalingrad, the Warsaw Ghetto Uprising, or the defense of Ukraine. These are just a few historical examples of efforts (many of them failed) to chase off the wolves when no other means were available. On the other hand, "self-defense" is a notoriously slippery concept often as useful to oppressors as to the oppressed. Certainly, armed resistance by oppressed peoples has always been used as a pretext for military aggression by the powerful. Furthermore, the mode of the lion is easily co-opted by radical ideologies. It is undeniable, for instance, that Confederate generals and racist lynch mobs believed their actions were justified on the basis of protecting their people and culture. In our contemporary world, the same goes for terrorist cells, ultra-right nationalist parties, or criminal narco-states. Each may use lions to chase off wolves, but there is nothing essentially virtuous about a lion or sinister about a wolf. Ultimately it depends on which side one happens to be on at the time. The only thing that is consistent about lions is the use of force.

Still, there remains a way of reconciling reason and force in Machiavelli that opens up a possibility for a more normative assessment. This is because all modes of leonine force are not created equal; some are better than others. For him, there was a very clear distinction between *good arms* and *bad arms*. Unlike today's usage, "arms" did not only refer to weapons like swords and crossbows; it also referred to the people wielding them. Consequently, to seek to possess one's "own arms" (as Cesare Borgia had done) was to recruit soldiers to your side who were both effective and loyal. As Machiavelli defines them, "one's own arms are those which are composed of either subjects of citizens or your creatures; all others are either mercenary or auxiliary."[77] Which of these three categories are "good" arms is obvious. Machiavelli at length condemns both mercenary and auxiliary arms as "useless and dangerous."[78] Mercenary arms (private soldiers who fight for pay) are lazy, untrustworthy, and often criminally duplicitous; auxiliary arms (professional soldiers borrowed from another state) may be effective in the short term but over time become threats in their own right as occupying forces. Only one's own arms, which fight out of a sense of honor and duty, can be relied upon to secure a state.

The reconciliation between reason and force thus appears in Machiavelli in the form of the relationship between good laws and good arms. Machiavelli introduces this subject in his treatment of military matters, arguing that "the principal foundations that all states have, new ones as well as old or mixed, are good laws and good arms."[79] Of the two, good arms appear to take precedence in Machiavelli's thought over good laws, because "there cannot be good laws where there are not good arms, and where there are good arms there must be good laws."[80] Regardless of priority, however, Machiavelli clearly places the good laws and good arms in a cooperative relationship. Far from being opposites, law (which is the civic institutionalization of reason) and arms (which is the civic organization of force) are complementary. Good laws require good arms in the same way that lions must protect reason by chasing off wolves. But good arms benefit from good laws by a different logic. Good laws protect the people, secure their property, provide opportunities for glory, and guarantee justice. As clearly demonstrated by the Ordinances of Justice in the early Florentine republic, a state with good laws therefore tends to inspire its citizens to take up arms willingly and openly in its defense, thereby providing the security a state requires to preserve its autonomy to develop better laws.

A Machiavellian approach to the use of force thus presumes an already established relationship between laws and arms. To use the modes of the beast does not necessarily corrupt the purity of the state, because the liberty of the state is dependent upon them. Where Levitsky and Ziblatt warn against the democracy going off of the rails through the introduction of violence, Machiavelli would say that problem is more specifically the *corruption* of arms, whether through use of mercenary forces or the shattering of unified civic arms into factional paramilitaries or forced conscripts. But whereas Levitsky and Ziblatt have little to say about what happens when this corruption occurs, Machiavelli has a very clear answer—one must respond by working to constitute one's own arms as a counterforce. What makes these arms "good" is that they come willingly from a people who share a common cause, are willing to follow a common leader, and consist of individuals with the will to sacrifice their individual lives for the sake of their collective prosperity. These are the kind of arms that eventually toppled Corso Donati and restored order to Florence.

Today, of course, is it not simply this or that state that is ensnared by traps or cornered by wolves. The entire planet has been trapped and cornered. The very lungs of the atmosphere in the Amazon rainforest are being burned out of existence along with the indigenous people who live there, and yet the forest and its people sit largely defenseless. Lacking both laws and arms, neither can resist the steady encroachment of fire and savannah. The same story can be told across the globe. As authoritarian regimes in collaboration with extraction industries strip what remains of available resources for profit, the rest of the global community looks on with anxious hand-wringing, unenforceable treaties, and well-intentioned charity. But decency is of no avail against great malice. Ultimately, a new mode of "good" arms must be developed in which people are empowered to defend themselves, renegotiate past contracts imposed through coercion, and promote justice sanctioned by international law. This does not mean the covert flooding of nations with weapons to orchestrate guerilla warfare; it means broadening, democratizing, and strengthening modes of coalition peacekeeping and defense. If we are to take seriously that our planet is on the verge of catastrophe, to reject the animalistic modes as essentially barbaric is to empower preexisting barbarism. We must consider all the modes of defense with frankness and honesty, recognizing that in our dependence on nature we also share kinship with the beasts.

CHAPTER 4

How Cruelty Makes and Then Unmakes Tyrants

NOTHING OFFENDS OUR HUMANITY MORE THAN THE SPECTACLE of cruelty. As Judith Nisse Shklar argued, any person of liberal temperament should "choose cruelty as the worst thing we do."[1] Cruelty, she reasons, effectively turns other people into mere objects made to suffer for our own pleasure or purpose. That is because cruelty represents "the willful inflicting of physical pain on a weaker being in order to cause anguish and fear."[2] Shklar's abhorrence of cruelty led her to propose making cruelty the worst of all vices. For her, this principle, when taken seriously, would even call into question cruelty committed for a "higher" aim, as in the type represented in that masterpiece of the early Renaissance, "Giotto's *Last Judgment*, where every conceivable instrument of physical torture is used against the damned."[3] To become more human, for Shklar, is to become less cruel. And we become less cruel the moment we stop seeing cruelty as a means to some higher aim or common good (including those acts done in the name of God) and begin treating it as a mode that results in the degradation of both the abuser and the abused.

But cruelty has a paradoxical character. Just as it dehumanizes its objects, it can also reaffirm the humanity of its perpetrators. Unlike the violence of the beasts, cruelty is a vice peculiar to symbol-using animals and is often performed to thing-ify the victim precisely so that the one committing cruelty can feel *more* human. Marina Levina, for instance, argues that "cruelty emerges out of an encounter between the self and the Other" and "is dependent on affective identification of a body as deserving cruelty."[4] Describing her own experience with Soviet anti-Semitism as a child, she finds cruelty to be not a sad passion but a joyous one. For her tormentors, "being cruel brought them joy—the glint in the eyes, the straightening of the posture, the smirk—the joy of the oppressor is what makes cruelty so effective as a tool of the oppression."[5] Similarly, Adam Serwer, when describing the faces of white men and women in photographs of lynchings, concludes that "their cruelty made them feel good, it made them feel proud, it made them feel happy. And it made them feel closer to one another."[6] This capacity for cruelty to bind people together by providing them a shared sense of superiority thus led Serwer to his pithy conclusion: "The Cruelty Is the Point."[7]

Machiavelli enters this debate as a particularly troubling figure for political ethics precisely because he accepted cruelty as a legitimate instrument for solidifying power and establishing order. That said, cruelty in Machiavelli is never joyful; it is always coolly instrumental. Machiavelli treated cruelty, in itself, as the violent subjection of another person or group to emotional, physical, and social suffering. Cruelty was an instrument used primarily to reduce the power or prestige of an opposing group through a shocking display. But Machiavelli warned against the use of continued cruelty of the type described by Levina and Serwer. Machiavelli accepted cruelty only under strict limits that made it acutely experienced rather than chronically endured. Machiavelli, in other words, strips cruelty of its popular association with racism and bigotry and turns it into a dispassionate tool for consolidating political power. Shklar describes the appeal of the Machiavellian outlook on cruelty this way: "The usual excuse for our most unspeakable public acts is that they are necessary. . . . To respond to danger is one thing, but necessity in the Machiavellian vocabulary means far more than that. It expresses a great confidence in controlling events once they have been intelligently analyzed. To master necessity is to rule. It is, together with the subduing of Fortune, quite within the power of an astute ruler. Once necessity has been mapped and grasped it is just a matter of plotting and executing. This is the utopianism of efficiency, with all the cruelty and treachery that it invites."[8] A better description of the tone of Machiavelli's realist style could hardly be found. Within his work, any means can be justified once they are incorporated into a Machiavellian political calculus that guarantees specific outcomes. Antonio Gramsci, for instance, explains this style as one that assumes an "effective reality" underlying our symbolic universe, a reality constituted by "a relation of forces in continuous motion and shift of equilibrium" that in turn is "the only realistic and historicist interpretation of reality, it alone is history in the making of philosophy in the making, it alone is politics."[9] Cruelty is simply one more relation of force to be calculated in the algorithms of politics. The only question then becomes one of comparative utilitarian analysis reminiscent of the familiar lifeboat ethics of catastrophe.

Machiavelli, therefore, does not celebrate cruelty in the abstract; he is not sadistic. He only praises specific acts of cruelty for their instrumental benefit while condemning others for their inefficiency. Cruelty in Machiavelli's thought thus means a form of violence that exceeds any purely practical function (like that of assassination or territorial war) in order to achieve its aims by explicitly producing pain, distress, shock, or terror in either the target or those witness to the act. For instance, Machiavelli praises the Greek tyrant Agathocles, who was known for his cruelty. Machiavelli holds him up as a model of imitation for those "who ascend to a principality by some criminal and nefarious path."[10] Agathocles emerges in Machiavelli's account as a model of self-reliance. Born in 361 BCE and enduring a mean and abject childhood, he kept to a life of crime, but "his crimes were accompanied with such a virtue of spirit and body that when he turned to the military, he rose to its ranks to become praetor of Syracuse."[11] Finally, he decided to become a tyrant through adopting the methods of violence and deception: "One morning he assembled the people and Senate of Syracuse as if he had to decide things pertinent to the republic. At a signal he had ordered, he had all the senators and the richest of the people killed by his soldiers. Once they were dead, he seized and held the principate of that city without any civil controversy."[12] Agathocles then displayed his skills as a military leader when he successfully defended the city against the Carthaginians. Using these modes, he established and secured his rule for over a decade until his death in 289 BCE, leading Machiavelli to conclude that "if one considers the virtue of Agathocles in entering into and escaping from dangers, and the greatness of his spirit in enduring and overcoming adversities, one does not see why he has to be judged inferior to any most excellent captain."[13] Agathocles is thus often paired with Cesare Borgia as two of the great examples of virtú that appear in *The Prince*.

The measure that Machiavelli uses to evaluate Agathocles's action reveals much about the way he calculated the effectual truth of actions. That standard is captured by his oxymoronic phrase, *cruelty well-used*. At this end of the same chapter, Machiavelli imagines that "someone could question how it happened that Agathocles and anyone like him, after infinite betrayals and cruelties, could live for a long time secure in his fatherland, defend himself against external enemies, and never be conspired against by his citizens."[14] His answer: "I believe that this comes from cruelties badly used or well used."[15] To utter "cruelty well-used" would be in conventional usage akin to saying an "evil good" or a "good evil." Machiavelli uses the apparent paradox to his advantage: "Those can be called well used (if it is permissible to speak well of evil) that are done at a stroke, out of the necessity to secure oneself, and then are not persisted in but are turned to as much utility for the subjects as one can. Those cruelties are badly used which, though few in the beginning, rather grow with time than are eliminated."[16] He then proceeds to give clear criteria for evaluating the modes of cruelty and sums up the mode of action this way: "In taking hold of a state, he who seizes it should review all the offenses necessary for him to commit, and do them all at a stroke, so as not to have to renew them every day and, by not renewing them, to secure men and gain them to himself with benefits."[17] Agathocles committed evil when he lured the leaders of Sicily to their death and rose to power on the terror evoked by the sight of their corpses; yet he proceeded to secure his state for over a decade through relying on self-restraint and greatness of spirit to maintain order.

The core of Machiavelli's radical and terrifying novelty is his brutally evenhanded treatment of cruelty that measures its value according to the totality of costs and benefits that accrue as a direct result of its enactment over a specific period of time. Yet this evaluation must also be done in comparison with its alternative, which in this case might be generosity, tolerance, and mercy. Notably, Machiavelli also gives voice to this opposing position. Although Agathocles managed to cling to power, Machiavelli writes, he cannot fully praise him for his virtú. For "one cannot call it virtue to kill one's citizens, betray one's friends, to be without faith, without mercy, without religion; these modes can enable one to acquire empire, but not glory."[18] Consequently, despite the fact that Agathocles might be considered among the most excellent captains, "his savage cruelty and inhumanity, together with his infinite crimes, do not permit him to be celebrated among the most excellent men."[19] Typical of Machiavelli's dialectical mind, he begins by recommending imitation of Agathocles's tactical use of cruelty but concludes by condemning the overall quality of both his character and his rule. Whatever benefits Agathocles gained with cruelty could not compensate for his loss of glory—which is to say his enduring reputation for honor, greatness, and virtue among the people. As Shklar wryly observes, "even Machiavelli had noted that an indiscriminate butcher was not likely to enjoy the best of reputations in history, even if he should have succeeded in all his enterprises."[20]

In addition, Machiavelli acknowledges a limiting condition to cruelty. This limit is reached when it produces a counterforce of hatred. According to Winter, Machiavelli defined hatred as a "general hostility" that takes the form of "a kind of vengefulness, a desire to retaliate."[21] One arouses hatred when acts of cruelty leave lasting memories of pain, suffering, and humiliation in their wake that sow seeds of vengeance. More than just sudden anger at the injustice or offense of a particular action, hatred represents a burning contempt and disdain for the character of an individual or group, combined with a desire for their cruel annihilation. The ways of avoiding hatred are quite specific in Machiavelli: "This he will always do if he abstains from the property of his citizens and his subjects, and from their women; and if he also needs to proceed against someone's life, he must do it when there is a suitable justification and manifest cause for it. But above all, he must abstain from the property of others, because men forget the death of a father more quickly than the loss of a patrimony."[22] Interpreted as a literal recommendation to indiscriminately kill people's fathers, these rules appear to conform to the profile of Machiavelli as little more than a gangster; yet I believe they are best interpreted as efforts to *limit* cruelty by princes all too willing to massacre enemies at a stroke. Understood this way, Machiavelli strictly condemns the modes of rape and extortion while limiting lethal punishment only to cases in which there is a suitable justification and manifest cause. Such actions certainly do not produce affection for the perpetrator; but in Machiavelli's view, they do leave open space for an eventual reconciliation and the possibility of restoring the rule of law.

The constraints that Machiavelli places on cruelty has led some scholars to find in his attitude a useful corrective to the absolutism of Shklar's abhorrence for cruelty. For instance, Thomas Osborne argues that "Machiavelli can also be a positive resource for such a liberalism, on the one hand in providing a nuanced account of a kind of calculus of fear and cruelty in political life, and on the other in laying down some of the rudiments of a prudentialist take on politics."[23] From this perspective, Machiavelli represents the objective attitude of a political strategist who must evaluate every mode action, regardless of traditional labels of "good and evil"; he recommends adopting those courses of action appropriate to the situation, relative to one's end, and most importantly in recognition of shifts and changes in the times. A good leader therefore must constantly be prepared to change modes when the situation demands it. Machiavelli makes this need for constant adaptation clear in a personal letter, explaining that "because times change and the pattern of events differs . . . the man who matches his way of doing things with the conditions of the times is successful; the man whose actions are at odds with the times and the pattern of events is unsuccessful."[24] For instance, "cruelty, treachery, and impiety are effective in providing a new ruler with prestige in that region where human kindness, loyalty, have long been common practice, just as human kindness, loyalty, and piety are effective where cruelty, treachery, and impiety reigned for a while, for just as bitter things irritate the taste and sweet things cloy it, so men become impatient with the good and complain about the bad."[25] Most often, situations call for a mix of the two modes, each targeting different audiences. Thus, the most prudent choice falls somewhere in between.

Strauss characterizes this "in between" position as the "Machiavellian mean." Although Strauss ultimately rejects this position as a debasement of higher morality, he nonetheless accurately captures its character. Using the example of fraud and cruelty, Strauss writes, "According to Machiavelli, the right course regarding fraud is the middle course between the unqualified rejection of fraud and its unqualified approval. Humanity is praiseworthy and makes a man loved whereas cruelty is detestable and makes a man hated; yet the 'true way' consists in not desiring 'too much' to be loved and therefore in not being too humane; it consists in a certain combination of humanity and cruelty . . . The true way consists therefore in the alternation between virtue and vice: between gravity (or full devotion to great things) and levity, constancy and inconstancy, chastity and lasciviousness, and so on . . . That alternation is a movement guided by prudence and sustained by strength of mind, will or temper."[26] Machiavelli provides, through his method of calculating the effectual truth, a framework whereby all possible paths and destinations can be evaluated according to the same measure and then compared and contrasted without prejudice or contempt. The acquisition of virtú is dependent on acquiring the mastery of this calculus. And from the perspective of political realism, this is a demanding ethic. Machiavellian virtú demands a total accounting of the possible impacts of our actions on ourselves and others before committing oneself to a specific mode.

As much as he often praised "impetuosity," for instance, this should not be confused with impulsiveness. The bold and impetuous came to their decisions only after perceiving that the latter were the only courses capable of overcoming great necessity. Similarly, one who adapts a strategy closer to a "mean" has (ideally at least) done so in careful consideration of multiple audiences and their complex relation of forces. Nothing in Machiavelli demands that we must always choose cruelty over love. What is important is to be able to arrive at one's choice only after having been open to all alternatives through critical analysis. The Machiavellian mean is not an absolute target, as if one must always fall between good and evil; it represents a method of thinking and inquiry whose first tenet is that every option should be on the table. The subsequent evaluation of alternatives then must be guided by prudence and sustained by strength of mind, steadiness of temper, and force of will.

Before passing judgment on Machiavelli's position, I find it useful to think, for a moment, of the ways in which the dispassionate, calculating attitude of his political realism finds expression in our own time. And we must admit to ourselves, particularly in light of its popularity in film and entertainment, that many of us are attracted to its methods. On the one hand, nothing arouses our anger as much as acts of cruelty. Mass shootings, terror attacks, mob violence, honor killings, genocidal wars—the images of these events make us despise the perpetrators and condemn their methods. On the other hand, these acts of cruelty inspire in us the desire to enact cruelty in turn. The suffering of innocents often provokes a desire to unleash cruelty against those who preach and commit cruelty. This is the logic of punitive and redemptive violence. The decision to be peaceful is simple when one lives with security and well-being; it becomes something quite different when it seems that the only way to resist being a victim of cruelty is to commit it against those who we feel are evil. Turning the other cheek may seem noble when the one who suffers is oneself; but a part of us feels responsible if our refusal to enact cruelty results in the suffering of others. Who among us would not wish, at some level, to enact cruel vengeance upon those who tortured and killed our loved ones? We flock to the theaters to witness these acts and live vicariously through the vigilantes and action heroes whose cruelty redeems suffering. The temptation is there. Let us not flatter ourselves by condemning Machiavelli for what we often contemplate in our own hearts and imaginations. If we are not to thoughtlessly enact or sanction cruelty, we need a better mirror with which to see ourselves.

The starting point for this method of judgment is to clearly define the nature of the modes being considered. Cruelty, for instance, should not be understood simply in terms of the pain inflicted on another. Cruelty as a mode of political action has a fundamentally *rhetorical* nature. As Winter argues in his critique of Machiavelli's orders of violence, "it is worth looking at Machiavelli not just as a practitioner of rhetoric but also as an analyst of the rhetorical and performative dimension of violence" who highlights "its theatrical and communicative aspects."[27] In Winter's analysis, Machiavelli uses three distinct terms to identify three distinct modes. First, force (forza) represents a purely instrumental application of force, as in the deployment of military arms for attack or defense. Second, violence (*violenza*) refers to a force that commits an injustice; it is "associated with criminal behavior, with a lack of legitimacy, and with unjust force used against free cities and institutions."[28] Finally, cruelty (*crudeltà*) is reserved for "an essentially offensive, provocative, and often scandalous mode of violence" that "involves a transgression that strategically elicits shock and awe."[29] Whereas both force (as in a military assault on a city) and violence (as assassination of an opponent in the dark of night) can achieve their ends without publicity, cruelty of the type that brought Agathocles to power requires an audience to achieve its political ends. According to Winter, cruelty represents a form of distinctly *political* violence that represents "a performance, elaborately staged, and designed to be perceived, experienced, remembered, and narrated."[30] For instance, Dante's *Inferno* is written by the pilgrim author to retell the terrors he witnessed so that the living might keep alive in their memory the fateful end of unrepentant sinners. Machiavelli simply applies to political inferno the lessons of cruelty that Dante attributed to God the Maker. One saves the lives of the many through the shocking violence against the few or the one.

When Machiavelli describes cruelty as well or poorly used, he does not simply refer to whether force or violence has been instrumentally deployed to eliminate opponents or punish the opposition; he refers to whether an act of political violence has communicated the right kind of message by producing an effective public spectacle directed for or against specific audiences. According to Winter, "cruelty is a type of physical violence that traffics in appearances and deploys such appearances in a calculated manner: It is indissociable from the imagination, and it constitutes strategic acts of violence disguised as irrational and senseless."[31] What makes it so powerful, however, is that these apparently irrational and senseless acts are specifically intended to challenge aspects of the established order. Consequently, "cruelty produces its effects by violating a social expectation, by breaching a certain presumption of privilege" in a way that produces "the phantasmatic images that evoke passionate responses."[32] Cruelty is effective not just because it uses violence but also because it violates the norms and privileges that are intended to preserve and protect the dignity of certain classes of persons. For instance, when Mark Antony executed Cicero and nailed his hands and tongue to the rostrum, he did not simply offend Cicero's reputation; Antony offended the entire *class* of senators to which he belonged and its accompanying rights, privileges, and honors.

A vivid metonymy Machiavelli uses to reduce the abstract character of cruelty to a concrete object or action is the phrase "cut to pieces." As John McCormick notes, "Machiavelli uses this image repeatedly; indeed one might think it to be his favorite recourse against elites."[33] For instance, in the *Discourses* he describes how in the fourth century BCE the aristocrats of the city of Heraclea on the Black Sea invited the exiled tyrant Clearchus back to the city in order to suppress the people from whom they had taken their freedom. Yet on returning, Clearchus found himself trapped uncomfortably "between the insolence of the aristocrats, whom he could not in any mode either make content or correct, and the rage of the people, who could not endure having lost their freedom."[34] Caught in the middle, Clearchus sought a mode to "free himself at one stroke from the vexation of the great and the win over the people to himself."[35] The answer was the mode of cruelty: "Having taken a convenient opportunity for this, he cut to pieces all the aristocrats, to the extreme satisfaction of the people."[36] To have simply eliminated them would not have been enough to earn the people's support; Clearchus had to show his disregard for aristocratic privilege by cutting them into small pieces. By this mode, he not only eliminated the aristocracy through instrumental violence but also satiated the yearning of the people by allowing them the spectacle of being avenged upon their oppressors. Similarly, Machiavelli describes how, when the tyrant Hiero took control of Syracuse in the fifth century BCE, he was suspicious of the loyalty of the mercenary military used by the prior regime. Knowing "he could neither keep them nor let them go, he had them all cut to pieces, and then made war with his arms and not with alien arms."[37] The cruelty he showed to the mercenaries communicated hatred for the entire class of foreign soldiers and solidified his loyalty to native Syracusans' arms. In both cases, Clearchus and Hiero used cruelty as a tactic of political violence carefully designed to have rhetorical impact on a popular audience of witnesses.

To more properly stimulate our historical imaginations, however, I believe we must move beyond these familiar and ancient examples found in Machiavelli. It is too easy to dismiss such tactics as holdovers from a more savage age or simply treat them as almost comic-book examples. We need to better identify with people both suffering and enacting cruelty in order to put ourselves in their position. I believe we find an ideal case in the experience of the Florentine people in the fourteenth century. Almost four decades after the death of Corso Donati, cruelty reappeared in Florence with the arrival of Walter of Brienne, the "Duke of Athens," in June 1342. During this time, cruelty was suffered and enacted by both sides. Walter of Brienne followed the authoritarian playbook by using cruelty to divide and oppress the people, causing humiliation and fear to one population while gratifying and empowering another. But Walter's tyranny was finally brought down by a populist backlash that used cruelty against what the people saw as the sources of their oppression. We find, therefore, a complex narrative that dramatizes the limits of cruelty when imposed by a tyrant while suggesting that cruelty can be a source of liberation when done "well." The question Machiavelli poses to us is whether "well" can ever be used to describe cruelty.

This period in Florentine history shows how rapidly catastrophe can fall upon a city. Indeed, the greater the prosperity before a catastrophe strikes, the more the event is felt to be catastrophic. As Machiavelli recounts in his *Florentine Histories*, the duke's arrival came after several relatively prosperous decades for Florence. From 1328 until 1340, the city "remained quiet inside and attended only to the affairs of their state outside," thus giving Florentines the time and resources to adorn the city with new buildings, including what it now known as Giotto's Tower in the Duomo complex.[38] Yet "when the year 1340 came, new causes of change arose."[39] Contemporary chronicler Giovanni Villani (1275–1348) laments, for instance, how "God, for our sins, inflicted on our city so many punishments in so short a time: flood, crop failures, famine and sickness, defeats, failed ventures, loss of capital, failure of merchants, [and] unpaid debts."[40] These sufferings and humiliations once again inflamed tensions between the magnati and the popolo, with the traditional ruling class blaming the people for poor governance while the people blamed the powerful nobles for having exploited and squandered the city's wealth. Finally, a foreign policy disaster threatened to burn down the republic.

The event that sparked the catastrophe of 1342 arrived, like the previous catastrophe, from outside the city walls. The nearby city of Lucca, long coveted by the Florentines, had come up for "sale" by the departing lord of Mastino della Scala. The competitors were the Florentines and their hated rivals, the Pisans. Fearful that the wealth of the Florentines would carry the day, the Pisans took Lucca by force, with the assistance of the Milanese tyrant. Florence responded by giving authority to twenty prominent popolani (called simply the "Twenty") to conduct a campaign to free Lucca from siege and selected Malatesta da Rimini as captain—but to no avail. The Twenty were incompetent strategists and Malatesta was a weak captain. Machiavelli remarks, "After a long war the Florentines were driven off with loss of money and acquisition of shame, and the Pisans became its lords."[41] The defeat was catastrophic for the merchant elite ruling class of the popolo grasso: "The loss of this city, as always happens in similar cases, made the people of Florence indignant against those who were governing, and in all places and through all the piazzas they defamed them publicly, accusing them of avarice and wicked counsel."[42] In an effort to save their reputations, the "Twenty, seeing the people indignant, thought to renew their hope by electing a new captain and with that election either to check or to remove the causes for the slanders against themselves."[43] Appealing to Robert of Anjou, king of Naples, for assistance, they welcomed with open arms the arrival of Walter of Brienne and 420 soldiers with the hope of restoring order to the city and propping up their own rule.

The rise and fall of the duke of Athens (a largely empty title referring to his lost patrimony in Greece) acts as a perfect microcosm by which to explore the uses and abuses of cruelty and deception in both undermining and restoring civic liberty. Unlike Charles of Valois, Walter of Brienne did not come simply to loot Florence. He desired to permanently turn the republic into a principality under his rule. Florentine First Chancellor Leonardo Bruni (1370–1444) in his *History of the Florentine People* describes the events following Walter's arrival this way: "As though heaven's wrath sought to crush her, a tyrant was imposed on the city—something that had never happened before—who took away her liberty and lusted for the blood of her citizens."[44] In Bruni's account, the year that Florence suffered under the tyranny of Walter was both a trial and a turning point, the moment at which the Florentine citizens had to decide for themselves whether to be long-suffering victims of chronic cruelty or to restore liberty by any means necessary in order to live as a free people. The Florentines chose the second course. When Bruni penned his *History* in the early fifteenth century, he felt strongly that "the subject is worth putting on record both as a warning to citizens and as a reproof to rulers. For it will become clear that citizens should fear nothing more than servitude, and lords will learn that nothing is more ruinous than immoderate and uncivil arrogance."[45] What he also put on record, however, was an argument that defended the modes of cruelty and deception as necessary means by which those citizens cast off that servitude.

The account that most vividly captures the cruelties of this period, however, is the *New Chronicle* by Giovanni Villani, the first comprehensive history of the city. Just as Dino Compagni provided a firsthand account of the factional strife between the Blacks and the White at the turn of the fourteenth century, Villani provides the most graphic description of Walter's short-lived tyranny because he had lived through it. His *Chronicle*, in fact, provides the framework of the narrative that Bruni and Machiavelli imitated when composing their own histories. His motivation for composing a history can be traced back to the attitudes of his class. Villani was a prominent member of the mercantile Guelf leadership that controlled Florence during the thirteenth and fourteenth centuries, engaging in textile trading and banking all along the peninsula and up through France, Belgium, and England. According to Rala Diakité and Matthew Sneider, his immersion in this complex network of trade with distant cultures broadened his mental horizon and made him feel connected to a widening world. Consequently, "the world was worth exploring, knowing, and documenting precisely in order to maneuver better within it, and in his *New Chronicle* he collected and offered useful market research."[46] Villani, in short, produced his *Chronicle* as a Florentine patriot so that his fellow citizens "may exercise themselves in practicing virtues, and shunning vices, and enduring adversities with a strong soul, to the good and stability of our republic."[47] His explicit purpose in documenting the rise and fall of the Duke of Athens was therefore to "provide an example to people of future generations not to seek a perpetual or lifetime lord."[48] In the process, Villani also provided examples of cruelty both well and badly used that Machiavelli would carefully study.

What is so instructive about Walter's use of cruelty in his rise to power was that it did not emerge from any particular sadistic or evil temperament; he consciously deployed cruelty as a method of authoritarian rule because it was the most effective means of accruing power within a highly divisive partisan atmosphere. Typical of catastrophic situations, a superficially unified people quickly fragmented into competing factions, each blaming the other.

Villani is particularly sensitive to these divisions. Like Compagni, he identifies the core conflict as that between the *grandi* (the magnati, or "nobles") and the popolo, which in his usage "refers to a group identity forged in a number of contexts,—guilds, neighborhood associations, religious movements—which was positioned in opposition to the truculence of the *grandi*" and exerted its influence through "political councils to provide leadership and military companies to provide muscle."[49] But Villani identifies even more complex divisions within the popolo than had Compagni, dividing it into not two but three classes: "the *popolani grassi* ('fat *popolani*') who dominated the guilds, the *popolani mezzani* ('middling *popolani*') who were the majority of the guildsmen, and the *popolani minuti* ('little *popolani*') who were the artisans and laborers."[50] These divisions are essential to the success (and failure) of Walter's cruelty. For he arrived in a situation in which great hatred had been aroused against the failed leadership of the Twenty, who came largely from the ranks of the popolo grasso and *mezzani*. Quickly sizing up the situation, Walter realized that public spectacles of cruelty against the elite classes of the popolo could create an unlikely alliance between the grandi and the popolo minuto, both of whom had largely been excluded from the power in the guild republic. His authoritarian rhetoric thus co-opted popular resentments against what the Florentines saw as a corrupt republican leadership. Villani summarizes how these hatred and schisms within the Florentine republic were directly responsible both for Walter's rise to power as well as his adoption of cruelty:

> This gentleman, seeing the city divided and being greedy for money, which he needed because he was a wayfarer and pilgrim—although he held the title to the duchy of Athens, he did not possess it—was seduced by certain grandi who were constantly seeking to destroy the ordinances of the popolo, and by certain rich popolani, who wished to be lords of the city and avoid repaying their debts to their creditors . . . These people went continually to Santa Croce, by day and night, advising him to take the lordship of the city entirely into his hands. The duke, for reasons stated above, and longing for lordship, began to follow this wicked advice. He became cruel and tyrannical, with the excuse that he was doing justice . . . in order to make himself feared, and make himself wholly Lord of Florence.[51]

We can see through Villani's account a vivid example of how the modes of cruelty can be used to solidify the power of a prince over a republic. Only a month passed before he began publicly executing and humiliating members of elite popolani (the wealthy merchant families) to the delight of the grandi and the popolo minuto. The first act was perhaps the most dramatic. In July 1342 during the Feast of Saint James, a son of a prominent popolani family and citizen of Prato by the name of Rodolfo arrived at the gates accompanied by a few dozen soldiers from exiled families seeking admittance to the city. Instead of greeting them, Walter had Rodolfo and the others arrested. His subsequent act set in motion all of the cruelty that was to come: "The duke released our exiles, over whom he had jurisdiction, but wrongly cut off the head of this Rodolfo, who was neither his subject nor an exile from Florence. This was the first act of justice he did in Florence, and he was much blamed by wise men for his cruelty."[52]

But these wise men also understood quite clearly the logic behind Walter's violence: "Just as the proverb says of tyrants: 'he who offends one, threatens many.'"[53] Making sure his threat was communicated clearly, Walter then arrested and beheaded Giovanni de' Medici (under the accusations he had conspired with the Pisan forces at Lucca) and also cut off the head of Guglielmo Altoviti (from whom he extracted a confession of corruption under torture), both leaders of some of the "greatest *popolani* houses of Florence."[54] Finally, he arrested several members of other prominent families, accusing them of corruption and treason, sparing their lives only after they made public confessions. Even then, they were imprisoned and had their money confiscated. The impact of this practical political violence was immediate: "The *grandi* grew quite bold, and the *popolo minuto* was very happy, because the duke had dared to touch the rulers, and they glorified him, crying out as he rode his horse to the city: 'Long live the Lord!' And the citizens had his coat of arms painted on nearly every corner and every house in Florence, some to curry favor and some out of fear."[55] Cruelty against the popolo grasso had paid its dividends; reinforcing the connection between cruelty and joy, the grandi and the popolo minuto took pleasure in seeing the offense done to their so-called rulers and felt empowered in the wake of their humiliation.

The modes of deception and force then followed in the wake of cruelty to strike fear into the ruling popolani and embolden their opponents. First, the duke created an alliance between numerous factions united against the rule of the popolo grasso—almost all the great houses of the grandi who "wished to destroy the Ordinances of Justice," a contingent of the popolo grasso "on account of the poor state of their companies, since the duke was propping them up," and virtually all "the lower artisans, who disliked the recent rule of the Twenty and the *popolani grassi*. All offered him their armed support."[56] Second, he choreographed a spectacle that would grant him the appearance of legitimacy and provide an opportunity for his supporters to make a show of strength. On September 8, 1342, he called a *parlamento* to be held, "an assembly of the entire citizenry, to approve the creation of a *balìa* [emergency counsel] with special authority to defend the regime."[57] With the *parlemento* looming, he then went to the reluctant priors to negotiate a new position in order to mask his authoritarian aims with republican clothes. The priors, fearing "that they were neither strong enough nor sufficiently prepared and that this *parlamento* might bring discord, clamor, and tumult to the city," agreed to a one-year lordship of the city with guarantees that he would maintain "the liberty of the *popolo*, the office of the Priors, and the Ordinances of Justice."[58] Finally, the duke arranged for soldiers to arrive unexpectedly at the parlamento and, with the support of the grandi and the popolo minuto, break down the doors of the palace, at which point he had himself proclaimed lifetime lord: "In this way and by this treachery, the Duke of Athens usurped the liberty of our city and annulled the *popolo* of Florence—[a government] that had lasted about fifty years in great liberty, estate and power."[59]

Yet here is the crucial moment in this narrative that exemplifies the difficulty in any straightforward reading of cruelty as a successful tool of authoritarian power. For just when the modes of cruelty appeared to have solidified Walter's smooth ascendency to perpetual lordship, they began undermining his authority and power. In seeking to establish a true *signoria* in Florence (that is to say, a one-man lordship of a signore, not to be confused with the republican Signoria of the priors), Walter knew he could be beholden to no single class—especially not the grandi. Consequently, he wasted no time in humiliating and undermining his former allies. As Villani explains, "This was the way the duke pandered to and then deceived the citizens—he took away all the arrogance of the *grandi* who had made him lord, and he took away the liberty, power, and duties—all but the names—of the Priors, and he did the same to the *popolo*. He dissolved the office of the standard-bearers of the companies of the *popolo* and took away their banners, and he dissolved every other ordinance and officer of the *popolo* that did not please him."[60] He confiscated palaces and fortresses, levied heavy fines on his enemies, created corrupt courts of justice, freed prisoners and welcomed exiles hostile to the republic, negotiated peace with the Pisans, and "created a place for women of easy virtue from which his marshal drew much profit."[61] The only class left that supported him was the popolo minuto, whom he satisfied by offering greater pay for their work while associating with "the butchers, the wine cellars, the wool carders, and the lesser artisans, giving them consuls and rectors at their pleasure."[62] Yet even they eventually suffered his cruelty. Walter, as like most aspiring tyrants, quickly grew intolerant and paranoid, and "many people of little importance were wrongly killed with cruel tortures by his executioner and *conservator* of evil deeds."[63] As a result of these acts, "the very same *grandi* and *popolani* who had made him lord began to conspire against him."[64] The very modes that had brought him to power were now working to destroy him out of hatred.

Fittingly, it was the spectacle of an act of cruelty "badly used" that unified the Florentines against the duke's tyranny. As a means of flattering the popolo minuto, Walter had created new priors mostly drawn from the artisan classes (even though at the same time he had reduced their authority to almost nothing). One of these men had been "a certain Bettone Cini da Campi, one of the ox drivers of the ancient *carroccio*" (the cart that carried the city's standard into battle).[65] The duke even allowed him to be dressed in scarlet because of the dignity of the *carroccio*. But Walter's treatment of Bettone soon showed his appearances of respect for the popolo minuto to be completely hollow; his act of cruelty against the once dignified prior showed that no class of people were to be spared degradation and humiliation. Villani writes, "When his term in office was over, Bettone complained, saying some idle words regarding the tax imposed on him by the duke. The duke had his tongue torn out all the way to the roots, and had it carried around the city on a lance for laughs; he then exiled Bettone to Pesaro, where he died shortly thereafter from the cutting of his tongue."[66] The impact of this cruel treatment of Bettone had the opposite of the intended effect: "The citizens were greatly upset by this punishment, and everyone realized they could neither speak nor complain about wrongs and outrages."[67] The fact that Bettone was "a cruel *gabelliere* [customs tax collector] and had the worst tongue of any man in Florence" made no difference.[68] Following the logic of cruelty, the act had been committed not against Bettone the greedy, pitiless, loudmouth; it had been committed against a representative of the popolo minuto and former prior of the city. Villani concludes that even though one might blame the alignment of Mars and Venus in the heavens as bringing Walter to a shameful end, he attributed the true cause of his downfall to "more his bad rule and the evil works that flowed from his depraved free will, badly used."[69]

Machiavelli unambiguously agrees with Villani. In his own history, Machiavelli treats the duke of Athens with contempt. Nothing in his use of arms, deception, or cruelty is worth imitating; aspiring leaders should rather shun every mode he employed during his short rule over Florence. Although clearly drawing from Villani's account, Machiavelli narrates the duke's actions using his own distinct vocabulary. He describes, for instance, how "the assessments he levied on citizens were heavy and his sentences unjust, and the severity and humanity that he feigned were converted into arrogance and cruelty, whence many great citizens and popular nobles were either fined or killed, or tortured in new modes."[70] The citizens lived "full of indignation as they saw the majesty of their state ruined, the orders laid waste, the laws annulled, every decent being corrupted, all civil modesty eliminated."[71] And "above all else, what displeased was the violence that he and his men did, without any respect, to the women."[72] And when the duke "had the tongue of Bettone Cini cut out with such cruelty that he died of it . . . This increased the indignation of the citizens and their hatred of the duke, for the city was accustomed to do and speak about everything and with every license and could not bear to have his hands tied and his mouth sealed."[73] The result was a resurgence of populist rhetoric against authoritarian rule that united the formally divided classes against Walter's tyranny: "In three parties of three sorts of citizens three conspiracies were made: the great, the people, and the artisans. They were moved, apart from universal causes, because it appeared to the great that they were not getting back to the state; to the people that they had lost it; and to the artisans that they were losing their earnings."[74] Rather than consolidating his gains and seeking to establish a new order that satisfied multiple interests, the duke had chosen to disempower and humiliate every class interest in the city. His cruelty had made him universally hated.

In the end, the shared hatred of former enemies for the common source of their suffering brought them together in conspiracy and rebellion. This fact inspired Villani to quote another "old and coarse proverb: 'Florence doesn't move until she hurts all over.'"[75] Only when every class suffered the same cruelties and hurt in the same way were they able to finally overcome their differences and bind together as a unified power. In a final ironic turn, the duke attempted one last deception by inviting a list of three hundred prominent citizens to the palace under the pretext of consulting with them. The citizens, employing the cunning of the fox to detect a snare, let the invitation go un-answered. But the list of invitees, as Machiavelli narrates this episode, had its ironic effect: "Because each had read the list, they sought each other out and inspired each other to take up arms, preferring to die like men, arms in hand, then to be led like cattle to the slaughterhouse."[76] The duke's hit list became the medium of consolidating power against him: "In a few hours, all three conspiracies were revealed to each other and they resolved to start a tumult in the Mercato on the following day, which was 26 July 1343, and after that to arm themselves and to call the people to freedom."[77] The catastrophe of Walter's rule had led to a populist rhetoric that called for mass deployment of violence and cruelty to liberate the city.

Just as Walter's cruelty and deception had destroyed the republic, the same modes were now to be used by the conspirators to overthrow his tyranny and restore freedom. They decided to organize a tactical deception on July 26, 1343, during the Feast of St. Anne. They planned that when "the work-ers left their shops, certain rascals should feign a scuffle in the Mercato Vec-chio and in the Porta San Piero and cry out, 'to arms, to arms!' And so they did."[78] On this cue, citizens organized themselves around their banners and cried out, "Death to the Duke and to his followers, and long live the *popolo* and the Florentine commune and liberty!"[79] Initially the duke's men made a show of force on their mounted horses while his remaining allies gathered in the Piazza of the Prior "shouting 'long live the duke!' But when they realized that almost all the citizens were moved to fury against him, they returned to their homes and followed the *popolo*."[80] This show of power was impressive. Villani in particular was struck by what he saw gathered in the city square: "There were more than ten thousands citizens armed with cuirasses and hel-mets like knights, not to mention the armed *popolo minuto*, and not counting foreigners or the people from the *contado* [the countryside]—this *popolo* was something most admirable to see, powerful and united."[81] Faced with the people wielding their "own arms," the remainder of the duke's forces fled in-side the Palazzo dei Priori. Deception and arms had forced the duke and his soldiers to retreat; now only the spectacle of cruelty could overcome his re-maining resistance.

The subsequent actions described by Villani are more horrific than any-thing found in Machiavelli. The people attacked the palace by day and hunted down Walter's officials by night. First they found a notary of Walter's regime, "a man who had been cruel and criminal, he was cut into morsels."[82] Then they found a man "who had been a treasury official for the commune, a man who had cruelly tortured and condemned many citizens, some rightly and some wrongly, and he was also cut to pieces."[83] Another notary and captain of the duke's sergeants, "a cruel and criminal man, was cut into morsels by the *popolo*."[84] Seeing the cruelty brought upon other members of the duke's entourage, the man in charge of collecting customs' taxes "fled from the Church of the Servites in a friar's habit [but] was recognized at San Gallo; he was killed and his naked body was dragged by children through the whole city; finally, he was hung by his feet in the piazza of the Priors and gutted and impaled like a pig."[85] The sight of his mutilated corpse had its intended effect. From inside the palace walls, men from Burgundy who had worked for the duke abandoned him, negotiating with the popolo for their release if they betrayed the duke and his leadership. Quickly sizing up his situation, the duke persuaded the Burgundians to satisfy the hatred of the people by giving them their most hated object—the conservator who had orchestrated the torture, imprisonment, and death of so many citizens. Villani narrates:

> On Friday, 1 August, around dinnertime, the Burgundians seized Messer Guglielmo d'Assisi, the conservator of the duke's tyrannies, and his eighteen-year-old son, whom the duke has recently made a knight, but truly he was criminal and treacherous in his torturing of the citizens, and they pushed him through the gate of the palace into the hands of the angry *popolo*, into the hands of the relatives and friends of the man his father had punished . . . In the presence of the father, to cause more pain, these men took the son and cut him limb from limb into tiny pieces right before his father's eyes. This done, the conservator was pushed out and they did the same to him. People carried pieces of their flesh through the city on lances or swords, and some were so cruel—filled with bestial fury and hatred—that they ate their flesh raw and cooked. Such was the end of the traitor and persecutor of the *popolo* of Florence. And note that whoever is cruel, cruelly must die *dixit Domino* ["thus sayeth the Lord"].[86]

Adding color to his own version of this incident, Machiavelli adds the sensual component to the act of cruelty that gives this mode is unique intensity: "And so that all their senses might be satisfied in revenge, having first heard the wails, seen their wounds, and handled their torn flesh, they still wanted their taste to relish them; so as all the parts outside were sated with them, they also sated the parts within."[87] The duke's desperate stratagem had its intended effect. In Villani's words, "As soon as this furious vendetta was carried out, the anger of the *popolo* was soothed and satisfied."[88] Having assented to the cruel rendering into pieces of his closest allies, the duke revealed himself to be powerless. And in Machiavelli's final analysis, rightly so: "As his governing demonstrated, this duke was avaricious and cruel, difficult in audiences, arrogant in replies; he wanted the slavery and not the good will of men; and for this he desired to be feared rather than loved."[89] Thus, on the third of August, he negotiated the surrender of the palace and safe passage from the city. Villani concludes this history by writing, "Such was the end of the lordship of the Duke of Athens, usurped through trickery and treachery from the commune of the *popolo* of Florence, and such was the end of this tyrannical rule—just as he betrayed the commune, so he was betrayed by the citizens."[90]

Cruelty as described by Villani had a power unmatched by any brute force or deceptive appearance; it had the capacity to penetrate city walls and strike terror directly into the souls of its targets. Cruelty had only one precondition—it had to be directly witnessed for it to do its persuasive work. The morsels and pieces that were once human beings had to be piled up before the walls or hurled over the battlements; the bowels and organs hidden inside the magistrate had to spill out over the city square below the sliced-open carcass; the father had to watch his own son torn to pieces before the entire city bore witness to their Dionysian dismemberment and participated in the subsequent feast. These spectacles rival anything found in Dante's *Inferno*. The duke and his men peering through the windows suffered vicariously the fate of their former friends and allies and undoubtedly placed their hands on their guts to assure themselves their bodies remained intact. But most importantly, the spectacle of cruelty disabused them of hope. There would be no restoration of the duke's power in Florence. He could not wait for reinforcements or for the rage of the people to subside. These acts of cruelty definitively communicated to the duke that there were only two ways out, either as a humiliated and penitent exile or in pieces that would eventually work their way through the people's digestive tracts. He chose exile. And by finally forcing his departure, cruelty had restored liberty to the city.

Machiavelli's treatment of the Florentine rebellion of 1343 demonstrates that all cruelty is not created equal. The cruelty of Walter, orchestrated by authoritarian rhetoric, may have won him short-term control but at the price of destabilizing the city and bringing about the duke's own ruin. Machiavelli condemns every action taken by the duke of Athens, adding a rather comic note that he also "had a long and sparse beard, so that in every way he deserved to be hated."[91] Walter had not sought to establish a new order of justice in Florence; he had come to destroy a functioning republic and install himself as signore. He had betrayed every constituency, exploited for his own gain every division, and used cruelty indiscriminately until he had destroyed the state and become universally hated. In contradistinction, both Villani and Machiavelli agree that the cruelty employed by the people of Florence successful reestablished their republic and saved hundreds of citizens from being extorted, raped, exiled, and killed. The people had gathered their forces, rebelled en masse at the right moment, and employed cruelty with just vengeance and tactical prudence in one spectacle designed specifically to overthrow a tyranny. Machiavelli, in his cool-headed rationality, tries to strip cruelty of its evil and turn it into simply another mode of action. But Villani goes further by praising acts of dismemberment and cannibalism as a punishment by God. For Villani, Walter had been sent as divine punishment for Florence's sins and the people had in turn acted as the arm of God's vengeance upon Walter's transgressions.

That both Villani and Machiavelli took the time to observe the pleasure the people took in cruelty should not be overlooked. Even Machiavelli seems to take vicarious joy in describing how the mob tore their persecutors into morsels, dismembering a child before his own father and literally eating the flesh of their enemies. Yet he leaves this aspect out of his political calculus. We cannot afford to do so. Machiavelli, for his part, correctly theorizes the nature and function of cruelty, identifies its limits, and shows the consequences of its overuse. Cruelty, in his writing, is only "well-used" when performed all at once to eliminate an enemy, but it then must be replaced by more ordinary modes to avoid producing hatred. All of these principles play out in the rise and fall of Walter of Brienne. But while Machiavelli acknowledges the dangers in provoking hatred in the victims, he ignores the enduring effects of cruelty on the character of both perpetrator and victim alike. Cruelty may have forced Walter into exile, but at the price of extreme dehumanization that not only turned opponents into mere body parts but also transformed ordinary citizens into torturers and cannibals.

Just as Shklar's liberalism of fear describes, the Florentines' actions exposed and then reinforced the cruelty behind Villani's medieval providentialism. By making God the father of the feast, the cruelty of men turns God into a monster. Cruelty thus had effects far beyond those calculated in Machiavelli's political realism, not least of which is the corruption of the human personality. In reflecting on this narrative, therefore, I am left with mixed feelings. I cannot help but celebrate the successful resistance of the Florentines to their oppressive ruler, and I must even admit a certain satisfaction in witnessing the people's execution of their own torturers. Yet I am troubled by the fact that this extreme cruelty likely had ethical and political consequences that endured long after their tactical victory. To achieve power through cruelty, no matter the nobility of the aim, establishes cruelty not only as a legitimate mode but as a joyous one. And particularly in today's mediated environment, when joy is paired with cruelty and sanctioned by culture, religion, and politics, one is never without an available justification to see oneself as the instrument of God's vengeance. Machiavelli tends to look at these moments as isolated outbursts of passion. But today, cruel passions can be systematically stimulated and organized through propaganda, resulting in a normalization of cruelty enacted for its own sake. Should an event such as the liberation of Florence from Walter of Brienne occur today, it would not mark the end of drama but the beginning of a nightmare.

Therefore, if we understand cruelty strictly in terms of violence against the bodies of others for the purpose of terror and humiliation, Shklar is justified in calling cruelty the worst thing we can do. In this sense, I believe that in our contemporary life there is almost no justification to follow Machiavelli's recommendation to cut one's enemies into morsels, even if they should be genocidal dictators. I say this not out of some categorical imperative but from the calculus of effectual truth. The ease by which such cruelty is disseminated today creates the potential for chain reactions of unforeseen consequences that inevitably creates an atmosphere of terror. And as Albert Camus once warned, when terror reigns, it inevitably transforms people into either executioner or victim—usually both. Yet to understand this effect is also to understand the logic of terror itself. By making it clear, Machiavelli provides a way to resist the psychological impact of terror by anticipating its strategy and blunting its impacts. Cruelty feeds off of spectacle. We defeat cruelty not by returning it in kind but by suffocating and denying it.

Yet if we understand cruelty as *any* form of humiliation, quite apart from acts of violence, I do not believe cruelty can ever be avoided in times of radical change. Humiliation, as we have seen, involves a symbolic kind of cruelty that harms one's sense of pride and integrity by exposing oneself and one's "class" to public criticism and ridicule. In our everyday life, of course, humiliation in the form of things like racism, misogyny, bigotry, and hate speech is rightly condemned. But there is also the humiliation that comes from social change itself. Consider, for instance, the movement to deface, destroy, or dismantle monuments and memorials to historical figures whose accomplishments have today been condemned by a new generation. Slaveowners, colonialists, and captains of industry are all targets of what its critics call "cancel culture," a term meant to condemn the humiliation suffered by those people who still defend the traditions and culture established by these past "heroes." The violence may no longer be done to flesh and bone but to bronze and stone, yet the humiliating effects are the same. If we think about humiliation as *symbolic* cruelty, then it must now be understood not as a violent assassination of one's enemies but as a method of targeting and undermining the irrational and unearned privileges of class, race, religion, and nationality built on a history of injustice and exploitation. In this sense, "cruelty well used" means the sweeping and sudden change in orders that upends traditional social hierarchies. But to do this is inevitably to assault someone's "way of life." And there is no way to criticize a way of life without being cruel.

That said, we must also accept the fact that the contemporary social media environment makes it almost impossible to ever enact cruelty "well used," symbolic or otherwise. Machiavelli had hoped to control cruelty by containing it, by making it something one could turn on and off like a spigot. But today, nothing can be stopped once it enters the current of cyberspace. A single cruel or humiliating event, which in the past was done and gone, can today have eternal life if captured on a smartphone and posted on Twitter. Recall Machiavelli's insight that "men forget the death of a father more quickly than the loss of a patrimony."[92] That is not true if their father's murder was recorded and broadcast on state propaganda or posted on the dark web. It is worth speculating on how Machiavelli might have altered his calculus if Agathocles's slaughter of the city elite had been uploaded on YouTube. And the same goes for humiliation. Consider, for instance, how often the Confederate flag is defaced at rallies and protests. There is no escape from humiliation for people whose identities are wrapped up in these symbols. No wonder that our political environment seems fraught with division. In a time of radical change, acts of symbolic cruelty proliferate, spread widely, and endure forever, meaning that cruelty is both inevitable and inevitably badly used. It is tempting to hope that perhaps that means that the only way to overcome this atmosphere is to become less susceptible to humiliation by learning to hold our identities lightly, to see everyone as mistaken, and ultimately to find pleasure in laughing at oneself. But it is more likely that symbolic cruelty will become more widely deployed even as it becomes more loudly condemned. Such is the irony of cruelty that the more we seek its eradication, the freer we are with its use. Cruelty may be the worst thing we can do; but for better or worse, it may also be the most human.

CHAPTER 5

Why Love Is the Foundation of Republics and Hatred Their Ruin

W HEN READ THROUGH MACHIAVELLI'S REPUTATION AS THE *EVIL Machiavel*, these narratives of the early Florentine republic appear to support the crass political realist worldview that the primary instrument of politics is force. The twin catastrophes of the tyrannies of Charles and Walter demonstrate the ability for authoritarian rhetoric to exploit divisions and for populist rhetoric to mobilize violent and sometimes cruel opposition. But thus far republican rhetoric has appeared largely helpless to resist the authoritarian assault on civic freedoms. Indeed, little in either of these case studies has provided any basis for republican politics at all. Instead, their narration has demonstrated quite clearly that catastrophes stoke latent factional divisions, invite authoritarian rule, and reach a resolution only after an entire city has suffered so much that it violently shakes off tyranny. Given the apparent incapacity of Florentine citizens to reach consensus through rhetorical deliberation based on a sense of mutual tolerance and institutional forbearance, there would seem little hope that they would be able to reestablish a free society after such civic strife.

Understood this way, Machiavelli's world seems to be one of constant struggle between the modes of force, fraud, and fear in which the virtue of love has no role to play. According to Michael Harvey, when Machiavelli effectively overturned a "whole tradition of moralizing political thinkers, narrowing their concerns to the elemental question of survival, he removed love from the political equation."[1] For Harvey, the characteristically Machiavellian actor is one both always alone and always ready for war, such that

"Machiavellian *virtú* is nothing more than the skill and art of the warrior, in the armed camp that is the world of men."[2] Politics here is simply an extension of force. Harvey concludes that "there is virtually no place for love in Machiavelli's view of human affairs. He seems to delight in stories that violate our expectations about the power of love to soften human relations."[3] Even in his fictional works, such as his poems and plays, "instead of the romantic of familial love that one might expect, one finds in so many of Machiavellis's stories baser, crueler emotions: lust, malice, ambition, pride, and terrible aloneness."[4] What goes for his stories also goes for his political histories. His narratives of the early history of Florence convey the impression that the city's times of unity were mere accidents that masked the true state of affairs—an underlying strife ready to erupt into violence at any time.

Harvey is right that we find little romantic or even filial love in Machiavelli. But we do find the basis for another form of love that provides a powerful foundation for republican politics. This is the love of country of the type expressed by Machiavelli in one of his last letters before his death: "I love my native city more than my own soul" (*amare la patria piú dell'anima*).[5] And this kind of love, in his writing, was unique to republics. As Viroli explains, any "*patria* always inspires love and attachment, but, when the *patria* is joined with republican liberty, citizens love it in a special manner."[6] Love of country, for Machiavelli, was therefore a founding political passion for all free peoples and the necessary relation that bound together both citizens and leaders within a republican political order. In Viroli's description, this kind of love refers to more than just the place of one's birth or the people to whom one belongs; it is love "of a concrete way of living under particular republican institutions in places filled with memories, culturally dense, historically situated. It is love not just of republican institutions and laws, but of . . . the political and social practices they permit and encourage."[7] As we shall see in the narrative that follows, this love of country not only creates the possibility of freedom but also could be deployed effectively in republican rhetoric to constitute power in the face of catastrophe. In fact, the ability to be able to speak freely at all would be a source of that love.

In this chapter, I revisit the conflict between Walter of Brienne and the representatives of the Florentine republic by focusing on Machiavelli's reconstruction of the republican rhetoric of the priors. Although in this case they failed to prevent Walter's takeover of the city, their arguments warning him against this course of action were prophetic. In Machiavelli's history, the duke's fate was foretold by members of the Florentine Signoria just prior to the spectacle of the *parlamento*. In one of the first major imagined speeches of Machiavelli's invention, the priors first warn the duke that "amidst universal hatred one never finds any security, because you never know from whence evil may spring, and he who fears every man cannot secure himself against anyone."[8] And so it came to pass that once Walter became hated, he could not even trust the men of Burgundy not to betray the duke to the voracious mob gathered outside the palace walls. But the priors also explain that free people are particularly unsuited to rule by force because they are deprived of what they call "the sweetness of free life" (*la dolcezza del vivere libero*).[9] Even if the republican institutions could not withstand Walter's initial assault of force, fraud, and fear, their legacy endured in the people's mind as an important source of freedom, glory, and belonging. And the suppression of these institutions created in the people a capacity to act in concert to regain them, by cruelty if necessary. The love of country is nothing to be taken lightly.

Yet to claim that Machiavelli advocates for cultivating and respective love of country appears to flatly contradict one of his most infamous maxims—that "it is much safer to be feared than loved."[10] This maxim is so adored by what Stephen Holmes calls "Bush-League Machiavellians" that they "recite 'it is better to be feared than loved' as if it were a wedding vow."[11] Undeniably, there is justification for their belief. Machiavelli advocates for relying on fear rather than love based on what he might call his "realistic" view of human nature. One cannot rely on love, he explains, because men in general "are ungrateful, fickle, pretenders and assemblers, invaders of danger, eager for gain. While you do them good, they are yours, offering you their blood, properties, lives, and children, as I said above, when the need for them is far away; but, when it is close to you, they revolt."[12] These qualities do not make human beings evil. They make them unreliable. Fear is therefore safer than love because "men have less hesitation to offend one who makes himself loved then one who makes himself feared; for love is held by a chain of obligation, which, because men are wicked, is broken at every opportunity for their own utility, but fear is held by a dread of punishment that never forsakes you."[13]

The dread of punishment thus has a solidity and reliability that love, constructed merely on words, completely lacks: "That prince who has founded himself entirely on their words, stripped of other preparation, is ruined; for friendships that are acquired at a price and not with greatness and nobility of spirit are bought, but they are not owned and when the time comes they cannot be spent."[14] When paired with Machiavelli's realistic appraisal of human nature, it seems quite logical to assume that because people cannot be trusted to keep their word in times of crisis, we must sometimes threaten them into compliance. And that is why he argues that it was cruelty, not love, that allowed Cesare Borgia to bring order to the Romagna and reduce it to "peace and to faith," noting that "it is impossible for the new Prince to escape a name for cruelty because new states are full of dangers."[15] Better accept blame and secure the state through cruelty than to earn the love of a people who will then betray or flee from you at the slightest danger.

Given these strong claims, it is not surprising that the centrality of love to Machiavelli's political theory is downplayed by his interpreters. Winter, for instance, acknowledges that in Machiavelli, love functions as one of the "regime preserving" political passions grounded in loyalty, fidelity, esteem, and gratitude and even grants that "it plays a central role as a generator of political unity."[16] But he does not investigate that role. Instead, Winter diminishes its importance, citing Machiavelli's comment in the *Discourses* that "most often whoever makes himself feared is more followed and more obeyed than whoever makes himself loved."[17] This leads Winter to conclude that "despite the vital role of love in the formation of political unity, Machiavelli considers fear a more potent force."[18] Similarly, Strauss recognizes a place for love in Machiavelli's thinking, noting how "the government must try to gain the love of the governed by paying a price, i.e. by acts of liberality and gentleness."[19] But then he negates its importance by concluding that "the bond of obligation is felt as a burden and therefore it is broken on every occasion on which it restrains the self-interest of the obliged."[20] In fact, Strauss goes so far as to characterize Machiavelli as an Antichrist who argues that "the primacy of Love must be replaced by the primacy of Terror if republics are to be established in accordance with nature and on the basis of knowledge of nature."[21] Based on his reading of Machiavelli's privileging of fear over love, Strauss concludes that his work represents something akin to a diabolical call to arms, "as a war of the Anti-Christ or of the Devil who recruits his army while fighting or through fighting against the army led by God or Christ."[22] In Strauss, we must choose between the Christ of Love and the Antichrist of Terror. There is no "middle."

I don't find these strong readings of the role of fear in Machiavelli convincing. I tend to agree with Benner's comment that "this intemperate passage is often plucked out of context and treated as an unambiguous expression of

Machiavelli's bleak view of human nature."[23] To me, Machiavelli was saying something perfectly obvious—that love alone isn't enough. Fear of punishment is required to produce compliance, especially in a large population. There is nothing controversial here. Every parent and teacher would agree. Besides, Machiavelli makes it perfectly clear he is not making a universal claim of priority between being loved and feared. The ideal response, in fact, is that "one would want to be both the one and the other."[24] Indeed, right after praising Cesare Borgia's cruelty he notes of his ideal prince that "nonetheless, he should be slow to believe and to move, nor should he make himself feared, and he should proceed in a temperate mode with prudence and humanity."[25] Undoubtedly, Machiavelli defends cruelty and fear as legitimate and necessary modes of action in specific circumstances, especially those faced by a new prince. As he explains through a quote from Virgil's *Aeneid* in the mouth of Dido, "'The harshness of things and the newness of the kingdom compel me to contrive such things, and to keep a broad watch over the borders.'"[26] But that is the essential point—*in the specific circumstances of harshness and newness.*

What forces a leader to make a dramatic show of fear (outside of the ordinary enforcement of law) is a combination of circumstances. First, like Dido, the prince must be a "new" prince facing harsh conditions and the possibility of invasion from across the borders. This new prince would lack both an established order and the respect and honor that comes from long acquaintance with what Machiavelli calls "greatness and nobility of spirit."[27] As a result, the prince would have to use fear and dread of punishment to create unity and obedience through threat of force. Second, the resort to force in this circumstance often arises because of the prince's own *lack* of greatness and nobility of spirit—that is, of virtú. Machiavelli codes his language in such a way that the imagined prince facing this tragic choice had brought it on himself, being so naive as to believe he could establish a new rule "entirely on their words" having neglected "other preparation." [28] Any new prince ascending to leadership of a mass of strangers would be an absolute fool to trust that these people would have one's back in a fight, no matter their promises. To recommend relying on fear rather than trusting in love in such a context is not diabolical but common sense.

I prefer a reading of Machiavelli that interprets fear and love as complements rather than opposites. The forced choice is completely artificial. The natural opposite of love is not *fear* but *hatred*. Not only does he say quite clearly that one ideally should wish to be both feared and loved, but even when he acknowledges that love may not be possible, he argues that "being feared and not being hated can go together very well."[29] One might redefine "not hated" in this context along a spectrum ranging from being tolerated, accepted, to even respected. Stern parents, disciplined generals, or impartial judges might be feared because of their power to inflict punishment when their codes or laws are violated, but the very same characteristics may earn them love for having created a system of order that allows for justice and the flourishing of human creativity within a secure household, military, or state. Fear only generates hatred when the modes employed are indiscriminately cruel and when those who employ them lack any appearance of goodwill or justice. But a "well-used" fear, such as employed by the police, the courts, the army, or one's "own arms," may be instrumental in creating order and obedience within a chaotic situation. The stability imposed by fear would then make possible institutional reforms that might produce loyalty to the state and the order of justice it might embody.

Love in this context is not love of a ruler but the type of love that Machiavelli felt toward his native city—that is, love of country. This may not be the love of Christ, that is true, but it is a kind of civic love Machiavelli feels to be absolutely essential for establishing political unity in republics. Love for a ruler means the feelings of respect, gratitude, and loyalty between follower and leader; love of country means the bonds of affection, duty, and pride between citizen and republic. In both forms of love, one finds a sense of obligation understood as something akin to the feeling of responsibility to keep one's promises. According to Robert Kocis, "the obligation would not be seen as originating in an act of God but in a person's decision, at a point of time, that life could be made fuller and more rewarding by making and keeping such a pledge."[30] But love for a ruler tends to be highly individualistic, contingent on the particular personality of the ruler. Love of country is more collective and institutional, bound up with the laws and orders of the state. Citizens feel obligated to the state insofar as making and keeping pledges is rewarded through security, prosperity, and glory. The state, in turn, keeps its promises in order to maintain the support of the people. Love of country thus does not contradict the conflictual nature of Machiavelli's political realism. It is rather a form of identification that provides a unifying counterforce to factional division and strife.

As we see in Machiavelli's narrative of Walter's rise to power, love of country is no weak reed. Particularly under threat, it can function as a republican source of power capable of rallying people to act in the face of catastrophe. We find the appeal to love of country in one of the speeches Machiavelli puts in the mouth of the historical actors of his *Florentine Histories*. In this case, the speech that defines the role of love in republican politics is the one delivered by the priors to the duke of Athens prior to his coup, warning him against tyrannical overreach. When Machiavelli composes the priors' oration, he adapts it to the constraints of a particular type of rhetorical situation that demands an appropriate response.

In this case, representatives of a divided city must find a way to persuade an aspiring tyrant to respect civic freedoms and rule within a republican order. Wasting no time, they identify the exigence immediately: "It appears certain to use that you want to obtain extraordinarily that which we have not granted to you in the ordinary way" and that "you are seeking to enslave a city which has always lived free."[31] Realizing that the republic lacked both the unity and the arms to resist the duke's ambitions, they pursued a rhetorical strategy that sought to persuade the duke that it would serve his own interests to respect Florentine freedoms. Appealing to the duke's own impulse for self-preservation, they claimed that their intention was not "to oppose your designs with any force, but only to point out to you how heavy a weight you are taking on your back, and how dangerous the course you are selecting."[32] The remaining portion of the oration then exploits every Machiavellian resource to defend the notion that, at least within a republic, a rule that respects traditional order and relies on the modes of tolerance and love is more secure than one that adopts extraordinary modes of force and fear.

The most practical (and by now familiar) argument the priors make against enslaving a free city is that it will stoke divisions and evoke hatred to such a degree that it will bring the ruin of both the prince and the city. First, the prince must evaluate the degree of resistance faced by a free people to being enslaved: "Have you considered how important this is in a city like this, and how vigorous is the name of freedom, which no force can subdue, no time consume, and no merit counterbalance?"[33] Second, the force required to suppress such resistance would only serve to multiply resentments among his current allies and make them ready to usurp his authority at the first opportunity: "Think, lord, how much force will be necessary to keep such a city enslaved. Foreign forces, which you can always keep, are not enough; those from inside you cannot trust because those who are your friends now and who encourage you to select this course, just as they will have fought their enemies with your authority, will seek as they can to eliminate you and make themselves princes."[34] Third, even a violent campaign of cruel suppression would backfire, for hatred has a way of spreading like wildfire beyond the immediate target: "If indeed you try to do it, you aggravate the dangers, because those who remain burn more with hatred and are readier for revenge."[35] In the end, no number of citadels, guards, and friends could secure such a prince against the hatred of the people, such that ambition to take the city by force and fear "must necessarily fail with the greatest harm to yourself and to us."[36] Seeing that events played out precisely as the priors had warned, we should not interpret these arguments ironically. The words Machiavelli puts in the mouth of the priors clearly are meant to impact the reader of his history, "so that you can always remember our advice."[37] In Machiavelli's hands, the situation outlined by the priors will inevitably be recurrent, so that their proverbs be remembered.

Yet their most powerful and original argument points to love of country as an enduring and mobilizing source of political unity. Specifically, the object of this love is for the republican institutions that guarantee political freedom. By "freedom" Machiavelli means not individual license but the capacity to enact self-legislation and pursue collective goals through the modes and orders of an independent state. Here we discover the true foundation of republics and the source of its binding obligations—the uniquely republican "benefit" of allowing citizens to share in the pride of self-determination, the honor of recognition, and the glory of accomplishment. The priors appeal to this love of country when they argue that free citizens (which here means free men of proper station) prefer glory over any material benefit that compensates for slavery: "Which deeds of yours do you want to be a counterweight to the sweetness of free life [*la dolcezza del vivere libero*] or to make men lose their desire for present conditions? Not if you were to add all Tuscany to this empire, and if every day you were to return to the city in triumph over our enemies; for all the glory would not be its but yours, and the citizens would not acquire subjects but fellow slaves in whom they would see their own slavery aggravated. And even if your habits were saintly, your modes benign, your judgments upright, they would not be enough to make you loved; and if you believe that they would be, you would be deceiving yourself, for to a man used to living unshackled every chain weighs and every link binds him."[38] Cruelty can be expressed in more ways than dismemberment; it can also take the form of benign paternalism that provides material benefits accompanied with a condescending smile. Humans may be grasping and fickle, but they also crave what Raymond Belliotti calls the "external validation" that "hunger for recognition that endures beyond their lifetimes."[39] When republican orders provide the opportunity for that validation, they bestow benefits that begin forging the chains of obligation that unify the citizens and bind them to the institutions of the state. For someone like the duke of Athens to destroy these institutions in exchange for material gain is a poor trade; once citizens have tasted glory, the love for the republic that made this possible will overwhelm any fear of punishment if they still have hope it can be recovered.

The desire to recover the freedoms that make possible the attainment of glory is so powerful, in fact, that it permeates the very stones of the city. The priors here draw upon what Winter refers to as a type of "political memory" that "sustains regimes when it is continuous with the present—thus republics benefit from an ensconced memory of political freedom."[40] In their warning to Walter of Brienne, the priors pay homage to the recalcitrance and endurance of this memory of political freedom by leveraging it as a threat to the duke's rule. They argue, "That there is not enough time to consume the desires for freedom is most certain, for freedom, one knows, is often restored in a city by those who have never tasted it but who loved it only through the memories of it left to them by their fathers; and thus, once recovered, they preserve it with all obstinacy and at any peril. And even if their fathers had not recalled it to them, the public palaces, the places of the magistrates, the ensigns of the free orders recall it. These things must be recognized with the greatest desire by citizens. Which deeds of yours do you want to be a counterweight to the sweetness of free life or to make men lose their desire for present conditions?"[41] The basis for their threat is the same principle Machiavelli had defended in *The Prince*—that a tyrant wishing to possess a free city had no more secure mode than to ruin it. The maxim is often carelessly cited as a recommendation, but to me it makes more sense to read it as both a warning against tyrants and indirect celebration of civic pride. For as he explains, "whoever becomes patron of a city accustomed to living free and does not destroy it, should expect to be destroyed by it; for it always has a refuge in rebellion the name of liberty and its own ancient orders which are never forgotten either through length of time or because of benefits received."[42] An aspiring tyrant thus had to contend with the fact that "in republics there is greater life, greater hatred, more desire for revenge; the memory of their ancient liberty does not and cannot let them rest."[43] And this conclusion is precisely how the priors end their speech. Because of the public memory of freedom in Florence, the duke has only two options: "You have to believe either that you have to hold this city with the greatest violence (for such a thing the citadels, the guards, and friends from outside many times are not enough), or that you have to be content with the authority that we have given you. And we urge you to this, reminding you that that dominion is alone lasting which is voluntary."[44] In other words, the only way Walter could maintain his authority would be to abandon his ambition for lordship and become a republican.

When threatened by fear and force, the priors defend their city with memory and love. These are not idle threats. Machiavelli shows how a distinctively republican love of country becomes embedded not only in practices but expressed in the very built environment. To the extent that the buildings, squares, memorials, and streets function symbolically to remind a people of the continuity between past, present, and future, they function to unify them through the binding force of memory. As Winter explains, for Machiavelli, "the political past lives on in the present in three modes: as institutions [*ordini*], as practices [*modi*], and as memory [*memoria*]."[45] Power in republics, in short, is built upon loving memories, for republics are "narrative constructs: They rely on recurring narrations and dramatic reenactments of stories about their origins and their history."[46] But memory is distinct from institutions and practices because of its essentially *narrative* quality that relies on imaginary reconstruction of past events. According to Marie Gaille, "Machiavelli grants a central role to memory and imagination in the relationship linking passions to civil conflict. Memory and imagination maintain the passions: memory, by drawing support from past experience, and imagination by fictitiously transposing into the future events that are likely to occur."[47] The type of public memory in republics, of course, does not imply that each citizen directly witnessed or even experienced some past event; rather, it relates to what Winter terms *mnemopoiesis*, or the "cultural activity of creating memories."[48] Through often ritualistic representations and performances of civic power and authority, republican citizens come to share imagined narratives of their origins, character, and destiny. The love of citizens for a free republic is thus not an obligation to a specific person but a commitment to fulfilling a promise to a political order that promises them glory in return. The expulsion of the duke of Athens from Florence in the year 1343 was thus a spectacle that left a lasting impression on the public memory of the city and bound its citizens even stronger together in chains of obligation.

In rhetorical terms, the love of country produced through republican institutions, rituals, and practices represents what Kenneth Burke designates as a powerful form of *identification*, which he believes is the foundation for all rhetorical persuasion. For Burke, any particular act of persuasion always draws upon more fundamental and often unspoken sources of unity. Identification stands for those shared interests, qualities, values, and practices that make people feel joined with one another as if they possessed the same "substance." Drawing from Christian terminology, Burke connects identification with a doctrine of "consubstantiality" that he argues "may be necessary to any way of life. For substance, in the old philosophies, was an *act*; and a way of life is an *acting-together*; and in acting together, men have common sensations, concepts, images, ideas, attitudes that make them *consubstantial*."[49] In other words, we are persuaded to adopt a course of action not just out of a purely utilitarian calculus of future benefits; we are persuaded because that course of action conforms with our sense of belonging to a collective identity grounded in common substance. But because we can never all share the same properties with all people, rhetoric as an art always navigates between identification and division, of belonging and exclusion, of unity and conflict. Rhetoric "deals with possibilities of classification in its partisan aspects; it considers the ways in which individuals are at odds with one another, or become identified with groups more or less at odds with one another."[50] Yet just as Machiavelli recognizes that a republican unity can emerge out of a political realism of conflict, Burke sees that even a kind of love can exist despite strife. In fact, for Burke, love and strife are always bound together, just as identification is compensatory to division: "We need never deny the presence of strife, enmity, faction as a characteristic motive of rhetorical expression. We need not close our eyes to their almost tyrannous ubiquity in human relations; we can be on the alert always to see how such temptations to strife are implicit in the institutions that condition human relationships; yet we can at the same time always look beyond this order, to the principle of identification in general, a teministic choice justified by the fact that the identifications in the order of love are also characteristic of rhetorical expression."[51]

In the context of Florentine republican politics, we might interpret this "order of love" that is Machiavelli's love of country as a rhetorical expression of what Burke calls "piety." For Burke, piety is no more a specifically religious category than consubstantiality. It refers simply to that sense of "loyalty to the sources of our being," whether those sources come from family, culture, geography, religion, or the state.[52] Piety derives from our emotional connection to some past origin to which we feel not only grateful retrospectively but which we also use prospectively as a model for how to act. For instance, the pieties of family and state might converge. In this way, the "connection between our pieties and our childhood should seem clear, since in childhood we develop our first patterns of judgment, while the experiences of maturity are revisions and amplifications of these childhood patterns."[53] Similarly, a potter might act on the basis of piety "when the potter moulds the clay to exactly that form which completely gratifies his sense of how it ought to be."[54] In short, for Burke, "piety is a system-builder, a desire to round things out, to fit experiences together into a unified whole. Piety is *the sense of what properly goes with what*."[55] But as such, piety stands in tension with a "purely utilitarian attitude."[56] Piety cannot be easily overridden by a cost-benefit analysis. To challenge piety is to face an entire fabric of identifications that people use to build their identities and make meaning of the world. And that is why a prince would have to destroy a republic to rule it.

From a Machiavellian perspective, therefore, the republican rhetoric of love of country is an important factor in his political realism because it forms the basis of a distinctly republican form of power. By "power," I mean the ability for a group of people who share a common identification to act collectively toward a shared goal. Power therefore represents not an individual possession but shared "capacity to act in concert through communicative understanding, using available resources, technologies, and mediums, to overcome resistance in pursuit of an imagined good."[57] The aim of rhetoric is the creation of this unity of purpose through symbolic action. As Machiavelli's predecessor, Collucio Salutati, once wrote, rhetoric represents the art by which one masters "how to stir the public with his indignation and use dignified remonstrance to win their sympathy for persons and circumstances, getting them to favor his side and be outraged at his opponents."[58] Rhetoric, as I have argued previously, thus "produces power when it creates the capacity to act in concern through the medium of symbolic action; it undermines power when it dismantles the same capacity in others, and it transforms power when it shifts from one form of collective action to another in response to contingencies and possibilities."[59] When we speak of someone "possessing power," we mean that some actor stands at the center of a network of established relationships, shared understandings, and institutional structures that allows their will to be enacted through the agency of others. In this way, republican love of country thus creates a wider basis of power than a principality. Through piety to a state that provides them opportunities for self-advancement, recognition, and glory, the citizens of a republic become consubstantial by acting together through republican institutions.

Yet it is important to emphasize that republican rhetoric in Machiavelli constitutes and directs power by almost exclusively relying upon the honors and benefits that come with participation in civic offices. And part of those benefits is the ability to participate in and enact what Hariman calls a "republican style" of politics. Drawing inspiration from his reading of Cicero, Hariman argues that "the republican style begins with a relish for the pleasures of composing and delivering persuasive public discourse, it includes other modes of exchange and becomes a more focused mode of action by defining consensus as the foundation means and end of governance, and it culminates in a mode of leadership that features personal embodiment of the civic culture."[60] For Machiavelli, part of the pleasure of republican orders is the sheer ability to argue, deliberate, perform, and express one's reason in public. More than even the actual attainment of consensus, the value of republican orders can be found in the habits and practices of the offices themselves, namely the way that republican orders involve citizens in the workings of the state and provide them clear, ascending paths toward greater honors and privileges. Viroli captures this institutional republicanism in his description of how the love of country translates into power. Writing of Machiavelli, Viroli argues that "love of country was for him a synonym of what we call civic virtue—that is, love of the common good of the citizens which translates into acts of service and care for the republic. It is a passion which makes the individual's soul both generous and strong. As such, it gives ordinary citizens the motivation to discharge everyday duties, and resist tyranny and corruption; it inspires magistrates and rules in their commitment to justice; it sustains legislators in their wisdom; and it gives redeemers and saviours the strength to restore liberty."[61] As Viroli shows, love of country is not some kind of weak-kneed passion or soft-hearted sentimentalism; it is a source of generosity, strength, pride, and courage that justifies sacrifice for the cause of justice, freedom, and glory. Furthermore, when love confronts those who would attack or exploit the common good, love becomes the very *source* of vengeance, cruelty, and hatred necessary to defend oneself. As Machiavelli observes after narrating the cruelty done to

Walter's allies, "Without doubt, indignation appears greater and wounds are graver when liberty is being recovered than when it is being defended."[62] And so the Florentines, out of love of country, ended up taking out their indignation upon their tormentors through cruelty.

The concept of love of country provides the essential foundation for the republican generation of power. Without being grounded in this type of love, Machiavelli's concepts float free and become a mere tactical handbook for individuals seeking personal gain. But once situated within a broader republican context, Machiavelli's tactics can be seen as a part of a larger strategy of constructing and securing a republican order. Love of country is essential to this construction. When bound together through common narratives of origins, a shared vision of the future, and most importantly collective channels of communication that allow individuals an opportunity for recognition and even "glory" within an established system, people come to see themselves as part of a wider community. As much as people demand material satisfactions, they also crave to be a part of a state that grants individuals and their children a sense of dignity.

That said, love of country is not always an unalloyed good. Particularly today in an era of nationalistic revival, the love of country can easily be exploited by an authoritarian rhetoric that sows division between peoples and sets nations, religions, tribes, races, and genders against one another. In this case, love and terror are not opposites but complements. Just as the Florentines cut their enemies into morsels and literally devoured their enemies, those who take vengeance on others out of love of country can produce horrors. Sometimes this terror is unleashed on a target seen to be a foreign aggressor; other times it is unleashed on "internal enemies" within the city itself. As in Dante's time, the ruin of a republic arrives when competing visions of patriotism divide people into factions who, in mutual hatred, unleash terror against each other. Burke calls this outcome a pervasive and troubling "*disease of cooperation*," namely that "men are brought to that most tragically ironic of all divisions, or conflicts, wherein millions of cooperative acts go into the preparation for one single destructive act."[63] That act is war. And the tragic fact is that republics, for all their love of country, have shown themselves to be no less susceptible to this disease than any other order.

Nonetheless, there is no question that we cannot meet our current catastrophe without cultivating a new order of the love of country that seeks a wider circumference of identification. In the first place, so much of our current environmental devastation and resource depletion has in large part been due to the belief that a few privileged nations could treat the Earth as their birthright, heedless of the impact such extractive practices would have on future populations of the globe. That is to say, love of country for colonial nations justified anything from slavery to genocide if they served to increase their wealth and power. In the second place, the COVID-19 pandemic, in particular, has shown how latent tribal divisions, large and small, inhibit the international cooperation necessary for acting in concert. One's "love of country" ironically was used as justification for flaunting international guidelines and championing an odd kind of freedom to get oneself and others sick while stigmatizing and blaming outsiders. This same type of reaction is common, especially among the privileged nations, whenever they are asked to accept limits or make sacrifices as a necessary part of coordinated international responses to crises. If there was one positive outcome to the pandemic, it was the dawning realization that our health, economies, and security are bound inextricably together through supply chains and communicative networks that rely on global cooperation.

Paradoxically, I believe this conclusion is wholly Machiavellian even as I recognize that it flies in the face of his actual foreign policy recommendations. As we shall see, contemporary Machiavellian political realism has, with textual justification, often argued that international politics should simply be treated as a balance of power in which each nation should strive against competitors to acquire what it can and sacrifice as little as it must. And I cannot deny that this counsel has often been the only prudent choice for nations trapped in zero-sum logics that punished compromise as weakness. I am not suggesting, therefore, that when faced with rapacious opponents, nations should rely on empty promises or act selflessly out of a moral duty. I am not talking about foolishness or altruism. I am talking about the prudential realism of collective self-interest. To adapt the old Florentine proverb, the nations of the globe will not cooperate until they hurt all over. Tasks like managing water resources, integrating refugee populations, controlling pandemics, and reducing carbon emissions cannot be done by individual nations in isolation. Protecting one's "own" people now necessitates understanding and assisting others. The global "public" comes into being when all nations realize they must work together. I do not believe this violates any tenet of Machiavelli. It simply broadens their application.

A Machiavellian approach to global cooperation therefore goes beyond conventional pieties that demand that we "think globally" out of moral duty. For Machiavelli, love of country is impotent if it simply remains an attractive but empty ideal of goodness. I see two preconditions as necessary for widening the scope of our political identification. First, the people of each nation must come to see themselves as part of a global community of peoples each sharing a common home. Interestingly, this argument was made strongly by Pope Francis in his encyclical *Laudato si'*, whose opening chapters are grounded in a wholly empirical study of our catastrophic times.[64] Second, and perhaps more importantly, people from every nation must be able to participate, at some level, in the emerging international orders of state. Part of the backlash against institutions like the European Union, for instance, has been a pervasive feeling (whether justified or not) that its leaders are detached and elite bureaucrats and that ordinary citizens have no place within its order. For Machiavelli, an international republic limited to closed-door meetings by heads of state to negotiate watered-down treaties will lack legitimacy and produce familiar nationalistic backlash. The only viable republican internationalism, from a Machiavellian standpoint, is one that people would defend with their own arms because they identify it with their own freedoms and access to honors and glory. I believe if Machiavelli looked at today's political divisions, he would say that founding a new order of a global republic requires constituting a global citizenry that is active, empowered, and armed. In that case, people would seek international cooperation not out of "goodness" but out of self-interest and pride, two modes that can be relied upon in any Machiavellian calculus designed to produce a unified response to a common threat.

CHAPTER 6

When Tumults Can Serve
the Health of the State

T HE TWIN CATASTROPHES THAT BESET THE EARLY FLORENTINE
republic culminated in the institution of a foreign tyrant as the method
of confronting catastrophe through authoritarian control. These catastrophes
originated in a combination of internal and external pressures, while the suffering brought about by disease, famine, and war exacerbated preexisting
class divisions. Exploiting crisis as an opportunity, members of the great families used authoritarian rhetoric to scapegoat their enemies and inflame social divisions as a pretext for imposing de facto tyrannies, which soon created
the conditions for even greater catastrophes. In both cases, republican rhetoric, while defending the integrity of the republican orders, lacked sufficient
power, arms, or cunning to prevent politics from running off the guardrails.
Yet the memory of republican liberties lived on in the people even after they
had been eliminated, making possible the success of a populist rhetoric that
could translate this republican piety into power. Appealing to a love of country, this populist rhetoric was able to create a wider identification among previously antagonistic classes, uniting them against a common enemy. In the
name of defending the republic, they then combined the modes of the beasts
with very human cruelty to chase off the wolves that terrorized them. The result was a restoration of the republican order, albeit still based on an unstable
hierarchy of classes in which wealth and nobility ruled.

The remainder of the *Florentine Histories* provides an opportunity to explore different genres of the rhetoric of catastrophe that are in many ways
more directly relevant to our own challenges. After Machiavelli narrates

the exile of Walter of Brienne, he dedicates the remainder of his history to largely internal political conflicts in the city leading up to the death of Lorenzo the Magnificent in 1492. Consequently, the types of strategic action he describes are more continuous with forms of contemporary politics, including social protests, revolutionary movements, counterinsurgency, political orchestration, and propaganda. Furthermore, the nature of the catastrophes is far more complicated than the made-for-movie scripts of popular resistance against a foreign tyrant. These later catastrophes grow out of all-too-modern conflicts rooted in class divisions, disparities in wealth, religious fanaticism, and resource scarcity. In short, they are catastrophes that concern not only questions of power but matters of distributive justice.

That Machiavelli would be concerned at all about justice might be surprising for those under the sway of Bush-League Machiavellians. Yet one can clearly find a working definition of justice in his work. As Machiavelli wrote in *The Prince*, "victories are never so clear that the winner does not have to have some respect, especially for justice (*iustizia*)."[1] For Benner, this passage reinforces what she sees as "a central argument of the *Prince* . . . that brute force is seldom enough to underwrite political power."[2] Any population or individual might be intimidated into silence, exiled, or killed so that a tyrant or faction might gain ascendancy in the short term. But the prince who wishes to rule with peace and security for more than a brief time must have some respect for justice. According to Benner, "the word 'justice' for Machiavelli refers to standards, procedures, and judgments that are derived from reasoning about the conditions for ordered existence among free agents."[3] And Zuckert, too, finds in Machiavelli a Socratic notion of justice that seeks "worldly knowledge of how to protect the lives of most people and enable them to live not merely prosperously, but freely."[4] Neither of these definitions is idealistic. They simply observe that a state ordered by justice is more efficient and powerful than one governed by force. When both the people and the nobles can agree upon common modes of action and cooperate in pursuing what Machiavelli termed the "common good," they develop a shared love of country that makes them voluntarily obey its orders and defend its borders. As he frequently says, no state can be ruled for long through fortresses alone.

But Machiavelli's contribution to republican political theory does not reside in his rather commonplace recognition that stable, long-lasting, and powerful orders require the institutionalization of justice. That simply makes his theory realistic. His originality lies in the means by which justice is secured and renewed within a republic. Traditional Ciceronian conceptions of republican politics, both in Machiavelli's time and in our own, hold that the perfect republic is always a peaceful republic. As Hariman describes it, in the republican ideal, eloquence is the only acceptable instrument of conflict resolution while the norm of "civility is a *sine qua non* of political life."[5] And this notion of civility includes such habits as "refraining from violence, recognizing social status, observing parliamentary customs, and acting as if oneself and one's opponents always were motivated at least in part by civic virtue and the duties of public office."[6] Anything else represents an obstruction to the path of reason. But Machiavelli dramatically departs from this ideal. For him, republics need civility and eloquence to thrive in ordinary times, but they also require something more. They require periodical tumults during extraordinary times. Indeed, Machiavelli argued that the longest and most successful republics thrive not by suppressing tumultuous expressions of political tensions but by fostering them. For Machiavelli, tumults promoted the health of the state.

Machiavelli's positive assessment of tumults as a legitimate mode of popular action makes him a rather unexpected participant in the debate over the nature and function of civil disobedience. Perhaps more accurately, Machiavelli suggests that our conceptions of disobedience should also include what Jennet Kirkpatrick calls *uncivil* disobedience. For Kirkpatrick, uncivil disobedience refers to the actions of "groups of citizens who commit illegal and violent acts while claiming to uphold democratic ideals and serve justice."[7] As indicated by her choice of case studies, including the contemporary militia movement, southern lynch mobs, frontier vigilantism, and militant abolitionism, not all such groups should be considered vanguards of republican virtue. But Kirkpatrick's purpose in studying uncivil disobedience is not to praise it as an unqualified good in all cases. Her purpose is to stress that despite the republican ideal of universal obedience to the rule of law, uncivil disobedience is not an aberration; it should rather be considered as a predictable and recurrent mode of action even in modern democracies. Understanding its origins and function means we should seek to understand the motives behind uncivil disobedience rather than simply condemning it as an illegitimate choice of means. Very often, for instance, "angered by a disjunction between law and justice, uncivil disobedients are convinced the law can be redeemed by direct civic activism outside of established legal channels."[8] Just like their nonviolent counterparts, "many violent uncivil disobedients are also committed to civic empowerment, believing that citizens in a democracy can and should change laws they believe are unjust."[9] Although Kirkpatrick acknowledges that uncivil disobedience can often serve unjust ends and produce suffering, she also emphasizes that it often serves as an opportunity to address real corruption within a democracy, potentially leading to a "reformation of political institutions, making them more efficient, responsible, competent, and honest."[10]

Machiavelli would agree. As David Polansky argues in the popular periodical *Foreign Policy*, a timely case of uncivil disobedience that invites a uniquely Machiavellian perspective is the assault on the US Capitol building by a popular mob on January 6, 2021. Enraged by what they felt to be a "rigged" election that stole a second term from President Donald J. Trump, rioters stormed the halls of Congress, violently overcoming Capitol Police in order to impose what they felt to be the will of the people. Polansky writes that although "pundits ransacked their dictionaries" for terms like "coup d'état," "putsch," and "insurrection," "there's a more apt word both for what occurred in Washington and for the spates of violence and destruction across the country in 2020 and early 2021: 'tumult'—a humble word with a classical pedigree, once used to describe the public disturbances that were a recurring feature of political life in ancient Rome."[11] And this was also the word favored by Machiavelli. Only, for Machiavelli, tumult had a potentially positive connotation. As Polansky explains, Machiavelli "treats tumult as a useful outlet for the people to vent their displeasure against their political and economic superiors. Provided that they do not turn violent, they can be healthy ways for the people to press their interests and let off steam where normal institutional channels no longer work."[12] Consequently, Polansky finds a Machiavellian lesson to be learned in the wake of the January 6 tumult: "Machiavelli would say this is a dangerous time," but he would also counsel "that in corrupt republics—like the United States—one may prevent the rise of an unscrupulous leader and simultaneously mitigate tumults by satisfying certain grievances of the people and depriving potential demagogues of the means to gain political power."[13] Echoing Kirkpatrick, Polansky argues that we need not celebrate every tumult as an achievement, but we must attend to the causes of tumults and consider how to use them as an opportunity for reform.

In the rhetoric of catastrophe, tumults play a particular central role in both ancient and modern republican contexts. We have already seen, for instance, how political and economic catastrophes in the early Florentine republic created an alliance between the great and the popular parties against the ruling mercantile republican elites. Both Charles and Walter provoked popular tumults as a way of orchestrating their rise to power, thus putting populist rhetoric in the service of authoritarian rule. Conversely, the catastrophe of Walter's tyranny created such widespread suffering that both republicans and popular parties rose up in tumult against him, employing vicious cruelty to overturn his regime. However, neither of these episodes captures the spirit of most modern tumults that arise more from pervasive conditions of injustice within established republican orders, particularly those connected in some part to economic exploitation and political marginalization. In the twenty-first century, events like the January 6 tumult, regardless of their particular politics, are often inspired by a perception that existing republican orders are irredeemably corrupt, inefficient, and irresponsible. This feeling that only popular action, civil or uncivil, can redeem the state is captured by the movement Extinction Rebellion, whose participants argue that "when government and the law fail to provide any assurance of adequate protection of and security for its people's well-being and the nation's future, it becomes the right of citizens to seek redress in order to restore dutiful democracy and to secure the solutions needed to avert catastrophe and protect the future. It becomes not only our right but our sacred duty to rebel."[14] Machiavelli's treatment of tumults may lack this modern democratic ethos, but it nonetheless addresses the same catastrophic rhetorical situation in which, during a time of crisis, the rule of law no longer reflects a significant percentage of the popular will.

Tumult in Machiavelli's work is defined purely as a mode of action. It is what Mansfield calls a "passionate and noisy clashing."[15] Tumults should thus not be conflated with contemporary social movements with coherent ideologies and organizations. In conventional terms, a tumult is a type of outbreak, riot, uprising, or disorder caused by a mass of people enraged by some state of affairs and usually targeting their rage at some institution, group, or individual. A tumult may be the result of a planned conspiracy or it may be a spontaneous event. Either way, tumults are always shocking spectacles of popular violence that provide an outlet for pent-up political passions. The most vivid description of a tumult in Machiavelli's theoretical writings appears in one of his descriptions of the periodic uprisings in Rome. During this event, the people used modes that "were extraordinary and almost wild, to see the people together crying out against the Senate, the Senate against the people, running tumultuously through the streets, closing shops, the whole plebs leaving Rome—all of which things frighten whoever does no other than read of them."[16] The images he employs of people running wild through the streets, closing shops, crying out against the state sound surprisingly modern, which makes his support of such modes all the more striking. Machiavelli then adds this comment: "I say that every city ought to have its modes with which the people can vent its ambition, and especially those cities that wish to avail themselves of the people in important things."[17] Machiavelli champions those modes of extraordinary uprisings that frightened his republican colleagues.

Even during his own time, Machiavelli's support for tumults directly challenged the orthodox republicanism pervasive among humanist writers. According to Quentin Skinner, "the belief that all civic discord must be outlawed as factious, together with the belief that faction constitutes one of the greatest threats to political liberty, had been one of the leading themes of Florentine political theory ever since the end of the thirteenth century."[18] And Machiavelli's rejection of this consensus would have an enduring impact on modern political theory. In fact, writes Gabrielle Pedullá, "the *Discourses* appear to be the decisive turning point in this grand narrative: the single work that opens the door to an original conception of political order breaking with the classical and humanist tradition of concord."[19] And Filippo del Lucchese argues that "it is this conflictualist theory of politics that constitutes the Machiavellian revolution in the history of political thought."[20] When Machiavelli compared Rome with his own time, he saw clearly that maintaining a free republic required the means of tumultuous politics.

For Machiavelli, his recognition of the value of tumults did not make his theory less republican. In fact, in his view, only tyrants or oligarchs promise absolute freedom from faction, which they then use as a justification to silence criticism and suppress political liberty. For instance, when Walter responded to the appeal from the priors, his authoritarian rhetoric appealed precisely to the republican intolerance for tumults. Walter argued that "it was not his intention to take freedom away from the city but to restore it; for only disunited cities were enslaved and united once free. And if Florence, by his ordering, should rid itself of sects, ambition, and enmities, he would be getting it liberty, not taking it away."[21] The predictable result was a reign of terror whose symbol became the severed tongue of Bettone Cini—the silencing of the Florentine people. Only when all of the different groups of citizens in Florence realized they were all targets "to be led like cattle to the slaughterhouse" did they made their fateful decision "to start a tumult in the Mercato Vecchio on the following day, which was 26 July, 1343, and after that to arm themselves and to call the people to freedom."[22] This tumult would save the republic. Walter had been invited into Florence to save it from its factions, but he pursued this goal by imposing tyranny. When all parliamentary methods of resistance had failed, he had been driven out of Florence by an alliance of citizens who restored freedom by rousing a tumult.

For Machiavelli, the lesson to be learned is that a free city that wishes to remain free cannot seek to rid itself completely of sects, ambitions, and enmities. That desire, when pushed to the extreme, invites the very authoritarianism that republics claim to despise. Republics can only seek to identify, balance, and allow expressions of these tensions. Classical republicanism, of course, advocates bringing conflicts into the realm of discourse so that they can be resolved through deliberation and eloquence. Machiavelli does not disagree. But he also recognizes that there are inevitably times in all states, however free they might have been in their origins, when systemic corruption within a republic excludes people from this discourse of power. In these situations, tumults erupt when grievances have accumulated to a point at which violent passions burst the dams of the rule of law in the demand for a higher justice. Yet unlike the type of tumults seen in the case of Walter of Brienne, these tumults are not intended to destroy a regime but to redeem it. The ideal tumult for Machiavelli therefore is one that operates with limits, in which violence functions rhetorically as a symptom of anger and an appeal for reform.

For Machiavelli, tumults functioned best as forms of populist rhetoric *within* a republican order. The most stable government is not one that denies and suppresses conflict but one that recognizes and integrates it. Ancient Rome was such a government. For Machiavelli, the genius of Rome was not its military discipline but its tumultuous politics. In his mind, those who condemned the tumults and praised the military thus had it completely backwards. Typical of narrow-minded critics, they praise the positive effects of things and damn their unseemly cause. They pretend that one can have order and law in a republic without division and conflict. Some even appeal to a strong military as a better way of keeping order without tumult. But Machiavelli argues that this claim, once again, confuses cause and effect. For "where the military is good, there must be good order."[23] In other words, having a disciplined and responsible military is not a cause of good order but an effect of it. So where does this good order come from? Machiavelli answers, "Good examples arise from good education, good education from good laws, and good laws from those tumults that many inconsiderately damn."[24] In short, the military functioned well *because* earlier tumults had made it so: "I say that to me it appears that those who damn the tumults between the nobles and the plebs blame those things that were the first cause of keeping Rome free, and that they consider the noises and the cries that would arise in such tumults more than the good effects that they engendered."[25] The tumults allowed the simmering conflicts in the republic to be openly expressed so they could be resolved through negotiation and enshrined in law. These laws and institutions, in turn, generated the love of country necessary to produce a military that was loyal not to an individual but to the state. Thus we see, once again, the connection between good arms and love of country.

However, only those who can see past the "frightening" appearances of tumults to understand their root causes and long-term effects can understand Machiavelli's radical position. Two characteristics, for Machiavelli, distinguish a tumult from an assassination, conspiracy, or military assault. First, tumults are relatively spontaneous, uncoordinated, and popular. They arise when one triggering event sparks a collective outpouring of thwarted desires and burning resentments. Second, tumults seek changes in law, not conquest through force. A tumult is a spectacle of appearances that provides the people with a form of leverage to affect alterations in political order. Tumults are an expression of grievance, not an instrument of insurrection. In Rome, for instance, Machiavelli explains that "when the people wished to obtain a law, either they did one of the things said above [engage in a tumult] or they refused to enroll their names to go to war, so that to placate them there was need to satisfy them in some part."[26] In this example, Machiavelli juxtaposes the two forms of social protest, tumult and draft avoidance, in order to demonstrate the different modes by which people seek to change laws, whether through instituting new laws they desire or abolishing laws they feel to be unjust. Despite their frightening appearances, tumults nonetheless occur within the boundaries of a republican order and have as their aim the reform of laws and the actualization of some form of justice.

The paradigmatic tumult, for Machiavelli, was the people's revolt in the Roman Republic that led to the creation of the position of tribune of the plebs. In Rome, the "plebs" referred to the class of plebeians, or the free citizens of the artisan and laboring classes who lacked noble wealth and distinction. Machiavelli narrates how after the defeat of the Tarquin kings in 509 BCE and the establishment of the first republican institutions by Brutus, there was a time of "very great union between the plebs and the Senate," for it appeared for a while that "the nobles had put away that pride of theirs, had taken on a popular spirit, and were tolerable to anyone, however mean."[27] But this appearance was deceptive. The nobles had simulated popular spirit while they had feared the plebs; but once "the Tarquins were dead and fear fled from the nobles, they began to spit out that poison against the plebs that they had held in their breasts, and they offended it in all the modes they could."[28] The people, by contrast, had to thwart this corruption by developing a new "check" on the nobility capable of maintaining a threat against their malignancy. They created this institution through a tumult: "After many confusions, noises, and dangers of scandals that arose between the plebs and the nobility, they arrived at the creation of the tribunes for the security of the plebs. They ordered them with so much eminence and reputation that they could ever after be intermediaries between the plebs and the Senate and prevent the insolence of the nobles."[29] As John McCormick explains, the tribunes of the plebs is an office "for which the very wealthiest and most prominent citizens are ineligible, and citizen participation is facilitated in plebian assemblies, which either exclude the most prominent citizens or at least minimize their influence."[30] The office of the tribune and the legislative power of the plebeian assembly were direct outcomes of tumults that affected changes in law that strengthened rather than weakened the power of the republic.

Tumults are thus quasi-rhetorical forms of protest. Even though they may often emerge from voiceless, impulsive grievances, they function instrumentally as rhetorical spectacles of popular violence that in a republic invite policy responses to satisfy those grievances in reason and law. Popular disruptions should thus not be dismissed as lacking any sense of reason or purpose. To lack a clear voice is not always a sign of irrationality; it may indicate rather a yearning for an appropriate language to satisfy desire. Characteristic of Machiavelli's tendency to find solutions in the virtú of a single individual, it is the republican rhetoric of a "good man" that ideally satisfies the inchoate but often sincere demands of the people. According to Machiavelli, the "desires of free peoples are rarely pernicious to freedom because they arise either from being oppressed or from suspicion that they may be oppressed. If these opinions are false, there is for them the remedy of assemblies, where some good man gets up who in orating demonstrates to them how they deceive themselves; and though peoples, as Tully says, are ignorant, they are capable of truth and easily yield when the truth is told them by a man worthy of faith."[31] While Rome remained a republic, therefore, "this lack of corruption—men having a good end—was the cause that the infinite tumults in Rome did not hurt and indeed helped the republic."[32] For Machiavelli, then, the populist rhetoric of tumults of the people alerted the state to the symptoms of corruption and conflict, while the republican prudence of "good men" diagnosed these symptoms and then responded to them through eloquence. In other words, tumults often originate in populist movements but their energy can only be captured and institutionalized through republican orders of justice.

To investigate the meaning of Machiavelli's theory of tumults in action, we can turn to perhaps the most iconic episode of tumultuousness in the early Renaissance, the Ciompi Revolt of 1378. As described by Winter, "during the summer months of 1378, the lowest stratum of the Florentine working-class [the *ciompi* of the popolo minuto] overthrew the governing elites and instituted a revolutionary regime. For the first time in history, Florence was ruled by a radical insurgent government that included both artisans and manual laborers, drawn primarily from the textile industry."[33] Yet like the later Peasants' Revolt of 1381 in England, the Ciompi Revolt can only be understood as a reaction to the buildup of tensions and contradictions in the economic and political order in the wake of the catastrophe of the Black Death. According to Norman Cantor, the breakdown of the medieval order had increased the opportunities for the accumulation of wealth in the survivors and led to the widespread "conviction that unrestrained greed is good."[34] Yet these opportunities tended to be concentrated among a few fortunate and opportunistic individuals. Across Europe, "the main consequence of the Black death was not the advancement of a workers' procommunist paradise but further progress along the road to class polarization in an early capitalist economy. The gap between rich and poor in each village widened. The wealthiest peasants took advantage of the social dislocations caused by the plague and the poor peasants sank further into dependency and misery."[35] A parallel effect occurred in Florence with its urban laboring class. As the profits of the wool industry tended to get further concentrated in the popolo grasso, the more the ciompi and the rest of the popolo minuto felt enraged by their exploitation and became ambitious to gain greater access to wealth and power.

Given Machiavelli's analysis of Rome, the structural oppression of the Florentine political and economic order at the time seemed ripe for tumult. "The ciompi" was the name given to those at the lowest rung of the wool industry hierarchy, including both unskilled laborers charged with washing and combing the wool as well as "subsequent manufacturing artisans of varying skill levels—spinners, weavers, fullers, stretchers, menders, and dyers—who operated their own shops and were paid by piecework."[36] The problem lay not only with the dire working conditions but also with the fact that they were denied fair political representation and adequate economic compensation. Just like the situation that caused the popolo minuto to initially support the lordship of Walter of Brienne, politically the ciompi were denied guild status by the greater and minor guilds, and hence any representation in the Florentine guild republic. As Winter explains, because "the guilds exercised substantial regulatory and judicial power in the commercial sphere in addition to their political role, the workers' exclusion from guild membership contributed directly to the maintenance and reproduction of the highly unequal relations of production that fed Florentine economic expansion."[37] In prosperous times, their wages remained fixed by the greater guilds dominated by the old Guelf merchant and aristocratic elite, meaning the ciompi lived barely above starvation levels while the popolo grasso got even fatter. These restrictions led to a situation in which "an unprecedented polarization of wealth separated the growing number of urban poor from a small plutocratic elite."[38] When the European economy faced another downturn in the 1370s, causing wool production to be cut dramatically, the ciompi bore the brunt of the suffering. By 1378 thousands of laborers were poor, starving, disempowered, and angry.

Just as he had attributed the ultimate cause of the tumults over the Agrarian Law to the greed and insolence of the Roman nobility, Machiavelli lays the blame for the Ciompi Revolt on the exploitation and suppression of the popolo minuto by the greater guilds. Just as the law in Rome had failed to both keep the public rich (because it drained state coffers) and kept the citizens poor (because it allowed the patrician class, that is, the "great citizens," to concentrate wealth), the laws in Florence had established divisions between the guilds that established an order of permanent dominance of certain noble classes at the expense of the people.

> From this division . . . arose the arrogance of the captains of the [Guelf] Party because those citizens who had been Guelfs of old, in whose governance that magistracy always revolved, favored the people of the greater guilds and persecuted those in the lesser guilds together with their defenders: hence arose the many tumults against them . . . But in the ordering of the guild corporations, many of those occupations in which the lesser people and the lowest plebs were engaged were left without guild corporations

of their own, but were subordinated under various guilds appropriate to the character of their occupation. In consequence, when they were either not satisfied for their labor or in some mode oppressed by their masters, they had no other place of refuge than the magistracy of the guild that governed them, from which it did not appear to them that they got the justice they judged was suitable.[39]

Inevitably, these structural inequalities generated and set opposing humors in motion. In McCormick's reading of Machiavelli's account, "the guild republic confronted circumstances in which its riches citizens were colluding with the arrogant, disenfranchised, but still quite powerful nobility to oppress members of the minor guilds and others, and the majority of the city's laborers were being exploited by their socioeconomic superiors within the major guilds, with no recourse to an appellate process that they deemed to be fair."[40]

Notably, Machiavelli points to the origin of the tumult not in the people but in representatives of the republic, namely two Florentine popolani, Salvestro de' Medici and Benedetto Alberti. Perceiving the strife within the people, they attempted to provoke a popular tumult as an instrument to bolster their own republican rhetoric of reform. Machiavelli describes their careful orchestration of events that culminated in the Ciompi Revolt, and Machiavelli's choice of words illuminates a great deal about how he evaluated the actions of the actors. For instance, Machiavelli narrates how, not being able to "bear that the people should be oppressed by a few powerful men" and designing a way "to bring an end to this insolence," they "secretly resolved on a law to renew the Orders of Justice against the great."[41] One can hear Machiavelli's inflection in these accounts, associating his favorite epithet, "insolent," with the new nobility of the popolo grasso, while showing how the two popolani sought reform through the institution of the law and the bolstering of institutional power. He then shows Salvestro turning to the mode of tumult to give him the power to push through the changes in law. At each step in this early history of the Ciompi Revolt, Machiavelli narrates actions in a way that mirrors his own general theory of political conflict, corruption, and resolution.

At this point, it is important to highlight a key element of Machiavelli's social theory that undergirded his support of tumults. For Machiavelli, the necessary tumultuousness of politics derives from the fact the two opposing humors are always contending with one another in any state, including a republic. Like the competing bodily desires for rest and activity, stability and adventure, forgiveness and revenge, or possession and conquest, the humors of the "people" and the "great" are always in tension and flux within the same body politic. By the "great," Machiavelli means those few with extraordinary wealth, power, and prestige within any community that gives them the autonomy and resources to act independently of or even antagonistically toward the state. By the "people" Machiavelli means the ordinary citizens of the popolo whose livelihood and possibility for advancement relies upon the resources and orders of the state. Machiavelli presents their conflict in the most extreme and simplistic way possible: "Without doubt, if one considers the end of the nobles [the great] and of the ignobles [the people], one will see great desire to dominate in the former, and in the latter only desire not to be dominated."[42] The humor of the great can thus be summarized as insolent but farsighted ambition for private honor; the humor of the people can be described as fickle but spirited protection of public freedom. Whereas the great often see the state as inhibiting their ambition (for instance, with legal necessities such as the Ordinances of Justice), the people find in the state the mode by which they collective exert power over the great and secure their freedom from exploitation (such as the magistracy of the gonfalonier of justice).

A republic is not an exception to this rule. Republics simply attempt to negotiate these competing tensions through some rational order of justice that overcomes the natural tendency toward corruption. For Machiavelli, laws developed by participation of the people and enforced by a republican state represent legal necessities that check the natural human impulse to seek private gain and direct their energies toward serving the common good. Without such necessities, corruption is inevitable. According to Kocis, corruption in Machiavelli can take many forms. *Politically* is means "the elevation of personal or familial interests over the common good"; *legally* it means "depriving a people of the power to make its own laws and to live in lawful and just order"; and *psychologically* it means "the absence of the conditions necessary for humans to develop their higher potential, especially their potential for *gloria*."[43] The common good, by contrast, represents the establishment of a just political order that serves the interests of the large majority of its citizens. Strauss describes such an order as "consisting of freedom from foreign domination and from despotic rule, rule of law, security of the lives, the property and the honor of every citizen, ever increasing wealth and power, and last but not least glory or empire."[44] The phrase "rule of law" is particularly important here for Machiavelli. As Viroli explains, when he speaks of the rule of law, Machiavelli "always means rule of just laws—that is, laws and statutes that aim at the common good."[45] These laws limit corruption by prescribing "that men's actions are to be judged on the basis of general rules which apply equally to all actions of the same type into all individuals of the group concerned."[46] By preventing individuals from exploiting the state for their own personal benefit, these laws channel energies toward actions, policies, and works that help expand the power of the citizens as a whole. The resulting order, understood as a stabilization of competing forces, is what Machiavelli means by "justice."

All of these elements are made to play a role within Machiavelli's dramatic narrative of the Ciompi Revolt, but they are most vividly on display in the speech he attributes to Salvestro as he seeks to instigate the people to tumult. The context of the speech is important. As the proposed law was being debated by the representatives of the elite councils in the Signoria known as the Collegi, Salvestro (who had recently been elected gonfaloniere) craftily left the chambers and entered the chambers of the signori and delivered an oration in the name of republican ideals of justice. The speech is a masterpiece of Machiavellian republican rhetoric. Salvestro contrasts the private with the common good, praises the people's civic virtue while exposing the malignancy of noble corruption, and perhaps most importantly places blame for the crisis on the blocking of institutional channels of deliberation to express the public humors. In the name of defending the republic, he condemns its corruption. Machiavelli describes the speech as follows:

> Here, having climbed up high where everyone could see and hear him, he said he believed he had been made a Gonfalonier not to be a judge of private causes, which had their own ordinary judges, but to watch over the state—to correct the insolence of the powerful and to temper those laws by the use of which one would see the republic ruined. And he said that he had thought diligently about both these things and had provided for them as far as it had been possible for him, but the malignity of men so opposed his just enterprises that the way to doing good had been taken from him, and the way not only to deliberating on it but to hearing about it had been taken from them. Hence, seeing that he was no longer able to be of any use in anything to the republic or to the universal good, he did not know for what cause he should any longer keep his magistracy, which

either he did not deserve or someone else believed he did not deserve. On this account he wanted to go home so that the people could put another in his place who would have either greater virtue or better fortune than he. And having said these words, he left the council to go home.[47]

The threatened resignation, of course, was a rhetorical move intended to provoke the people once they heard of his heroic defense of their liberty. By showing that he had done everything possible within the current regime to advance their cause, his resignation showed there was only one mode left open to them—that of tumult. And it had the desired effect. On departing the meeting, those in support of his "desired innovation raised an uproar," and soon the council was in "full tumult."[48] The council chambers became a site of cruelty, for "there many noble citizens were threatened with very abusive words, among them Carlo Strozzi, who was taken around the chest by an artisan who wished to kill him but was defended by the effort of bystanders."[49] Soon the uproar could not be contained and the popolani played their final card: "The one who excited greater tumult and put the city under arms was Benedetto degli Alberti, who at the top of his voice, from the windows of the palace, called the people to arms; and the piazza was quickly filled with armed men—so that which the Collegi had been unwilling to do when they were begged at first, they did when threatened and frightened."[50] By inciting the people to arms and threatening cruelty, Salvestro and Alberti had gained influence over the state and had won glory for the day.

Importantly, Salvestro's denunciation of his colleagues was defended through the same reasoning Machiavelli used to justify tumults. Machiavelli, like Salvestro, finds great value in "being able to accuse citizens to the people, or to some magistrate or counsel, when they sin in anything against the free state."[51] Just as tumults vent public energies by creating fearsome spectacles that instigate often necessary legal reform, public denunciations give the people an outlet "by which to vent, in some mode against some citizen, those humors that grow up in cities; and when the humors do not have an outlet by which they may be vented ordinarily, they have recourse to extraordinary modes that bring a whole republic to ruin."[52] Ironically, precisely those cities that prevent and suppress public accusations in the name of public order are the ones that give rise to what Machiavelli calls "calumnies," or the proliferation of defamatory rumors about someone in order to damage their reputation. The problem with calumnies is not the content of the accusation but the mode by which the accusations are handled. Lacking open and public trials, "calumnies anger and do not punish citizens, and those angered think of getting even, hating rather than fearing the things that are against them."[53] The result in every case is that on every side hatred surges, advancing from "division to sects; from sects to ruin."[54] Therefore, Machiavelli concludes "as much as accusations help republics, so much do calumnies hurt."[55] What is important in both cases, however, is that republican institutions are established and strong enough to limit these outbursts and energy and process them through legitimate modes and orders.

Machiavelli's support of both tumults and accusations thus reveals a latent progressivism in his overall thought, which is to say the belief that despite humans' vices, their behavior can be improved through knowledge, discipline, law, and effort. Machiavelli certainly did not assume that human beings, left to their own devices, were virtuous. He says quite clearly that "it is necessary to whoever disposes a republic and orders laws in it to presuppose that all men are bad, and that they always have to use the malignity of their spirit whenever they have a free opportunity for it."[56] Consequently, one must assume that "men never work any good unless through necessity, but where choice abounds and one can make use of license, at once everything is full of confusion and disorder."[57] But this latter passage can also be read as a positive prescription. Men may, in fact, be *made good* under pressures of legal and social necessity. Thus he follows the assertion of apparent pessimism with the observation that just as "hunger and poverty make men industrious . . . the laws make them good. Where a thing works well on its own without the law, the law is not necessary; but when some good custom is lacking, at once the law is necessary."[58] Here we confront an apparent contradiction. On the one hand, those who order laws in a republic must presuppose that all men are bad. On the other hand, those who design those laws should do so with the aim of making them good. But this contradiction is resolved by an appeal to process. Through the imposition of laws, the temptation of the bad can be turned toward the good. Machiavelli thus grants the case of the conservative about innate human depravity in a state of nature while accepting the progressive ideal of the possibility of human growth in a state of society. Like Aristotle, Machiavelli believes that human beings as political animals only achieve their potential through the institutions of the state.

From Machiavelli's perspective, the rhetorical challenge of republican and popular reformists, therefore, is to balance two opposing tendencies.

First, they must evoke and channel the anger and resentment necessary to expose corruption, challenge institutional inertia, and instigate legal reform. Second, they must never exceed the absolute limits of the republican orders that would necessitate a breakdown in the institutions themselves. Once the orders cease to be able to contain the energy unleashed by tumults and accusations, they invite the authoritarian solution that solves republican corruption by the destruction of the republic itself. But once these legal necessities are dissolved, politics goes off of the rails and there no longer is a check on the malignancy of spirit that ultimately leads to confusion, disorder, and ruin. In Machiavelli's republican ideal, authoritarian rhetoric is kept in check by an alliance between popular leaders and republican reformers, the one leading the people to tumult while the other pointing to their resentments as evidence of the need for institutional change. In the early stages of the Ciompi Revolt, for instance, Machiavelli shows many of the speakers appealing to his own political reasoning to advance radical reforms into the republic, some of them achieving quite significant short-term gains. Salvestro's actions masterfully exploited the opportunity to assert leadership of the people, seizing upon their grievances, exposing the corruption of the city's leaders, and using a tumult to force changes in the law. Soon the city of Florence would be the site of the most radical labor insurrection seen in Europe before the nineteenth century.

Yet we face difficulty in applying Machiavelli's idea of tumult in the twenty-first century. Machiavelli's entire theory was based on the ability to differentiate the potentially positive effects of tumult from the categorically negative outcomes of calumny. For him, a tumult's spontaneous, outgoing, and reformist nature made it an ideal catalyst for legal reform, whereas the orchestrated, insular, and corrupting nature of a calumny could only serve to foster suspicion, paranoia, and hatred among the people. In the twenty-first century, however, the method of tumult can no longer be easily disentangled from the method of calumny. When Polansky, for instance, interprets the January 6 attack on the capital as a "tumult," he downplays the degree to which many people participated in this riot because of their immersion in conspiracy theories like QAnon peddled by right-wing media outlets and President Trump himself. To assume there existed *legitimate* (and not simply *deeply felt*) grievances that justified the attack is to ignore the explicit intent of the occupiers of the Capitol, which was to use uncivil disobedience to overturn the election in the belief that President Biden's victory had been "rigged." This utterly false claim spread wildly over social media and was encouraged by prominent pundits on outlets like Fox News. Far from being a tumult, January 6 was quite clearly the result of orchestrated calumny. In the words of the Anti-Defamation League, the "events of January 6—and their far-reaching aftermath—demonstrate the toxic and dangerous impact of coordinated engagement between extremists and non-extremists, and illustrate the profound and far-reaching effects of ostensibly mainstream political leaders, media influencers and other high-profile figures who tolerate, flirt with and outright promote extremist ideology and conspiracy theories."[59] If anything, January 6 alerted many people to the existence of this network of extremist media influencers who profit from concocting and spreading fantastic lies. Rather than bolstering a republic, such an atmosphere can only serve to destroy it by eroding the entire basis of commonly accepted fact upon which any coherent public opinion must be founded.

The almost permanent presence of calumny in today's media environment puts the entire idea of uncivil disobedience under suspicion. One can imagine, particularly in Ancient Rome, that people often lacked any outlet for social or political expression. Just as Machiavelli speculated, the buildup of social, political, and economic stresses could lead in such conditions to the eruption of a tumult to make their presence felt. But that is not the case in today's media-saturated political environment. Grievances are not only easily expressed but also actively cultivated. Indeed, it is almost impossible to imagine an act of collective violence that isn't the result of conscious orchestration. This phenomenon leads, therefore, to the inevitable spread of extremist influencers who develop an audience of people eager to use violence as a means of self-expression and self-actualization. The ideal that inspires such uncivil disobedience often doesn't matter much, as it often consists entirely of abstractions and fabrications. The message of righteous violence in the name of some vague ideal of "liberty" is enough to recruit people to a cause. Whatever positive outcomes that Machiavelli associated with a violent tumult thus disappear when disorganized groups of Roman citizens are replaced by heavily armed citizen militias with body armor and coordinated logistics.

I believe, therefore, that the progressive and reformist character of Machiavellian tumults requires a renewed commitment to the active modes of *civil* disobedience practiced by traditional social movements. Violence quickly spirals out of control when it can so easily be co-opted by extremist elements, sometimes authorizing massive crackdowns by the state that suppresses rather than catalyzes reform. Nonviolent civil disobedience, by contrast, relies on shared idea and ideals to unite people in common cause and seeks, ultimately, to change attitudes rather than threaten bodies. Tumultuous civic disobedience may still involve loud, noisy clashing but not a clash of arms. It is the tumultuous clash of people gathered together to call attention to injustice and advocate for changes in law, and this motive is entirely Machiavellian.

Clearly, then, we are confronted with three different modes of action that seem to overlap considerably. First, the mode of the lion advocates using the force of one's "own arms" to chase off wolves and do whatever is necessary to confront an internal or external threat. Second, the tumultuous mode of uncivil disobedience uses a similar logic to deploy force to address systematic injustice within a republican order that has become corrupt. Third, the tumultuous mode of civil disobedience restrains from excessive force and relies on largely symbolic and rhetorical action to achieve just legal reform through persuasion. There is nothing contradictory here. One of Machiavelli's consistent recommendations is that one must adapt one's mode to the times and the situation. His political realism does not commit us, like a Kantian ethics, absolutely to one mode over the other in all situations. Effectual truth simply says we must evaluate our actions by their pragmatic outcomes. The prudential challenge is to fit the correct mode to the right situation according to the specific logic of circumstances.

The justification for the mode of the lion seems, at least on its face, to be clear. Today, we find natural resources and human populations under direct threat of exploitation, war, or genocide by superior military powers who operate in violation of human rights and international law. Sometimes these threats are from foreign aggressors, as with Russia's invasion of Ukraine. Other times people are subject to authoritarianism within the borders of their own country, such as the totalitarianism of North Korea. Suggesting that these populations should enact nonviolent modes of resistance is to send them straight to the prison or the killing fields. Machiavelli does not suggest that the mode of the lion should be pursued in all such cases. One should not instigate a battle that will bring even more suffering and ruin. But certainly we must acknowledge the right of any oppressed people to use force to emancipate themselves.

The line between civil and uncivil disobedience, however, is more problematic. Both types of tumults are suited for diverse civic populations operating within republican orders that have demonstrated past commitment to the rule of law. The goal of both modes is not to overturn these regimes but to reform them, and both modes employ a form of populist rhetoric that uses some form of coercion and persuasion to repair a republican order without ruining it. Civil disobedience therefore is fitting when the civic order is still responsive to change and when the freedom still exists to organize in the open and bring publics together to agitate for reform through democratic means. But when republics genuinely break the guardrails and drift toward authoritarianism, uncivil disobedience inevitably appears as a heroic and appropriate response. Certainly, many of those participating in the January 6 assault on the US Capitol saw themselves in the tradition of Sons of Liberty during the American Revolution. Ultimately, our choice of mode depends on how we understand the nature of our situation. That is why the challenge in an age of propaganda is to distinguish genuine threats from manufactured calumnies. For in the end, it is not tumults or lions that will ruin us but the widespread embrace of bigotry and lies.

CHAPTER 7

On Revolution

I N THE MODERN ERA, CATASTROPHE AND REVOLUTION ARE OFTEN counterparts. When catastrophe threatens to bring an old order to its knees, the dream of a new order cannot help but be born. As Hariman explains, "catastrophes can contain many of the features of the revolutionary ideal: a great rupturing of the established order, a sweeping process of change that affects all classes, enhanced solidarity as people create new modes of living together, and emerging awareness of a new horizon of meaning, with all of it exceeding prior practices of prediction and control."[1] But revolution, as a genre of rhetorical response, carries with it a more ambitious vision of possibility and a more fundamental optimism than the concept of catastrophe. In the modern worldview that largely followed in Machiavelli's wake, for instance, catastrophes were seen as opportunities to cast off the vestiges of the dying feudal order in order to advance "through perpetual revolutions" toward a state in which nature itself could be brought under complete control.[2] Catastrophe, by contrast, is "more pessimistic and more open to alternative forms of political agency."[3] Particularly today, when catastrophes have increased in scope and in scale, there is a "growing sense that modernity cannot delivery on its promises, that it can no longer ward off its negative consequences, that it is losing control of development on its own terms, or that it cannot be renewed and extended via revolutions."[4] Although the rhetoric of catastrophe therefore must include the rhetoric of revolution within its genre, it also must account for rhetorical responses that accept the limits on progress, that do not hope for wholesale renewal, and that accept the possibility that dystopia is as likely an outcome as utopia.

Machiavelli's work offers a surprisingly rich site for exploring the rhetorical complexities of revolution as a rhetorical response to catastrophe. In fact, political theorist Hannah Arendt identified Machiavelli as the founder of revolutionary thinking in the Western tradition. For her, the modern concept of revolution is "inextricably bound up with the notion that the course of history suddenly begins anew, that an entirely new story, a story never known or told before, is about to unfold."[5] In her reading, this modern concept has roots in the Renaissance. According to Arendt, "there exists in our political history one type of event for which the notion of founding is decisive, and there is in our history of thought one political thinker in whose work the concept of foundation is central, if not paramount. The events are the revolutions of the modern age, and the thinker is Machiavelli, who stood at the threshold of this age and, though he never used the word, was the first to conceive of a revolution."[6] What was revolutionary about Machiavelli, for Arendt, was that he was the first to become "aware of the contemporary beginnings of the birth of nations and the need for a new body politic . . . he therefore used the hitherto unknown term *lo stato* [the state]."[7] Unlike Plato, whose republic was more of a thought experiment, "he was the first to think about the possibility of founding a permanent, lasting, enduring body politic."[8] Machiavelli perceived that for modern states to endure, they had to move past the old feudal orders and develop institutions that were consonant with the emerging foundations of modern political power. His revolutionary call opens the *Discourses*: "Although the envious nature of men has always made it no less dangerous to find new modes and orders than to seek unknown waters and lands, and because men are more ready to blame than to praise the actions of others, nonetheless, driven by that natural desire that has always been in me to work, without any respect, for those things I believe will bring common benefit to everyone, I have decided to take a path as yet untrodden by anyone, and if it brings me trouble and difficulty, it could also bring me reward through those who consider humanely the end of these labors of mine."[9] By courage, nature, desire, and end, Machiavelli in this carefully wrought account claims himself to be the pioneer of the "new," in this case of new modes and orders. But as Arendt points out, we should not misunderstand this characterization: "Machiavelli's chief interest in the innumerable *mutazioni, variazioni*, and *alterazioni*, of which his work is so full that interpreters could mistake his teachings for a 'theory of political change,' was precisely the immutable, the invariable, and the unalterable, in short the permanent and enduring."[10] For Machiavelli, true revolutionary action instituted change in order to conform to what would never change. His revolutionary ideal was to innovate by adapting to what was permanent.

Machiavelli was therefore an ambiguous revolutionary. On the one hand, he speaks on behalf of the adventurous, the innovative, the reformed, and the bold; on the other, he warns that the pursuit of the perfect ideal of the completely fresh start, unhinged from the past, can only lead to a destructive tyranny. For instance, Machiavelli recognizes that any new prince seeking to institute a completely new order must make dramatic changes that necessitate violence and cruelty in order to break people from past habits and memories. In language that anticipates twentieth-century fascist regimes, Machiavelli writes that these princes must "make in cities new governments with new names, new authorities, new men; to make the rich poor, the poor rich . . . to build new cities, to take down those built, to exchange the inhabitants from one place to another; and, in some, not to leave anything untouched."[11] Taken out of context, this might seem like a recommendation. But I think he is simply stating a fact. Machiavelli presents this option in order to warn against it, noting that while achieving short term success, "these modes are very cruel, and enemies to every way of life, not only Christian but human; and any man whatever should flee them and wish to live in private rather than as a king with so much ruin to men."[12] A similar ambiguity can be found in his treatment of popular revolutions. Although Machiavelli often sympathized with the grievances of the people, he also argued that the mode of revolutionary action too quickly became violent and overreached any rational aims. For him, even large-scale innovation had to respect the limits of the possible.

What I wish to investigate in this chapter, therefore, is how Machiavelli dramatizes this more popular manifestation of the rhetoric of revolution that we find in the *Florentine Histories*, particularly in his narrative of the Ciompi Revolt. Although Machiavelli's conception of revolution technically applies also to the actions of reformist princes, the populist rhetoric of the ciompi revolutionaries resonates more closely with modern conceptions of revolution. For instance, Theda Skocpol defines revolution as "rapid, basic transformations of a society's state and class structures."[13] And Anthony Giddens argues that a revolution is "the seizure of state power through violent means by the leaders of a mass movement, when that power is subsequently used to initiate major processes of social reform."[14] Machiavelli largely ignores these types of revolutionary movements in his conceptual works, but in his description of the Ciompi Revolt they take center stage. What we find there is a narrative of catastrophe that shows republican leaders attempting to manipulate popular sentiments to enforce moderate changes only to find themselves overtaken by the populist energy they had unleashed.

We return, then, to the familiar challenge of how to direct reformist impulses into productive channels without lurching into violence and ruin. In the case of the Ciompi Revolt, the populist rhetoric that had achieved initial success quickly transformed into a rhetoric of revolution that cast aside an alliance with republican elites in the name of total transformation of the state through violence. Driven by hatred of the ruling class and a desire to emancipate themselves from social poverty and political powerlessness, the ciompi and their followers called for extreme forms of uncivil disobedience to replace the parliamentary rule of law by the direct will of the people. The collapse that followed was catastrophic. Machiavelli's narrative thus provides justification for Arendt's later conclusion that "the whole record of past revolutions demonstrates beyond doubt that every attempt to solve the social question with political means leads into terror, and that it is terror which sends revolutions to their doom."[15] Machiavelli's narrative of this episode in Florentine history provides a sympathetic account of the causes and the leadership of the revolt while ultimately making it a cautionary tale. When we are faced with catastrophes beyond our ability to completely control, pursuing revolutionary ideals without a sense of limit or respect for tolerance can quickly produce terror and bring ruin.

There are three reasons why the Ciompi Revolt provides the ideal case study through which to discern Machiavelli's revolutionary thinking in action. First, critical historians and theorists have often characterized the Ciompi Revolt as a landmark event in the development of modern class-conscious rebellion. According to Simone Weil, "this insurrection known as the insurrection of the Ciompi, is without doubt the earliest of the proletarian insurrections; and it is the more worthy of study from this point of view because it exhibits already in a remarkably pure form the specific features which appear later on in the great working-class movements."[16] Second, Machiavelli outdoes himself in the way he dramatizes these events. According to Anna Maria Cabrini, "the pages on the Ciompi Revolution are among the most memorable in the *Florentine Histories*, above all for the depth of their analysis of the motivations behind the hatred of the men of the plebs against 'the wealthy citizens and leaders of the guilds.'"[17] Third, Machiavelli includes what is arguably the most extraordinary example of eloquence to appear anywhere in his writings in the form of a rhetorical reconstruction of an oration delivered by an anonymous *ciompo* just before the insurrection. For Winter, this "revolutionary address reveals an untimely and not entirely self-conscious political radicalism, a plebeian politics that repudiates the logic of oligarchic privilege and is simultaneously not available for subsumption under the mantle of civic republicanism."[18] This address embodies the spirit of pure populist rhetoric so deeply that it stands alone in the literature of Italian Renaissance history.

Machiavelli makes his anonymous ciompo sound so persuasive, in fact, that many modern commentators have argued that the author of *The Prince* was a protosocialist. Gramsci, for instance, argues that Machiavelli writes his works from a distinctly class-conscious perspective in which he literally "becomes the people."[19] Althusser follows this line of argument by interpreting Machiavelli's work as a manifesto "addressed to the masses, in order to organize them into a revolutionary force."[20] Althusser goes so far as to argue that only by assuming Machiavelli's class position can we accurately interpret his work: "Outside this class position, his enterprise and his writings are inexplicable: to speak of the Prince as he does, one needs to be a man of the people, aligned with the class positions of the people."[21] Similarly, Antonio Negri finds in Machiavelli's work a "very radical image of a people capable of truth, equality, organized in its rallies, ethically sustained by civil religion, capable of arms and victory."[22] These are all inspiring images. Under these revolutionary interpretations, Machiavelli becomes a writer who superficially spoke the language of "princes" but actually cared for the power of the people. The truly Machiavellian revolution was thus not found in the redemptive leadership of Cesare Borgia but in the unfulfilled promise of the Ciompi Revolt.

Although I find these strong claims highly innovative, I am not persuaded by them. Machiavelli, after all, has a strange way of supporting his ciompi brethren—namely by repeatedly slandering them. At the very origin of the tumult, Machiavelli describes the three factions as follows: (1) the Guelfs, the ancient nobles, and the popolo grasso (including the names of Albizzi, Castiglionchio, and Strozzi); (2) the popolani, or "popular men of the lesser sort" (including the Ricci, Medici, and Alberti); and (3) "the rest of the multitude" who, "as almost always happens, adhered to the side of the malcontents."[23] The ciompi, in other words, represented a third faction of the mob of popolo minuto. And when the second stage of the revolt got under way, led by such "malcontents," Machiavelli immediately passed judgment that this second tumult "hurt the republic a good deal more than the first."[24] Rather than

Machiavelli supporting the participants in the Ciompi Revolt, the people are on the receiving end of his considerable scorn precisely because of their inability to see beyond their own interests. They act impulsively and almost destroy the state in the process. Strange praise for the people.

For instance, these types of passage were characteristic of how Machiavelli described the ciompi. On one morning, he tells us, "the impatient and fickle multitude came into the piazza under the usual ensigns with such loud and terrifying cries that they frightened the whole council . . . seeing such indecency in a multitude and such malignity or fear in those who could have checked or crushed it."[25] Machiavelli describes in detail how one of the popolani, Messer Giorgio Scali, became favored by the plebs for his insolence toward the nobles. Then just as quickly he fell out of favor for the same insolence. Typical of the fickleness of the multitude, they urged Benedetto Alberti to order Giorgio's decapitation—to which Alberti obliged. Machiavelli then makes sure his readers do not miss the point. He actually invents thoughts in Giorgio's head on the way to his execution, relating them this way: "As he saw himself coming to his death before that people which a short time before had adored him, he lamented his evil fate and the malignity of the citizens who, by injuring him wrongly, had constrained him to favor and honor a multitude in which there was neither any faith nor any gratitude . . . Then he lamented for himself that he had trusted too much in a people whom every voice, every act, every suspicion moves and corrupts."[26] The point was made. The people, while not evil, are prone to be fickle, ungrateful, eager for gain, and unreliable when not constrained by legal and social necessity.

That conditional phrase, "when not constrained by legal and social necessity," is the key to deciphering the seemingly contradictory attitudes that Machiavelli expressed toward the people. For instance, Machiavelli often spoke harshly of the ciompi but had largely praised the plebian tumults in Rome. At first this seems to be a contradiction. After all, the causes of the tumult in both were very similar. Furthermore, the conflict between the two humors in both cases contained the same reformist potential. For instance, Machiavelli repeats the principle he had already delineated in the *Discourses*, observing in his history that "the grave and natural enmities that exist between the men of the people and the nobles, caused by the wish of the latter to command and the former not to obey, are the cause of all evils that arise in cities. For from this diversity of humors all other things that agitate republics take their nourishment."[27] One would expect, therefore, that he would treat the two cases the same.

But he does not. Instead, he argues that what "kept Rome disunited" for its own benefit "kept Florence divided" to its detriment.[28] The key difference was that the strength of the Roman Republic stemmed from the fact that both the nobles and the plebs strove for the same aim, which was to be able to gain access to high office and receive honors from the state. Consequently, the result of the tumults was the establishment of a more stable (because mixed) political order, for as "men of the people could be placed in the administration of the magistracies, the armies, and the posts of empire together with the nobles, they were filled with the same virtue as the nobles, and that city, by growing in virtue, grew in power."[29] The Florentine situation was different. The revolutionary aims of the ciompi made them contemptuous of cooperation with the republican rulers they believed (with good reason) were corrupt. Hence, "the people of Florence fought to be alone in the government without the participation of the nobles."[30] The result was a zero-sum game for power, in which "the laws that were made afterwards were not for the common utility but were all ordered in favor of the conqueror."[31] And because the people initially conquered, the nobles were "deprived of the magistracies" to such a degree that they saw no recourse but to ready "greater forces for its own defense."[32] The seeds of class war had been sown.

Therefore, despite his clear sympathies with the plight of the ciompi, Machiavelli was no closet populist; he had as much contempt for their inconstancy, fickleness, and rage as he did for the greed and insolence of the grandi. In Machiavelli's account, although the grievances of the ciompi were justified, the modes by which they pursued their aims polarized class divisions and made any constructive cooperation impossible. For the "virtue in arms and the generosity of spirit that were in the nobility were eliminated, and in the people, where they never had been, they could not be rekindled; thus did Florence become ever more humble and abject."[33] For Machiavelli, revolution required more than violent tumult and naked aggression; revolution required a *political* foundation that integrated both humors into an order of *power*.

It is this emphasis on the politics of revolution that made Machiavelli a favorite of Arendt. For her, modern "revolutionaries" had consistently brought actual revolutions to their doom by celebrating the exciting but ephemeral violent phrase of liberation while ignoring the necessity of establishing a foundation for freedom through politics. Like Machiavelli, Arendt recognized that violence might be necessary to break the chains of oppression, whether through the essentially mute act of physical force or the symbolic act of cruelty. But to genuinely begin something new, to start a new story that builds upon a new foundation, requires bringing people together through acts of speech and binding promises. For Arendt, "violence is no more adequate to describe the phenomenon of revolution than change; only where change occurs in the sense of a new beginning, where violence is used to constitute an altogether different form of government, to bring about the formation of a new body politic, where the liberation from oppression aims at least at the constitution of freedom can we speak of revolution."[34] Interpreted in Machiavellian terms, revolution sparked by populist rhetoric must often use violence to break the oppression of the old order, but it must then embrace republican rhetoric to envision and implement the new modes and orders capable of withstanding the vicissitudes of fortune.

The Ciompi Revolt did not begin with revolutionary aims. It was motivated by a clear reformist impulse consistent with Machiavelli's concept of a tumult. As Winter explains, "despite the bold actions, the Ciompi's political and social demands were modest. They wanted the right to form a guild and demanded production increases for the wool industry to abate unemployment."[35] Given that Machiavelli had explicitly blamed their exclusion from political power by the popolo grasso as a cause of the tumult, it is unsurprising that he would take the time to list their demands. They wanted "three new guild corporations be formed, one for the carders and dyers, another for the barbers, doublet makers, tailors, and such mechanical arts, the third for the lesser people; and that from these three new guilds there would always be two Signori and from the fourteen lesser guilds three."[36] Nothing in these demands was at all unreasonable. Had these been all the demands that were put forward, it is possible (in Machiavelli's assessment, anyway) that the republican regime might have compromised in order to resolve the tumult through modifications in law.

But the ciompi did not stop there. And here we find ourselves again confronted with the ruin of tragic choices. Ironically, the ultimate failure of the Ciompi Revolt, in Machiavelli's view, was due precisely to its overreliance on the very modes that have come to be identified as "Machiavellian." Through the six-week insurrection, Machiavelli shows how the ciompi "badly" used fear, violence, cruelty, and duplicity to attain short-term satisfactions but then undermine what were otherwise rational and just demands. For instance, Machiavelli notes with clear disdain that "they demanded many other things besides these for the benefit of their particular supporters, and on the opposite side they wanted many of their enemies to be imprisoned and admonished. These demands, though dishonorable and grievous for the republic, were, for fear of worse, immediately decided upon by the Signori, the Collegi, and the council of the people."[37] Here we find the logic of political conquest at work that sets the private good against the common good. No compromise is possible. And despite their promise that all tumults would stop when this law was passed, the very next morning the "impatient and fickle multitude" rushed into the piazza and cried out "that all the Signori should abandon the palace or else they would kill their children and burn down their houses."[38] For Machiavelli, it was not the legal demands of the ciompi that were "dishonorable and grievous" to the republic, but the excessive, fickle, and inconsistent use of mob violence and fear to punish and humiliate enemies and thwart the implementation of law.

Machiavelli establishes the pattern of the ciompis' self-destructiveness by detailing a series of impulsive actions the day after the triumph of Salvestro and Benedetto. The tumult they had instigated outside the walls of the Palazzo della Signoria had produced the intended effect; the priors had agreed to changes in the law that were to be deliberated and approved in a general council (called a *balìa*) the following day. Yet passions once aroused are difficult to suppress. As the *balìa* was in session, the guilds and their banners once again filled the streets, and "some ensign bearers from the guilds and from those of lesser quality, moved by those who wanted to get revenge for the recent injuries they had received from the Guelfs, detached themselves from the others, and they sacked and burned the house of Messer Lapo da Castiglionchio," who "first hid in Santa Croce, then, dressed as a friar, fled to the Casentino."[39] Carlo Strozzi, not desiring to repeat his humiliation at the Signoria, also fled the city just in time: "When Messer Lapo's house had been burned—because evils begin with difficulty and grow with ease—many other houses were sacked and burned out of either universal hatred or private enmities. And so that they might have company with more thirst than theirs for stealing the goods of others, they broke open the public prisons and then sacked the monastery of the Agnoli and the convent of Santo Spirito, where many citizens had hidden their movables."[40] The sacking of the public treasury was only thwarted by one of the signori on a horse with armed men. Yet the priors knew they did not have the power to put down the revolt by violence; instead, they satisfied the people with more concessions, including the declaration of Messer Castiglionchio as a rebel to the state, the election of new priors, and the appointment of Luigi Guicciardini (ancestor of Machiavelli's contemporary, Francesco Guicciardini) as the new gonfalonier.

With the keen insight of a born rhetorician, Machiavelli at this point in the *Florentine Histories* focused all of his energies on rhetorical performances that would determine the course of events. For the fate of the revolution was balanced on the razor's edge. On the one hand, the nights of tumult, despite the damage to property, had instigated changes in law without a single death or act of irrevocable cruelty. With the new city leadership in place and the people still capable of leveraging the threat of arms, laws could be drafted that might integrate multiple constituencies into a more representative government that would provide more resources for the ciompi while preserving the honors of the grandi. But such an outcome required rhetorical leadership capable of uniting different classes under a common cause. On the other hand, the tumults had created widespread fear so that "the stores did not open, the citizens did not put away their arms, and there were heavy guards throughout the city."[41] For the whole city to erupt in uncontrollable violence required only one speaker to further incite passions and set one faction against another in the belief that one must either consume one's enemies or be consumed by them. And as Machiavelli points out, there was no shortage of leaders eager to initiate such a terror. The Signoria had consistently given in to the demands of the popolani who were instigating the revolt, "but because it is not enough for men to get back their own but they want also to seize what belongs to others and get revenge, those who put their hopes in disorders pointed out to the artisans that they would never be safe if their many enemies were not driven out and destroyed."[42] Into this rhetorical situation stepped two competing rhetors, Gonfalonier Guicciardini and an anonymous yet eloquent ciompo.

The oration Machiavelli attributes to Guicciardini perfectly embodies the principles of elitist republican rhetoric already articulated by Machiavelli's predecessors Leonardo Bruni and Coluccio Salutati. Within this ideology, any act of violence is antithetical to a just and free order; all conflicts are to be channeled through the ordinary modes of the state and negotiated by its official magistrates on behalf of the people. As Bruni expressed this view in his *History of the Florentine People*, the Ciompi Revolt "can stand as an internal example and warning for the city's leading citizens that they should not allow civil unrest and armed force to come down to the whims of the mob."[43] The very setting of Guicciardini's address expresses his conservative ideology, occurring as it does within the Palazzo della Signoria before a gathering of the magistrates of the guilds without a single ciompo present. Guicciardini sets the tone by praising himself and the virtues of the priors. Not only had they "suffered the recent riots with patience, especially as they were begun without blame on our part," but they had not fled the city out of fear because "we hoped to have to do with men who might have in them some humanity and some love for their fatherland, we accepted the magistracy willingly, believing that with our humanity we could conquer your ambition by any mode."[44] Guicciardini's oration perfectly embodies the stern paternalism of republican patriarchs. Scolding the guilds as if they were children, Guicciardini laments that "we see now by experience that the more humbly we behave, the more we concede, the more you grow proud and the more indecent things you demand."[45] Machiavelli clearly makes Guicciardini the very paradigm of patronizing nobles who view the state as their own private possession. Here is not a broad-based republicanism but a highly restricted one that sees virtue as belonging to the few.

But the most important part of the speech comes when Guicciardini reveals his noble contempt for popular tumults. In Machiavelli's hands, this rejection of the mode of tumult functions as a warning against short-sided political reasoning. Guicciardini once again sides with elitist civic republicanism, protesting that the Signoria has satisfied many of the demands of the lesser guilds, yet to no satisfaction. The only outcome of these constant discords will be a "disunion" that leads to servitude, hunger, and poverty.[46] Having established these core principles, Guicciardini closes his speech with the very epitome of the conservative civic republican ideal: "These Signori and I command you, and if decency permits it, we pray you to still your spirits for once and be content to rest quietly with the things that have been ordered through us, and if ever you wish something new, be pleased to ask for it with civility and not with tumult and arms. For if they are decent things, you will always be granted them, and you will not give occasion to wicked men, at your charge and to your cost, to ruin your fatherland on your shoulders."[47] According to Machiavelli, the speech humbled and satisfied the gathered leaders of the guilds, and "they thanked the Gonfalonier courteously for having done his duty to them as a good Signore and to the city as a good citizen."[48] Within the walls of the palace, at least, common quiet had been restored. But that is the problem with walls; they limit one's vision. And Machiavelli would show how mistaken they were.

This haughty insularity represents the limitation of elitist republicanism for Machiavelli; what is agreed upon inside the walls by the signori and their invited guests may have little bearing on the sufferings, passions, and desires of people outside in the street. Notably, it is precisely at this moment that Machiavelli explains in detail how the order of the Florentine Guild Republic had structurally disenfranchised thousands of workers, in effect leaving them to the mercy of the major guilds. It is no surprise, therefore, that Machiavelli begins the next section with a stark contrast: "While these things were proceeding, another tumult arose that hurt the republic a great deal more than the first."[49] Read out of context, this passage might seem to indicate that Machiavelli flatly condemned the tumult and thus aligned himself with conservative commentators like Bruni. Yet the reality is more complicated. Machiavelli clearly felt that the outcomes of the second major tumult ultimately harmed the republic; but he did not agree with Bruni that their "only goal was plunder, slaughter and the exile of citizens."[50] The ciompi, who had been systematically denied any ordinary form of representation and status within the state, found themselves caught in a trap: "The greater part of the arson and robbery that took place in the preceding days had been done by the lowest plebs of the city, and those among them who had shown themselves the boldest feared that with the greater differences quieted and composed, they would be punished for the mistakes committed by them and that, as always happens to them, they would be abandoned by those who had incited them to do evil."[51] Machiavelli clearly communicates the degree to which the ciompi felt forced into extreme action by necessity. From long experience, they saw how popolani like the Medici (or for that matter aspiring lords like Walter of Brienne) might use them as pawns to leverage influence over the state only to abandon them after they achieved power, thus reducing the ciompi to the same miserable condition from which they started. Having been instigated to violence once again by those same popolani, the ciompi faced a tragic choice—either accede to Guicciardini's demands in the name of civility only to be betrayed and then punished, or use violence and cruelty to take power for themselves and crush their enemies in the name of self-preservation.

Machiavelli put this logic in the mouth of one of the most charismatic and mysterious characters of his *Histories*—an anonymous ciompo. In Machiavelli's narrative, this man stepped forward to speak during one of the meetings the revolutionaries held at night to discuss events and "point out to each other the dangers in which they found themselves."[52] Emotions were running high during these meetings. The "plebs" (as Machiavelli called the ciompi) were both "full of indignation" at their historical mistreatment and full of "fear because of the arson and robbery they had done."[53]At one of these meetings, Machiavelli notes, "one of the most daring and more experienced spoke in this sense so as to inspire the others."[54] Machiavelli provides no further details about this individual beyond the speech itself. The text that follows can thus be assumed to be a Machiavellian invention in which he imagines what would be the appropriate response from such a daring speaker within an extraordinary set of events. Liberated from the constraints of historical fidelity, Machiavelli lets his rhetorical consciousness run free. The result is what Winter calls "a remarkable rhetorical achievement, blending sophisticated techniques of argument with emotional appeals, vivid examples, and evocative figures."[55] The degree to which Machiavelli actually sympathized with the arguments of the ciompo remains a matter of debate; but the manner in which he juxtaposes this speech with Guicciardini's makes very clear "his view that politics consists of confrontations, that it marks a battlefield where forces encounter one another."[56] Regardless of whether one agrees or disagrees with the ciompo, the fact that Machiavelli puts in his voice such masterful eloquence forces the reader to take him seriously as a political protagonist who demands to be heard and represented. Whereas Bruni saw only "the whims of the mob," Machiavelli imagined rational actors responding to the failures of an imperfect state.[57] The result was a masterpiece in popular revolutionary rhetoric.

Notably, the speech by the anonymous ciompo constructs an entirely different type of situation. Where the ruling elite see insubordination and whim, the people see an opportunity and necessity. In the context of revolutionary catastrophic situations, actors feel their choices to be starkly defined. They must either revolt or be dominated. In quieter times, the ciompo begins, he might have "put quiet poverty ahead of perilous gain," advising a more cautious approach when deliberating "whether to take up arms, to burn and rob the homes of the citizens, to despoil churches."[58] But necessity has forced their hands. Many evils have been done and the possibility for compromise has passed: "You see this whole city full of grievance and hatred against us: the citizens meet together; the Signoria is always on the side of the magistrates."[59] The modes of the fox and the lion have been thrust upon them, for "traps are being set for us" while "new forces are being prepared against our strongholds."[60] The path of "quiet poverty" has thus been blocked; in its place is the certainty of humiliating sufferings of "prisons, tortures, and deaths."[61] The only path left to them is therefore one of perilous gain, namely a course

in which they use force, violence, and cruelty to subdue their enemies and become "princes of all the city."[62]

For the ciompo recognizes what the Greeks called the kairos of the situation, or the timely moment of action. In the moment they faced, he said,
there cannot be "a greater occasion . . . offered us by fortune than this one,
when citizens are still disunited, the Signoria irresolute, and the magistrates
dismayed so that they can easily be crushed before they unite and steady their
spirits."[63] And here the ciompo addresses the plebs as Machiavelli addresses
a prince: "I confess this course is bold and dangerous, but when necessity
presses, boldness is judged prudence; and spirited men never take account of
the danger in great things, for those enterprises that are begun with danger
always end with reward, and one never escapes a danger without danger."[64]
Like all great founders of new orders, the plebs must confront the realities of
their situation and make the tragic choice of accepting the unavoidable evils
that accompany revolutionary renewal. In having the ciompo describe the
situation this way, Machiavelli outlines the contours of every revolutionary
action to follow in the coming centuries. Revolution appears as a desperate
possibility when individuals are confronted with almost overwhelming necessity. Yet out of catastrophe might come innovation.

But as Machiavelli lets the ciompo continue, more sinister elements appear within the speaker's revolutionary spirit. When unhinged from the constraints of social norms and orders, the modes of revolution can quickly
plumb the depths of vengeance. A few of the more shocking arguments in
the ciompo's speech stand out. First, the speaker does not seek to achieve virtue but rather to avoid punishment, arguing that "it is to our advantage . . .
if we wish that our old errors be forgiven us, to make new ones, redoubling
the evils, multiplying the arson and robbery."[65] Second, in order to achieve
this "forgiveness," he counsels having "many companions in this, because
when many err, no one is punished, and though small faults are punished,
great and grave ones are rewarded."[66] Third, he forbids any consideration of
moral conscience or fear of infamy, both because "those who win, in whatever mode they win, never received shame from it" and "where there is, as
with us, fear of hunger and prison, there cannot and should not be fear of
hell."[67] Lastly, he replaces a moral universe with the code of nature red in
tooth and claw, "from which it arises that men devour one another and that
those who can do less are always the worse off."[68] In the view of Mansfield,
a more concise portrayal of political inferno as a living hell could hardly be

imagined: "To be in the midst of a plebeian rebellion is not exceptional but reveals the essential situation of man: all of us stripped naked, exposed to danger and wickedness."[69] To accept the premises of the ciompo's speech at face value is to inhabit a universe of unspeakable cruelty, constant betrayal, and inevitable anarchy.

This logic is as simple as it is tragic—*all or nothing*. In the words of the ciompo, "Whichever of us is first to take up arms again will without doubt be the conqueror, with ruin for the enemy and exaltation for himself."[70] Based on a long history of suffering and betrayal, the ciompi had lost all faith in republican virtue committed to compromising in the name of the common good. They saw only a faithless world in which people "are exposed more to rapine than to industry and more to wicked than to good arts."[71] With such a debased view of human nature, promises are meaningless, and trust is an illusion. Even virtue has no real existence; it is just a hollow label as much as any false title: "You will see that all those who come to great riches and great power have obtained them either by fraud or by force; and afterwards, to hide the ugliness of acquisition, they make it decent by applying the false title of earnings to things they have usurped by deceit or by violence."[72]

However, none of these attitudes or positions articulated so far, whether attributed to the ciompo or to Machiavelli, can be characterized as "revolutionary." The *all or nothing* logic by which one's enemies must be vanquished entirely through violence in order to install one's own party or leader as tyrant is hardly a novel idea. It may, in fact, be one of the oldest political ideas. No, the revolutionary character of the ciompo's speech is not found in its violence but in what Kenneth Burke would call its "nudism." According to Burke, "nudism represents an attempt to return to essentials, to get to the irreducible minimum of human certainty, to re-emphasize the *humanistic* as the sound basis above which any scheme of values must be constructed."[73] Fittingly, Burke defined nudism in the context of discussing the drama of permanence and change in human societies. Nudism comes about after the pieties of the old order have collapsed, and the priests of the vestigial structure are about to give way to prophets who "seek new perspectives whereby this vestigial structure may be criticized and a new one established in its place."[74] Nudism represents a transitional stage between the priesthood and the prophets, a time when the clothing of the old structure is being stripped off in order that people can begin looking "for some immovable 'rock' upon which a new structure of certainties can be erected."[75] And this is precisely what we find in Machiavelli's account of the ciompo's speech, delivered as it was to a fearful and indignant gathering of fellow laborers who were dreaming of something new.

The revolutionary nature of this novelty is evidenced by three revolutionary ideas that Machiavelli inserts into this remarkable, if shocking, address. The oration Machiavelli composes for the ciompo includes three prophetic passages that herald the birth of the modern revolutionary spirit. First, despite the repeated calls for and justifications of the use of force and cruelty to conquer their enemies, the ciompo stresses that one of the two primary ends they must seek is "to be able to live with more freedom."[76] Although what this means in practice remains unclear, the very fact that he appealed to freedom and not simply power is indicative of a burgeoning political imagination in which, according to Arendt, "the idea of freedom and the experience of a new beginning should coincide."[77] Second, the ciompo clears away the ramshackle accumulations of medieval hierarchies with one revolutionary imperative: "Do not let their antiquity of blood, with which they will reproach us, dismay you; for all men, having had the same beginning, are equally ancient and have been made by nature in one mode. Strip all of us naked, you will see that we are alike; dress us in their clothes and them in ours, and without a doubt we shall appear noble and they ignoble, for only poverty and riches make us unequal."[78] Here we find the articulation of the modern idea of innate human equality, a natural unity that underlies apparent differences. Third, he strips away the hierarchical trappings both of culture and religion. Not only does he dismiss fear of Hell but he recognizes how the "conscience" of established religion functions to inhibit the freedom of the political imagination, noting that "it pains me much when I hear that out of conscience many of you repent the deeds that have been done and that you wish to abstain from new deeds."[79] In the ciompo's hands, to abstain from new deeds because of an emotional desire for "repentance" is to submit to the hegemonic domination of the old order and "suffocate in servitude or poverty."[80] In the rhetoric of popular revolution, only through a radical impiety can one truly imagine the new modes that will provide the foundation for the new order. Only by stripping humanity nude can it fully remake itself.

Yet despite their grandiose ambitions, the ciompi quickly find their initial spectacular successes followed by overreach, reaction, and ruin. Characteristic of sudden revolutionary movements at their heroic beginnings, the ciompo's speech had its intended short-term effect in constituting and directing the power of the ciompi to act in concert within that tumultuous moment.

Machiavelli comments, "These persuasions strongly inflamed spirits that were already hot for evil on their own, so that they decided to take up arms after they had secured more companions to do their will; and they swore an oath to help one another if it should happen that one of them were overwhelmed by the magistrates."[81] Soon, the *all or nothing* logic he employed became a self-fulfilling prophecy. As the ciompi were preparing to seize the republic, the signori had captured a ciompi named Simone dalla Piazza, who was tortured in order to extract details of their conspiracy; immediately, the forces of the popolo grasso began organizing armed companies to suppress the ciompi. But the pledge of the ciompi to support one another held true; one Niccolò da San Friano, charged with maintaining the palace clock, became aware of the signori's plans. After returning home, he raised a tumult of one thousand armed men. Soon they were joined by "another multitude," and any hope of resisting them through arms was extinguished.[82] To force the release of prisoners from the Signoria, the first house to burn was that of Luigi Guicciardini. Having recovered the prisoners, the multitude acted without any coherent leadership or plan according to the whim of the moment: "They burned the houses of many citizens, hunting down those who were hated either for public or for private cause. And many citizens, to avenge their private injuries, led them to the houses of their enemies; for it was enough that a single voice shout out in the midst of the multitude, 'to so-and-so's house,' or that he who held the standard in his hands turn toward it. They also burned all the records of the Wool Guild."[83] Yet they also sought to reward their allies, and so that "they might accompany the many evils they did with some praiseworthy work, they made Salvestro de' Medici and many other citizens knights," including Benedetto degli Alberti and, ironically, the same Luigi Guicciardini whose house they had just burned.[84] By the end of the evening, they had forced the Signoria to concede to the formation of the new guilds and mandate the imprisonment and punishment of their enemies.

Then a key moment in the revolution occurred that would ultimately decide its fate. For Machiavelli, a revolutionary movement without a head turns to anarchy. And here we locate Machiavelli's version of elitism—not so much republican as rhetorical. He put his faith not in a class of nobles but in a class of leaders, namely those with virtú capable of leading the people while satisfying the great. Such a leader appeared just when the situation risked getting out of control. Impatient for the Signoria to finish deliberating, the plebs filled the piazza and stormed the palace. But on gaining entrance, they were checked only by the sudden and charismatic appearance of Michele di Lando, a wool carder, who "barefoot and scantily clothed, climbed up the stairs with the whole mob behind him, and as soon as he was in the audience chamber of the Signori, he stopped; and, turning around to the multitude, he said, 'You see: this palace is yours and this city is in your hands. What do you think should be done now?' To which all replied that they wanted him to be Gonfalonier and lord, and to govern them and the city however seemed best to him."[85] Described by Machiavelli as "a sagacious and prudent man who owed more to nature than to fortune," he immediately sought to satisfy the rage of the people through cruelty well used; he suggested they seek out Messer Castiglionchio's handpicked replacement, Ser Nuto, who was equally hated by the people. They quickly found him: "Ser Nuto was carried by the multitude to the piazza and hung on the gallows by one foot; and as whoever was around tore off a piece from him, at a stroke there was nothing left of him but his foot."[86] Then to impose order, "he had it publicly commanded that no one burn or steal anything; and to frighten everyone, he had a gallows erected in the piazza."[87] Other changes to the Signoria and the guild system followed. Once again it seemed that the ciompi had won the day, only now led by a bold and far-sighted prince of the popolo who understood that cruelty had to be done in one stroke, and no more, as a precondition to establish peace.

Tragically, however, the people would not be led. The unlimited ambition of the ciompi combined with a lack of any clear foundation for a new order of justice quickly brought about their ruin. Michele di Lando had attempted to play the role of founder by mediating between the two humors of the state, abandoning popular harangue for republican deliberation. But the *all or nothing* logic of the ciompi could not be checked. The ciompi felt he was being too "partisan toward the greater people."[88] For the fourth time, then, they took up arms and came in "tumult into the piazza."[89] When rebuffed from the palace, they withdrew to Santa Maria Novella and created their own government, indignantly removing all honors from Salvestro and Michele. Finally, a few of them returned to the palace and threatened "with great boldness and greater presumption" the signori with force.[90] This was to be the last card they played in a dangerous game: "Michele was unable to bear such arrogance; and, as he was mindful more of the rank he held than of his low condition, it appeared to him that he must check this extraordinary insolence with an extraordinary mode; and drawing the weapon he had at his waist, he first wounded them gravely and then had them bound and imprisoned."[91] The multitude on hearing this were enraged, but this time they met resistance. Rather than "wait for the enemy within the walls and to have to flee, as did his predecessors, with dishonor to the palace and with shame for himself . . . he gathered a large number of citizens who already had begun to reflect on their error, mounted his horse, and, followed by many armed men, went to Santa Maria Novella to fight them."[92] The ciompi had no chance. As Winter summarizes events, "On August 31, they were brutally slaughtered by a coalition of major and minor guilds with the reformist forces under Michele di Lando. It was one of the bloodiest days in Florentine history."[93] In the coming days, most of the radical changes to the government were negated by the alliance of the popolo grasso and the minor guilds. By 1381 every achievement by the ciompi had been reversed. The revolution had passed through terror to its doom.

Despite Machiavelli's contempt for noble insolence and his sympathy with the plight of the plebs, he was unsparing in his condemnation of the ciompis' tyrannical ambitions and overreliance on violence and cruelty. Unlike the paternalistic civic republicanism of Luigi Guicciardini, however, Machiavelli did not condemn the tumult simply because it employed political violence to attain its ends; he condemned it rhetorically for *having* no clearly defined ends that could mobilize the people's resentments and productively direct their energies. Unlike the tumults in Rome, the Ciompi Revolt lacked any sense of limit; every time it achieved a proximate goal, a new tumult would break out and override the possibility of any unified agreement that established a balance between the two humors. The revolutionary potential latent within the ciompo orator's nudism was left undeveloped because of the multitude's impulsive desire to simply usurp the position of the great. In Machiavelli's account, therefore, the Florentine state was only saved by the actions of Michele di Lando, who emerged in the *Florentine Histories* as something close to the ideal prince:

> The campaign having succeeded, the tumults were settled solely by the virtue of the Gonfalonier [Michele di Lando]. In spirit, prudence, and goodness he surpassed any citizen of his time, and he deserves to be numbered among the few who have benefited their fatherland, for had his spirit been either malign or ambitious, the republic would have lost its freedom altogether and fallen under a greater tyranny than that of the duke of Athens. But his goodness never allowed a thought to enter his mind that might be contrary to the universal good; his prudence led him

to conduct things in such a mode that many yielded to his party and others he was able to subdue with arms. These things caused the plebs to lose heart and the better guildsmen to reflect and to consider what ignominy it was for those who had overcome the pride of the great to have to bear the stench of the plebs.[94]

In his encomium to Michele, Machiavelli demonstrates his ultimate preference for elitist republican order over any radical experiment in populist one-party rule, regardless of the legitimacy of its grievances. For Machiavelli, any revolutionary action must be pursued in the spirit of the common good, which for him is not an abstract ideal but an empirically determined balance of powers within an ordered network of forces. The stinging cruelty of his remark about having to "bear the stench of the plebs" naturally evokes in modern ears our sharp condemnation for his lack of sympathy, but it nonetheless reflects a core Machiavellian principle—that one cannot simply override inherent conflicts through force and terror alone. For just as with the Guelf factions that suddenly appeared after the defeat of the Ghibellines, even if one succeeds in completely subordinating or even eliminating one class of the great, another hierarchy will arise in its place. In Machiavellian politics, unity can only be produced by accepting and even embracing disunity, namely by integrating it within a flexible order guided by law that limits injustice while allowing equal access to glory.

Today, the rhetoric of revolution remains a thriving industry, for good or for ill. When the impact of such things as climate change, pandemics, population shifts, and supply chains are often felt immediately and globally, each modern catastrophe invites another vision of totalizing political reform. Pulitzer Prize–winning *New York Times* columnist Thomas Friedman, for instance, argues that the three dominant challenges of our time, "global warming, global flattening and global crowding—are like three flames that have converged to create a really big fire, and this fire is boiling a whole set of problems" that "are really going to shape the 21st century and a new era of history."[95] His preferred response is what he calls a "green revolution" in which people elect leaders who believe that "clean power, clean energy" and "clean tech has to be the next great global industry in a world that's hot, flat and crowded."[96] But Friedman's revolution is not a revolution in political structure but of technological innovation and technocratic policymaking. He assumes a functioning global republican order in which ideas on their own merits can overcome all constraints and create worldwide cooperation. For Machiavelli, however, the more pressing revolutionary question is whether we need to institute new modes and orders prior to making such a green revolution possible. Certainly, groups like Extinction Rebellion question Friedman's optimism. But even their embrace of extralegal means of protest and obstruction are more in line with how Machiavelli defines the mode of tumult.

Tragically, the contemporary movement that most closely imitates Machiavellian modes of violent revolution is what today goes by the name "eco-fascism." According to Peter Staudenmaier, eco-fascism involves elements of "nature mysticism, pseudo-scientific ecology, irrationalist anti-humanism, and a mythology of racial salvation through return to the land."[97] Unlike other right-wing political movements, therefore, eco-fascists do not deny climate change. According to Naomi Klein, they recognize that in "an age of massive disruption, that many hundreds of millions of people are going to be forced from their homelands, and that huge swathes of the planet are going to be uninhabitable."[98] But instead of working toward a revolution in global sustainability and social justice, they embrace what she calls "climate barbarism," in which the wealthier countries of the world say to themselves. "look, we simply believe we are better, because of our citizenship, because of our whiteness, and our Christian-ness, and we are locking down, protecting our own, pulling aid."[99] The revolution of eco-fascists thus uses violence and cruelty to oppress and/or expel foreign and marginalized populations while seeking to control and exploit remaining resources for the benefit of who they believe to be the Chosen Ones. Here we find the all-or-nothing logic of the ciompi applied on a nation or global scale, only with largely white Christian nationalists taking on the mantle of both oppressed victim and popular hero. In their revolutionary movement, violent modes can be used to transform republican states into authoritarian regimes in a last great war of all against all.

The revolutionary ideal can be mobilizing, unifying, and justified. But it must also be inclusive, limited, and humane. There is much to admire, for instance, in the anonymous ciompo's oration, expressing as it does many noble and modern sentiments that connect Winter and McCormick's populist labor politics. But Machiavelli's warning against romanticizing revolutionary violence should also be heeded. Although revolutions often begin by responding to genuine grievances and articulating utopian ideals, they are just as often quickly overtaken by militant groups and extreme ideologies. This happens even more rapidly today. In a network society, any idea or ideal can become quickly absorbed within the propaganda of militant politics in which violent rebellion becomes virtually an end in itself. We must therefore distinguish between revolutionary ideals and revolutionary modes. A revolutionary ideal is a vision of an end that brings people together in shared desire and unified commitment. To that extent, revolutionary ideals operate not as an end but as a means—namely the means of forming publics dedicated to pursuing a common good. This populist rhetorical mode of revolution is essential in making change possible. In contradistinction, a revolutionary mode is an extraordinary form of collective action that uses popular violence to overturn existing orders and institute popular rule. More aggressive and totalizing than a tumult, it does not limit itself to reform. What it desires is wholesale replacement of the old by the new, even if that means ruining a state to save it.

That said, what if we feel, like the ciompi, that we have no choice? The impacts of the three challenges that Friedman identifies—global warming, global flattening, and global crowding—are only accelerating. What happens when people feel they have no alternative to suffering under heat domes, having their lands drowned by rising sea waters, being forced into migration because of overpopulation, or simply starving due to drought and resource depletion? For Machiavelli, this isn't really even a question. Revolution is simply the necessary outcome. What he or anyone else might recommend or desire at that point is irrelevant. Like the ciompi, people forced into a corner will simply act out of anger and desperation, reaching out for any hope and adopting any means that might offer an escape. Eco-fascists, of course, count on this fact. So perhaps what Machiavelli "actually" felt about revolution is irrelevant. For him, revolutionary modes are a necessary (which is to say, unavoidable and irresistible) response to corrupt regimes facing catastrophe. If we wish to avoid following eco-fascists into our collective ruin, our current republican institutions must not only expand their political imaginations but also radically increase their popular base. The walls of money and power that distort political communication and widen class divisions can only increase the potential for self-destructive violent rebellion. Warning against revolution is a futile endeavor. Revolutions simply happen. But we can work to transform elitist republicanism into something closer to the actual ideal of democracy as a means of managing change intelligently and cooperatively, namely by allowing people like the anonymous ciompo to have a name and speak as citizens in the halls of power.

CHAPTER 8

On the Comic Nature of
Republican Power

DESPITE HIS REPUTATION FOR COLD-BLOODEDNESS, MACHIA-velli speaks with a modern accent less because he is cruel and more because he is funny. In fact, to his friends, Machiavelli was something of the life of the party, always entertaining his social set with exaggerated stories, poetic creations, and savage self-mockery. For instance, when Machiavelli was second chancellor and a major player in Piero Soderini's republican regime, he took the time to write a satirical guidebook for the social elite for no other reason than that he thought it was humorous. Machiavelli titled it *Rules for an Elegant Social Circle* and included in it such rules as "anyone attending mass who does not keep looking around, forcing himself in a prominent position to be admired by all, will be punished," that "members of the circle must make a point of speaking badly of one another and revealing one another's sins to any and every stranger, trumpeting said transgressions without restraint," and that "no lady of the company may have a mother-in-law."[1] Machiavelli would have felt at home in today's world of memes, tweets, and late-night satire. In all of his writings, Machiavelli displayed a wry humor that encouraged his interlocutors to take themselves less seriously, perhaps recognizing that deflating our pretensions was often a precondition for being able to work together cooperatively.

Importantly, the connection between Machiavelli and comedy is not simply a matter of temperament. In the last years of his life, Machiavelli achieved notoriety not as the founder of modern politics but as a comic playwright. Only one of his serious books, the thin and rather dry *The Art of War*, was published before his death and had a narrow readership. By contrast, around 1519 Machiavelli composed and performed his comic masterpiece *The Mandrake*. In 1520 "the excitement stirred up by a Florentine production of *The Mandrake* caused Pope Leo X, the former Giovanni de Medici, to insist that the same scenery and actors used in Florence be transported to his court in Rome."[2] Records show performances in Venice during the Lenten carnival season in 1522, in both Venice and Faenza during carnival in 1526, and for a private party in Florence in 1524.[3] In 1514 Machiavelli translated and adapted the comedy *Andria* from the Roman comedian Terrance, renamed *The Woman from Andros*. In 1525 he wrote and performed the play *Clizia*. Although not as acclaimed at *The Mandrake*, according to one Florentine contemporary, the "fame of the play 'inspired everyone with the desire to see it,' so that 'all the leading citizens' of Florence as well as 'the highest ranking members of the government then in power' came to the performance."[4] Given his plays all revolved around the desires, deceptions, and seductions of lovers, one can imagine Machiavelli testing out his racy jokes and provocative plotlines with the butcher and the miller over drinks and cards.

But Machiavelli's late-career success as a comic playwright does more than simply humanize his reputation as a villain; it also reveals the essentially comic orientation of his republican political philosophy. Although Machiavelli in his writings recognized the necessity of making tragic choices in catastrophic times, he largely rejected the appeal of tragic fatalism in politics. He never gave up hope for a happy ending. Consequently, he expressed what Vickie Sullivan calls a "comic view, in which his sometimes playful but always pointed challenges to previous authority illuminate the way to human beings' mastery of the forces that have hitherto thwarted their earthly endeavors."[5] And what made this approach distinctively comic was that Machiavelli understood that, ultimately, people had to work together in order to meet the necessities of Fortune. Even Strauss acknowledged that "the action of the comedy agrees with Machiavelli's claim that he was always moved by the natural desire to work for the benefit of everyone."[6] Although Strauss questions whether this desire was actually implemented in fact, the recognition by one of Machiavelli's harshest critics that his work had a comic strain is significant. For where there is comedy, there is communication and cooperation. And wherever the arts of discourse take precedence over the imposition of force, republican rhetoric may thrive. Because, as Thomas Farrell once wrote, "Rhetoric, after all, is a comic art."[7]

The connection Farrell makes between rhetoric and comedy extends an argument originally made by Kenneth Burke. For Burke, comedies are not simply stories that result in happy endings. In his view, comedy is a dramatic form whose primary attraction is the exposure, ridicule, and redemption of human frailties. Comedies narrate how multiple parties in conflict, each of them flawed in different ways, ultimately come to reconciliation not just *despite* their flaws but *because* of them. In comedy, whatever victories the actors achieve come about as much by admitting their own ignorance and arrogance as by employing cleverness and deception. Comedies thus traditionally have fulfilled an edifying function by identifying and exposing the vices of their characters. Machiavelli acknowledges this fact in the dramatic prologue to *Clizia*: "Comedies were invented to be of use and of delight to their audiences. It is indeed quite useful for any man, and particularly for young ones, to learn about the avarice of an old man, the frenzy of a lover, the deceit of a servant, the greed of a parasite, the indigence of the poor, the ambition of the rich, the wiles of a whore, and the bad faith of all men. Comedies are filled with such examples, and they all can be represented with the greatest decency. But if the audience is to be delighted, it must be moved to laughter, and that cannot be done while keeping our speech grave and austere; for speeches which evoke laughter are either fooling, or insulting, or amorous. It is therefore necessary to present characters who are foolish, slanderous, or love-struck."[8] Part of the pleasure of comedies, of course, is simply delighting in witnessing the foolish, insulting, or amorous portrayed on stage. But Machiavelli also acknowledges that comedies traditionally don't simply hold up foolish people to ridicule in order to flatter the virtues of the audience; they strive to make the audience *complicit* in the motives of the characters portrayed as fellow conspirators and thereby bring not only pleasure but also self-recognition.

According to Burke, what distinguishes comedy from tragedy is its cautious optimism. A comic orientation asserts that "the progress of human enlightenment can go no further than in picturing people not as *vicious*, but as *mistaken*."[9] Comedies dramatize this human condition by setting multiple actors at cross-purposes, each of them seeking to their own gain while at the same time exposing their blindness to the audience in a ridiculous fashion. But ultimately what drives the comic plot is the human capacity for humility and understanding. As dramatic events bring to light hidden facts and reveal the motivations of each actor, crisis and conflict give way to compassion and cooperation. For Burke, the great gift of comedy is self-awareness: "The comic frame should enable people to be observers of themselves while acting. Its ultimate would not be passiveness but maximum consciousness."[10] Rhetoric, therefore, channels the comic spirit when it persuades by promoting forgiveness over cruelty, consensus over division, cooperation over competition, and the common good over private gain. As Farrell remarks, rhetoric becomes comic when it does not foreclose options but instead promotes "preserving conversational continuity and making room for the possibilities of further choice."[11] It was under a similar motivation that Machiavelli wrote, for instance, the *Florentine Histories*; although obviously lacking the humor of his plays, its comic purpose was to hold a mirror up to Florence so that its political class might become observers of themselves.

That said, the comic element of Machiavellian rhetoric and politics must still be understood in the context of his political realism. In the first place, as we have already seen, not all crises can be resolved through the comic corrective. Often, they require tragic choices that demand the modes of the beast, the exercise of cruelty, or the spectacle of tumult. For Machiavelli, to forgive one's enemies when confronted with great malice is to invite destruction. In the second place, politics remains guided by self-interest and stabilized only through the balance of forces. From the perspective of political realism, a comedy can only achieve a happy ending when each party achieves a proximate goal and no longer feels threatened by opposing forces. Humility, forgiveness, and understanding are sources of goodness, but for Machiavelli they are insufficient for resolving conflicts on their own. Instead, they come after the fact as ways of facilitating acceptance. In the third place, not only Machiavelli's politics but also his plays lack the democratic character that Burke and Farrell attribute to comedy. Machiavellian actors do not play on a level playing field. Some of them are subjects to be manipulated, while others are the source of manipulation. In his plays, the characteristic comic hero is a single individual who directs every action in the plot. What appears hilarious to the audience is unknown to the other actors in the play. Similarly, virtuous republican leaders are often single heads in Machiavelli's narratives who orchestrate political power for the common good by manipulating the fears and desires of competing constituencies in different ways. For Machiavelli, the most effective republican rhetoric performs eloquence in public while imitating the tactics of the puppet master backstage. In the *Florentine Histories*, this was the type of rhetoric employed by the early Medici patriarchs of the fifteenth century who managed to stabilize the Florentine republic and bring it to its heights of power.

Before turning to this period of Medici republican dominance, a brief examination of Machiavelli's most famous play, *The Mandrake*, will provide a basis for understanding the comparison between Machiavelli's plays and his politics. With the satirical genius allowed only to a lifelong citizen of Florence, *The Mandrake* threads together a plot that exposes the hypocrisy, greed, ignorance, ambition, and duplicity characteristic of different social classes of his city, while at the same time showing how these different vices can produce happy outcomes if manipulated properly. The scheming ambition of the merchant class is represented by the main character Callimaco (a play on Machiavelli's own name), who recently returned to his hometown of Florence after twenty years of "studies, pleasure and business" in Paris.[12] His object of infatuation is Lucrezia, the very picture of feminine virtue of the type idealized by Petrarch and Dante. But she nonetheless harbors secret sexual desires that are unfulfilled because she must endure a childless marriage with her dull and stupid husband, Nicia, a lawyer and symbol of the boorish upper-guild ruling class. In Nicia's words: "All we're good for is going to funerals or to wedding parties, or sitting on the Proconsul's bench all day long watching the people go by."[13] Callimaco, aided by his loyal servant Siro and the grifter Liguro concocts a complex scheme to sleep with Lucrezia, namely by convincing both her and her husband Nicia that she should have sex with a stranger in order to make her pregnant and thus satisfy everyone's desires.

The rhetorical complexity of the plot involves getting all of the different parties to agree to go along with this absurd plan. The basis of the ruse is to have Callimaco pretend to be a doctor who possesses a magical cure (a mandrake root) for Lucrezia's presumed sterility that will ensure her pregnancy. The twist is that this root is said to have the unfortunate side effect of killing the first man to sleep with her. Not desiring to sacrifice his own life to guarantee an heir, Nicia agrees to find a sacrificial victim (also Callimaco in disguise) to "draw off all of the poison of the mandrake in one night."[14] But then comes the most difficult part—convincing the virtuous Lucrezia to sleep with another man in violation of her religious vows.

Now two more representative characters enter the play to act as rhetorical advocates for the scheme. One is Lucrezia's practical-minded mother, Sostrata, who is ready to try anything to secure her daughter's future. After all, without a son to inherit Nicia's estate, Lucrezia would be left completely defenseless should Nicia die. The other is the "shrewd and cunning" friar Timoteo, who agrees, on the promise of a large financial donation, to convince Lucrezia that her adultery would be blessed in the eyes of God.[15] The plan works out even better than expected. The clever Lucrezia discovers the plot but instead of condemning Callimaco, she judges that "divine providence" brought her seducer to her bedroom, and so "what my husband has willed for this one night, he shall have for good and ever."[16] The play closes with Nicia feeling so grateful for Callimaco (once again in the guise of the doctor) that Nicia gives him his own key to the house to come and go as he pleases to see his wife, while Timoteo invites them "all to go into the church, and there we will celebrate accordingly."[17] Exeunt.

The Mandrake presents in microcosm a comic theory of republican politics seen through Machiavelli's political realism. Machiavelli's realism recognizes and even celebrates the inescapably self-interested and amoral desires that inspire human passions. As sung by the nymphs and shepherds of the opening chorus of The Mandrake, "We live from day to day in search of pleasure, For he who seeks out ill, And clings to fear and grief as to a treasure, Regret it as his leisure."[18] Yet Machiavelli also recognizes that the unhinged pursuit of pleasure is often a source of ruin. Pleasures, just like ambitions, jealousies, and fears, only become sources of "good" when constrained and channeled by the various social, legal, and religious orders provide outlets and give appropriate cover for the expression of these passions. For instance, as Zuckert explains, "private individuals are not able to satisfy their desires unless they conceal their true motives and pretend to be serving others."[19] The republican value of institutions like the family and the church are that they provide ways of transforming our private vices into public virtues: "Like all well-conceived laws they direct or redirect human passions away from potentially destructive conflict so that they have not merely productive and stabilizing but even liberating results."[20] The Mandrake animates this principle through the intricate ironies of a comic plot in which, as Zuckert observes, "all participants in the conspiracy benefit."[21]

By the end of the play, not only has everyone attained their own desire but they have done so by appearing to satisfy public virtue. Indeed, they even go along with the deception in full knowledge of being deceived. As the friar Timoteo says to himself, "It's true that I've been tricked; nevertheless, this trick is to my benefit."[22] Timoteo, like all the other characters, evaluates the acts of deceiving or being deceived through a comic lens that turns imperfections into opportunities. In fact, it is in *The Mandrake* that we find the closest justification for attributing to Machiavelli the maxim "the end justifies the means." Something approximating this phrase is spoken by Friar Timoteo as he tries to convince Lucrezia to sleep with a man who is not her husband. In English translation, he is made to say, "We must always consider whether the end justifies the means. Your end is to fill a seat in heaven and to make your husband happy."[23] The Italian reads, "el fine si ha a riguardare in tutte le cose," or literally "the end should be regarded in all things," which is simply a restatement of Machiavelli's doctrine of effectual truth. But the meanings are close enough to be identical. In a republican context, it tells us that deception can be justified if everyone benefits from the outcomes.

The connection between Machiavelli's comic play and his conception of republican politics can be found in a shared conception of the relationship between rhetoric and power. According to Michael Hardt and Antonio Negri, Machiavelli more frequently viewed power as something springing up between people rather than being imposed upon them. For them, "the Machiavellian concept of power as a constituent power—that is, a product of an internal and immanent social dynamic."[24] In their conception, constituent power never belongs to a single individual or sovereign, no matter how divine; to think of power this way is to reduce it to a mere emanation of some single, totalizing force. The reality is the opposite. For "Machiavelli, power is always Republican; it is always the product of the life of the multitude and constitutes its fabric of expression."[25] Power is as much product as potential; like a comic play that impacts an audience only through the cooperation and improvisation of its writer, director, and performers, power finds its existence, its capacity, and its function coming into being all at once through the kairotic interplay of forces at an opportune moment. Power is never a singular unity but arises out of the play of differences and "is always conflictual. Power is organized to the emergence of the interplay of counter powers. The city is thus a constituent power that is formed through plural social conflicts articulated in continuous constitutional processes."[26] In this conception, republican rhetoric is the comedy of orchestrating constituent power. Through rhetorical manipulations, political actors inhabit sites of conflict and turn forces so that they collectively point in the same direction even as each individual believes they are pursuing his or her own aims.

As a mode of responding to catastrophe, this uniquely Machiavellian approach to republican rhetoric has advantages and disadvantages. On the one hand, the ability of leaders with forethought and vision to orchestrate constituent power allows them to forestall political catastrophes by resolving conflicts before they magnify into factional strife. As Machiavelli showed in the Florentine catastrophes of the thirteenth and fourteenth centuries, the tendency of republics to dissolve into extreme partisanship exposed Florence to the temptations of authoritarian rhetoric the moment the city was beset by crisis. In his view, had the republic been better orchestrated by a core set of leaders, it could have maintained the structure of the republican order while at the same time benefiting from the quick and decisive leadership of a virtuous head of state. On the other hand, a reliance on backstage rhetorical manipulation creates the conditions for private corruption and the slow disintegration of the legitimacy of the republic state. In Negri's language, it is in the nature of constituent power to solidify over time into "constituted power," or the constitutional power of a central authority whose "dynamics are imposed on the system from outside."[27] In such a situation, any benefits from the orchestration of constituent power quickly diminish under the influence of corruption. Eventually, even the veneer of a republic becomes, as Filippo Del Lucchese observes, "the rigid representation of a political and factual situation that does not exist any more."[28] In other words, what begins as a comic play of ironic happy endings soon degrades into a burlesque spectacle of exploitation and corruption.

Characteristic of Machiavelli's dialectical approach to history, he actually presents both sides of this conception of republican rhetoric in his narration of the Medici rise to power. The Medici played the game of politics better than their opponents because of their embrace of comic rhetorical tactics. Although they clearly sought to maximize their private ambitions, their political genius was to realize that their route to wealth and influence was to work *within* rather than *against* the republican order. By finding a way to gratify the desires and satisfy the ambitions of others, they made themselves the center of a network of forces and therefore the conductor of constituent power. As Zuckert explains, a Machiavellian prince rules in a comic vein not by force but "by persuasion. He seeks to secure his own life and liberty by showing others how they can best satisfy their desires."[29] In the case of Florence, as long as these desires and forces remained balanced, the republic was able to prosper while avoiding the catastrophic divisions that had led to the ruin of so many other late medieval Italian communes. Yet Machiavelli also clearly showed how Medici rule eventually led to the corruption of the Florentine state. As more and more people became reliant on Medici patronage, the integrity of the republic gradually decayed. Eventually, the republic became a mere shadow of its former self, a theater of courtly performance to mask the exercise of constituted power by de facto Medici princes. Although Machiavelli does not include this act in his *Histories*, the end of this drama would not be a comedy but a tragedy—or more properly a catastrophe produced by the very manipulations of its once comic protagonists.

The Medici who feature in Machiavelli's *Histories* were not, of course, comedians. They were the four serious and cunning Medici patriarchs of the fifteenth century—Giovanni di Bicci (1360–1429), Giovanni's son Cosimo the Elder (1389–1464), Cosimo's son Piero the Gouty (1416–69), and Piero's son Lorenzo the Magnificent (1449–92). These four generations of Medici men were the very embodiment of the "new men" of postplague Europe, a family that emerged from obscure ancestral origins by embracing the early modern maxim that greed is good. Their coat of arms of red balls (*palle*) on a field of gold (that to this day adorns buildings across Tuscany) indicates their nonaristocratic origins, representing either red apothecary pills (which would correspond with the literal meaning of their name, as *medici* is plural for *medico*, or "doctor") or simply coins (which would correspond to their later profession as bankers and money-changers).[30] They would rise to power as members of the popolani, those merchant elite who sought to create alliance with the popolo even as they strove for noble status.

It was Giovanni di Bicci who would be the first comic hero who orchestrated his family's ascent to power. After the suppression of the Ciompi Revolt and Salvestro de Medici's failed bold bid for leadership of the popolo minuto, the end of the fourteenth century saw the rise of the Albizzi faction of the popolo grasso, which quickly consolidated its power in the guild republic over both the plebs and old feudal magnati. But Giovanni di Bicci had not been idle. Eschewing the populist rhetoric of Salvestro, Giovanni quietly orchestrated his way into the networks of power. According to Christopher Hibbert, he "was a man of utmost discretion, acutely aware of the danger of arousing the Florentines' notorious distrust of overtly ambitious citizens, anxious to remain as far as possible out of the public eye while making money in his rapidly expanding banking business."[31] Brucker describes him as representing the "triumph of the mercantile mentality," typifying "the rational and calculating entrepreneur, the shrewd, tough-minded realist who had banished passion and emotion from politics."[32] This seemed hardly the type of character to feature as the comic hero of a political drama.

Yet just as all comic actors work best when wearing a mask, behind his calculating demeanor, Giovanni was a gambler with all the ambition of a Callimaco and the tactical genius of a Liguro. Machiavelli describes his character this way: "He had not much eloquence but very great prudence. In appearance he was melancholy, but then in his conversation he was pleasing and witty."[33] Giovanni used his wit to great advantage. Just after the year 1400, Giovanni befriended the embodiment of the comic mountebank, Baldassare Cossa: "Sensual, adventurous, unscrupulous and highly superstitious, Baldassare Cossa came of an old Neapolitan family and had once been a pirate."[34] Seeing an opportunity in Cossa, Giovanni fronted him money to buy his way into the Vatican as a cardinal. The gamble paid off. In 1410 Cossa became Pope John XXIII by the authority of the Council of Pisa, as part of the effort to put an end to the "great schism" that had divided the loyalties of the Catholic Church between the Avignon pope, Benedict XIII, and the Italian pope, Gregory XII. Cossa did not forget his friends; he immediately made the Medici the official bankers of the Vatican. Cossa was eventually deposed in 1414 for all manners of crimes, real or imagined (heresy, simony, tyranny, murder by poison, and "the seduction of no fewer than two hundred of the ladies of Bologna"), but the four years he was pope was enough to set Giovanni on a path to power.[35] According to Lauro Martines, Giovanni's "efforts had carried him to the top of the scale of wealth in Florence, which, in those years, ranking as the financial capital of Western Europe, was the home of more than seventy international bankers."[36]

The basis of Giovanni's republican rhetoric was his ability to use the influence of *financial* capital to build a complex network of *social* capital. According to Paul McLean, social capital in Renaissance Florence signified "a web of cooperative and trusting relationships (that is, social networks and the norms that inhabit and sustain them) that provide individuals with emotional and/or material support and opportunities and help to coordinate their several actions."[37] Giovanni's successful gamble, in other words, earned him enormous wealth and international connections that made him equal to other great families. By lending the city considerable amounts of money, Giovanni quietly used his wealth to build considerable social capital with ordinary people throughout the city. Machiavelli notes that "not only did he give alms to whoever asked for them, but many times he supplied the needs of the poor without being asked."[38] Thus when Giovanni began gaining quiet influence over the civic authorities, "this made for such joy throughout the generality of people in the city, since to the multitude it appeared that it had gained a defender."[39] In addition, Giovanni cultivated a humble demeanor that had allowed him, despite his family's association with the lesser nobility, to gain the trust of the greater nobles because they did not perceive him as a threat. As Machiavelli writes, "he never asked for honors yet had them all. He never went into the palace unless he was called."[40] In this way, Giovanni had also gained the trust of the great families. Because they didn't believe he had ambitions for political power, they saw his high standing with the plebs as an asset. If ever the people wanted to incite a tumult, the great families believed Giovanni could be called upon to pacify the people with a republican rhetorical style sure to make them adhere to the norms of civility and trust the rule of law.

Essential to the Medici family's early success, therefore, was Giovanni's comic ability to manipulate and satisfy people's desires in a way that benefited him while appearing to serve the interests of the great. In a passage from Machiavelli that perfectly captures his vision of the republican comedy, he says it is fortunate when "a wise, good, and powerful citizen" is able to rhetorical manipulate things such that the "humors of the nobles and the men of the people are quieted or restrained so that they cannot do evil, for then that city can be called free and that state be judged stable and firm."[41] Ironically, it is precisely because a single comic hero like Giovanni could orchestrate republic politics so masterfully that a city would no longer feel tempted by the authoritarian solution. For "a city based on good laws and good orders has no necessity, as have others, for the virtue of a single man to maintain it."[42] In clear reference to the prior Florentine experience with Charles and Walter, Machiavelli credits the city's relative political stability in the mid-fifteenth century to Giovanni's ability to reduce factional strife.

In Machiavelli's account, therefore, Giovanni's social capital came about precisely because multiple constituencies identified him as an essential stabilizing force in a Florentine republic that was under threat by yet another political catastrophe. This threat derived from a new kind of conflict that Machiavelli characterized as the competition between the "ministers of servitude" and the "ministers of license." The ministers of servitude were familiar. They were those nobles who possessed the resources, insolence, and authority to "do evil easily" and hence were insolent and eager to dominate.[43] But the ministers of license were a new breed. These were the "men of the people" who desired only pleasure and did not wish "to be subject either to the laws or to men."[44] Notably, Machiavelli here shifts the nature of the conflict to reflect the changing political environment of the fifteenth century, replacing the class division between the nobles and the plebs with the internal division in the nobility itself between the old magnati and the new popolani. The people and the plebs still had their traditional grievances, but now both their allegiances and their hostilities were divided between the old noble families and the rising merchant class. The popolani, eager to accumulate wealth and satisfy their demands of luxury, were contemptuous of the old feudal habits of the magnati, while the representatives of the old families found the stench of new money unbearable to their aristocratic sensibilities.

The catastrophe that loomed during Giovanni's rise to political power thus came from the reactionary forces of the magnati (the ministers of servitude) who were seeking to use their wealth to solidify their domination of the people and suppress the rise of the popolani (the ministers of license). At the head of the ministers of servitude was the Albizzi family, a traditional ruling clan that by the 1430s had become "insolent through unbroken dominion."[45] This insolence culminated in a costly and destructive war with the Milanese tyrant Filippo Maria Visconti. Although it was fought largely with mercenaries, the taxes necessary to fund the war fell heaviest on the lesser citizens, who "filled the city with complaints, and everyone condemned the ambition and greed of the powerful, accusing them of wishing to start an unnecessary war so as to indulge their appetites and to oppress the people so as to dominate them."[46] Tensions reached a breaking point after a disastrous defeat at Forlí created an opening for the popolani to ignite the rage of the people against the Albizzi and their class. Machiavelli clearly sides with popolani in this episode, his contempt for the magnatis' aristocratic elitism revealed by the words he puts into the mouth of Albizzi in defense of his catastrophic military campaign. Contradicting Machiavelli's insistence on evaluating events by their eventual truth, Albizzi insolently argues that "it was not prudent to judge things by their effects."[47] Needless to say, Albizzi soon lost control of the situation. Fearing a violent tumult that might topple his regime, he sought to use the mode of violence to "restore the state to the great and take away authority from the lesser guilds."[48] But Albizzi made one compromise; before employing the use of arms to take over the state, he would "get Giovanni de' Medici to agree to their will, because if he concurred, the multitude, deprived of a head and of force, could not offend them."[49] In other words, if Albizzi could get Giovanni on his side, the people would lose their champion. This compromise gave Giovanni the opening that all comic heroes need.

Albizzi had no chance against Giovanni's tactical mind; in a typical comic reversal, Albizzi entered Giovanni's house confident of one plan and exited, having agreed upon the exact opposite. Albizzi's original goal had been to persuade Giovanni that it was best to side with the ministers of servitude and to crush, with violence, the people's hopes of rebellion. By the time he left, Giovanni had convinced Albizzi that the best plan was, in fact, to impose a tax upon the greatest citizens, thereby allowing Albizzi to remain in power by satiating the people. His reasoning was clear. Any attempt to impose a new order through force upon a free citizenry would immediately incite rebellion. For Giovanni, "it is the office of a wise and good citizen not to alter the accustomed orders of this city," for in doing so "one must offend many, and whether many are left malcontent, one can fear some nasty accident every day."[50] The cost-benefit analysis of Albizzi's plan simply didn't add up. The people would lose much and the great would gain little. Employing a typically Machiavellian calculus, Giovanni explained to Albizzi that "men are naturally more ready to avenge an injury than to be grateful for a benefit, as it appears to them that gratitude brings them loss while vengeance brings advantage and pleasure."[51] Consequently, the prudent course was not to punish the people but to imitate the mode of Giovanni's father, "who, so as to get universal good will, lowered the price of salt, provided that anyone whose tax was less than half a florin might pay it or not as he saw fit, and that on the day the councils assembled, everyone might be safe from his creditors."[52] By giving the people justice rather than injury, they would be satisfied. In the end, Giovanni persuaded Albizzi to support what would later become the most progressive tax in Europe. Called the *catasto*, it funded Florence's wars primarily by taxing the goods of the wealthy merchants like Giovanni himself. The great retained their authority by paying such a tax, the people refrained from tumult because they were relieved of financial burden, and Giovanni gained influence by establishing himself as an evenhanded power broker. As in *The Mandrake*, everyone sacrificed a little but gained their desires.

If Giovanni was the master manipulator in private negotiations, his son Cosimo became the creative genius of the comic mask. In the second act of the Medici drama, Cosimo carried on his father's talents for backroom persuasion, but he added to the Medici repertoire a skill in crafting public appearances that could transform private vices into public virtues. After surviving a desperate effort by Albizzi to have him executed for treason, Cosimo suffered a short exile only to return to the city to a hero's welcome—after which he had Albizzi banished for life. For the next thirty years, Cosimo orchestrated constituent power in Florence from the elegance of his palace. He had no private army or hired assassins; he relied on no title or public office. Instead, he continued expanding his patronage network through interpersonal relationships. Machiavelli notes that at his death there was not a citizen who "who had any quality in that city to whom Cosimo had not lent a large sum of money."[53] But Cosimo also worked diligently to craft a public persona consistent with his posthumous title of *pater patriae*, or "Father of the Fatherland," by commissioning works of art and funding public building projects. His goal was for these objects to communicate what Hendrik Thijs van Veen calls the "central tenet" of Medici propaganda, that the Florentine "state belonged to the Medici rightfully and historically."[54] For with a keen sense of comic irony, "he knew how extraordinary things that are seen and appear every hour make men much more envied than those that are done with the deed and are covered over with decency."[55] Everywhere one turned in Florence, whether in sacred buildings, private palazzos, or public squares, there could be found a visible reminder that a good part of the beauty, health, safety, and prosperity of the city was due to Cosimo's generous patronage.

The comic lesson that emerges from Machiavelli's narrative is quite clear. Republics avoid catastrophes when comic protagonists like Cosimo do the hard and delicate work of balancing and synthesizing multiple interests. From inside the walls of his palazzo, whose courtyard displayed the erotic body of Donatello's bronze *David*, Cosimo made himself the center of a complex network of social capital that prospered for the same reason that Machiavelli's comic heroes prospered—because it served everyone's self-interest to for it to do so: "Hence not only did he conquer domestic and civil ambition, but he overcame that of many princes with such prosperity and prudence that whoever allied with him and with his fatherland would come out either equal or superior to the enemy, and whoever opposed him would lose his time and money or state."[56] Like his father, Cosimo knew how to play the part of the saint or the simpleton if he had to, masking shrewdness behind a veneer of respectability and channeling private ambition through publicly sanctioned modes of action. The republic under the leadership of Giovanni and Cosimo may not have lived up to modern standards of democratic egalitarianism, but in an age when many Italian city-states had become principalities under the rule of military condottieri (such as Milan under the Francesco Sforza or Urbino under Federigo de Montefeltro), Florence maintained itself as an imperfect but functioning republic. And Cosimo's Florence, while not representing the modern democratic ideal, nonetheless fostered an environment that balanced respect for tradition with the freedom of innovation. As Brucker summarized, "the achievement of Florentine artists and humanists in the early Quattrocento [1400s] constitute the most striking evidence for the creative possibilities of this felicitous combination of the old and the new."[57] The Medici support for great names like Donatello, Da Vinci, Botticelli, Masaccio, Brunelleschi, and Michelangelo is testament to the family's talent for recognizing artistic genius. Even if the Medici were not directly responsible for all of their achievements, their orchestration of Florentine politics with a comic touch helped establish the limited space of freedom that created the conditions for its flourishing at a time when other cities had succumbed to authoritarianism.

With the ascendency of Giovanni's great-grandson Lorenzo in act 3, however, the comedy of republican politics started coming to an end. After the brief rule of Cosimo's son Piero "The Gouty" from 1446 to 1469, the twenty-year old Lorenzo became the leading citizen in Florence. Intelligent, charismatic, and ambitious, Lorenzo reflected many of the virtues of his grandfather and great-grandfather, for "he was eloquent and sharp in discussing things, wise in resolving them, quick and spirited in executing them."[58] But in many other ways, Lorenzo departed from their example. Lorenzo had no patience for the mercantile mentality. Machiavelli writes that "he was very unprosperous in trade," and because he relied on unscrupulous agents to run the Medici business, he soon drove the bank into the ground so that "it was required that his fatherland help him with a great sum of money."[59] Far from being grave or modest in demeanor, Lorenzo was the very embodiment of a minister of license, luxuriating in pleasure and the arts, using both private and public funds to keep "his fatherland always in festivities" (hence the title "The Magnificent").[60] In short, he "delighted in facetious and pungent men and in childish games, more than would appear fitting in such a man."[61] Rather than carefully dissembling his private ambition behind a modest appearance, "Lorenzo, hot with youth and power, wanted to take thought for everything and wanted everyone to recognize everything as from him."[62] Lorenzo's ambition to subordinate the common good to his private good had made his regime the very example of corruption.

With the ascendancy of Lorenzo, the comic complexity of Medici rule began to give way to burlesque spectacle concealing civic corruption. By "burlesque," I mean a crueler drama than comedy, which stimulates licentious pleasure by reveling in exaggeration, ridicule, spectacle, and flattery. According to Burke, the burlesque represents a kind of "pamphleteering" that uses caricature to belittle and mock one's opponents.[63] In politics, the burlesque attitude translates all too easily into a rationalization for exploitation and massacre. In an event prophetic of the exploitative age of capital to come, in 1470, just a year after Lorenzo took power, an alum deposit was discovered in the region of Volterra, then a city under Florentine rule. In the fifteenth century, alum was an essential chemical used in the textile industry for cleaning and dying and consequently highly coveted by the Florentine textile industry. Lorenzo wasted no time exploiting this opportunity; even though the mine was on public land owned by Volterra, Florentine citizens in cooperation with local agents claimed it for their own private use. When the city of Volterra protested the injustice of this land grab, Lorenzo "decided to undertake a campaign and punish with arms the arrogance of the Volterrans," under the age-old rationalization "that if they were not set right by a memorable example, others without any reverence or fear would not hesitate to do the same thing for any light cause."[64] Lorenzo hired Federico de Montefeltro, lord of Urbino, who with twelve thousand troops surrounded the city. Realizing they were outnumbered, the city leaders negotiated a surrender and opened the gates under a promise of leniency. They did not receive it. Under Federico's command, "for a whole day [the city] was robbed and overrun; neither women nor holy places were spared."[65] The massacre was by design: "The news of this victory was received with very great joy by the Florentines, and because it had been altogether Lorenzo's campaign, he rose to very great reputation from it."[66]

Lorenzo's abandonment of Giovanni's comic touch produced an inevitable backlash. By 1466, Machiavelli writes, "the whole state had been so restricted to the Medici, who took so much authority, that it was required for those who were malcontent at it either to endure that mode of living with patience or, if indeed they wanted to eliminate it, attempt to do so by way of conspiracy and secretly."[67] On April 26, 1478, four assassins (including a priest and the archbishop of Florence) attempted to stab Lorenzo and his younger brother Guiliano to death during high mass at the cathedral; they succeeded only in killing Guiliano. Once the Medici partisans knew that Lorenzo had survived, the conspirators were quickly routed. The archbishop was hung naked from the tower of the palace, while the others were killed and "the limbs of the dead were seen fixed on the points of weapons or being dragged about the city."[68] In the coming months, Lorenzo would banish or execute all of his enemies and restructure the republic in a way that made it an instrument of Medici interests. Lorenzo had turned Florence into a principality in everything but name, and the result was to suffocate the innovative spirit of the city. In Machiavelli's words, "This new order put a check on the spirit of those who were seeking new things."[69] Authoritarianism has arrived. No one would challenge Lorenzo again.

One lesson from Medici rule is that for comedy to function effectively in a republic, the actions must also be performed also in public. In the case of Florence, however, the backstage came to replace the public stage. And when republican deliberation becomes a superfluous exercise to mask the self-interested accumulation of wealth and the exercise of power, it should be classified not as republican but as authoritarian. According to Hariman, in the republican ideal, "the achievement of good government at any time requires active participation by individuals successfully striving to overcome their private interests through common deliberation, and the stability of the republic through time depends on its ability to cultivate individuals possessing this virtuous character."[70] A genuine republican rhetoric thus always seeks the public stage in order to bring as many people as possible under the influence of eloquence, each member of the audience deciding voluntarily to assent to rational propositions performed with passion, character, and style. Consequently, the type of republican order orchestrated by the Medici, no matter their good intention, can only be seen as corrupt. For "as republican politics is thought to be an open process of persuasion among all citizens acting virtuously, the greatest threat to the public is imagined to be a secret arrangement by a few conspirators to manipulate or circumvent agreement."[71] In short, "in a political culture of oral argument, secrecy becomes the sign of subversion."[72] The energy of a republic derives from its republican style that promises glory and influence to those who can command an audience through rhetorical eloquence. But once the center stage becomes a mere sideshow, its heroic orators are replaced by sycophants and lackeys.

What Machiavelli demonstrates, in other words, is that for republican rhetoric to truly become a comic art in the way envisioned by Burke and Farrell, it cannot rely only on the tactics of the cunning puppet master of Machiavelli's plays. Rhetoric as a genuinely comic art is not just a way of manipulating the desires of others (although it is that, too); it is also a way of seeing oneself as a part of a wider comedy of human relationships. In Burke's terms, to adopt a comic perspective is to view human beings neither as *citizens of heaven* nor as *beasts of the jungle*; it is to view human beings as *members of a society* in order to make them *observers of themselves, while acting*. The essence of the comic corrective is thus our ability to engage in dialectical thinking, which means to place ideas or arguments or claims in relationship to their opposites and then set them in dialogue. There is no one voice to obey; "they are all voices, or personalities, or positions, integrally affecting one another."[73] The comic approach may not itself necessarily result in forethought or prudence (or else it would not, as a genre, be funny), but at the very least it sees a situation from many sides by considering multiple perspectives, which is a first step toward wisdom. In the ideal, at least, democracy requires a shared comic appreciation for the fact that we are all fallible, imperfect actors trying to make our way through trial and error toward a better life. But that requires that we all still *act* and are not just acted upon.

As a mode of confronting impending human catastrophe, however, we must acknowledge that comedy has clear limitations. The comic touch thrives in complex situations in which actors have the time and resources to bring multiple parties together in the pursuit of mutual self-interest. The success of the early Medici patriarchs, for instance, occurred during a time of Florence's greatest period of wealth and influence in Europe, when its greatest citizens had enough security and luxury to tolerate being manipulated for their own collective gain. And politically speaking, perhaps the greatest "comic" success of Lorenzo the Magnificent was in foreign policy, when he helped to craft the Peace of Lodi, which established a forty-year period of relative peace between Venice, Milan, Naples, Florence, and the Papal States between 1454 and 1494. But comic approaches seemed obsolete after the French invasion of the peninsula in 1494, which marked the beginning of the Italian "calamities." The catastrophes that beset Italy were so violent, irrational, and sudden that Machiavelli saw no alternative but to employ the type of extraordinary, aggressive, and impetuous modes of Cesare Borgia. As laudable as it might be to place different voices in dialogue during times of peace, to pursue such a mode when an army is closing around the city walls would be the height of foolishness. Comic approaches simply cannot function when one of the parties has the will and the resources to destroy the others.

Yet I believe that comedy has a central role to play in confronting natural catastrophes on a global scale. As seen in so many disaster films involving the potential destruction of humanity itself, whether from killer asteroids or zombie plagues or dying stars, nothing unites enemies in common cause more effectively than the threat of shared annihilation. The enormity of the catastrophe functions to diminish resentments and trivialize differences until they seem almost petty. Certainly, this happens in times of war as well, just as the Peace of Lodi was caused in large part by the fall of Constantinople to the Turks. But war is not a comic enterprise. Natural catastrophes, in contradistinction, have more potential to unite people not in common hatred but in common sympathy. Few challenges have produced as much effort at international cooperation (if not always success) than the two most present threats of global warming and global pandemic. Only outlier nations who have doubled down on denialism have remained outside these efforts at cooperation. Certainly, the level of accomplishment remains far below what is required to solve either crisis. But the fact that some degree of cooperation and goodwill exists at all at this level is at least a start.

I therefore find value in Machiavellian political comedy because it is wholly realistic. Each individual, party, or faction retains their ambitions, their limitations, and their biases. Everyone operates in their own self-interest. Talented protagonists will seek to manipulate the fears and desires of others, while the majority of people will inevitably allow themselves to be manipulated if they see benefits in following another's lead. Nothing in comedy requires its heroes to be anything other than flawed human beings. For Machiavelli, only people who believe they inhabit republics that never existed have confidence that they can count on the "comic" goodwill of others that springs up from the natural impulses of a generous heart. And those people inevitably pursue their own ruin. What keeps actions constrained, in Machiavelli's account, is not the inner goodness of the actors but the outer necessities of the situation itself. These necessities function to make people "good" much in the way that "hunger and poverty make men industrious."[74] Catastrophe does this by encouraging individuals to align their self-interest with the collective interest. Forgiveness, charity, and cooperation therefore become realistic modes of constituting power. Like all modes, therefore, the prudence of comedy is measured by the times. An opportune moment for political comedy arises when the necessity of confronting imminent catastrophe transforms enemies into allies. By reinterpreting trespasses as errors, former rivals can overcome the inertia of the past to meet a future challenge and emerge more unified—and therefore more powerful—than before.

CHAPTER 9

How Politics Requires the
Propaganda of Appearances

E VERY ASPIRING PROPHETIC LEADER PROMISES TO CONFRONT RE-
alities. They boast of their courage to take hold of realities, to see them
clearly and communicate their meaning to the people with bold sincerity so
that the world will be revealed in a new and vivid light. How things merely
"appear" is not their concern. Appearances are illusions, deceptions, and lies.
Only realities matter. And the form of communication they claim to practice
they call the "truth," a kind of frank speech that reveals the hard facts of the
world. Distorting the truth, according to these prophets, is mere rhetoric and
empty propaganda. Based on lies, flattery, and deception, they see the propaganda of appearances as representing a kind of dark magic that casts a spell
over the ignorant and the gullible, turning them from independent thinkers
into mere sheep to be led to slaughter. So these prophets send forth the call
to stop being seduced, to have the courage to face reality, to have the honesty
to hear the truth, and to reject the superficial and the spectacular. Those who
heed this call then become cloaked with the aura of goodness. Thus, the prophetic voice unites the Real, the True, and the Good in a battle against evil
in the name of freedom.

Machiavelli has a different recommendation for aspiring leaders: master the propaganda of appearances. To be sure, appearances are unreliable
guides. Machiavelli knew this very well. But he also recognized that political
power is built upon their surfaces. Even the prophet skates on them. By recommending this path, Machiavelli does not necessarily mean that one must give
oneself over to lies. Rather, he means that even if a leader possessed the truth

about reality, the only mode through which that knowledge could be disseminated would be through appearances, whether via the senses directly or the mental images evoked by language. That is why all prophets speak in stories, pictures, symbols, and signs. For Machiavelli, even the pursuit of the highest good requires the crafting of propaganda designed to satisfy the human craving for surfaces. For the sphere of politics, unlike the spheres of war or economy, is a symbolic battleground in which victory is determined by the capacity to turn words and images into weapons. The frequently heard complaint that some interest group is "weaponizing" some traditional virtue, image, maxim, or ritual simply reveals a lingering idealism about the nature of politics. But in Machiavelli's political realism, to engage in politics is by necessity to treat every symbol as a potential weapon. That has always been its nature.

Embracing the propaganda of appearances does not require the abandonment of virtue. It simply requires the acceptance of human finitude; that is, it requires accepting the fact that since no individual's imagination can encompass the complex details of the universe, we all must rely on appearances to make judgments. For Machiavelli, there is nothing "unreal" about appearances. The opposite of appearance is not reality but disappearance. Rather than judging appearances as a lesser type of existence, Machiavelli values them as instrumental objects or aesthetic events that make up the very substance of our everyday experience. A life without appearances would be either a meaningless void or a block universe. Appearances are vibrant precisely because they are constantly changing and on the move. To be sure, if we follow them blindly, they may guide us to ruin. But they can also inspire creativity and thought, evoke mystery and wonder, and generate solidarity and action. There is no other alternative in the sphere of politics but to appeal, in some way, to appearances. To lament this fact and seek refuge in "truth" is simply to lose. To acquire virtú, one must learn to fight wars with words or be ruined by them.

The recognition that appearances are essential to the art of rhetoric was hardly original to Machiavelli. Its origin can be found in Greek Sophists like Protagoras and Gorgias and later in Aristotle, who challenged Plato's contempt for appearances by making them objects of inquiry. According to Martha Nussbaum, Aristotle took what the Greeks called *phainomena* seriously. In common Greek usage, *phainomena* referred to "the world *as it appears to*, as it is experienced by, observers who are members of our kind."[1] For Arendt, too, an appearance referred to the way that things showed themselves. Things that appear, Arendt notes, "are meant to be seen, heard, touched, tasted, and smelled, to be perceived by sentient creatures endowed with appropriate sense organs."[2] Lastly, Farrell extends this Aristotelian respect for appearances to the realm of rhetoric. For him, appearances represent any "ensemble of objects, habitats, paths, tools, tasks, icons, and more or less recognizable characters that engage and reassure inhabitants of a locale through their emergent familiarity."[3] But Farrell also stresses that it is the task of rhetoric to give form, coherence, and meaning to this ensemble through the strategic manipulation of symbols. Rhetorical discourse thus "allows this plurality of appearances to be presented, witnessed, regarded, qualified, and subverted by the perspectives of others."[4] Rhetoric thus gives meaning to appearances in order to transform the flux of events into stable objects that can be witnessed, cognized, and acted upon.

The *propaganda* of appearances applies these rhetorical techniques on a wider scale through an organized, systematic campaign that explicitly targets the emotions, impulses, and senses more than it appeals to reason. Indeed, propaganda often is unconcerned with matters of rational belief. As Jacques Ellul stresses, propaganda seeks to produce not an *orthodoxy* (a unity of belief) but rather what he calls an *orthopraxy* (a unity of action). An orthopraxy is a type of "action that in itself, and not because of the value judgment of the person who is acting, leads directly to a goal."[5] Propaganda systematically manipulates appearances in a way that channels mass action toward a series of tangible, proximate goals while producing and reinforcing a passionate but largely trivial sense of identification. In a definition that resonates with Machiavelli's own perspective, Edward Bernays defines propaganda as "a consistent, enduring effort to create or shape events to influence the relations of the public to an enterprise, idea or group."[6] For Bernays, propaganda is not primarily a set of persuasive arguments that can be judged true or false; it is instead a way of symbolically shaping appearances so that events take on the contours desired by the propagandist. To encourage people to view events as threats or salvations, and then attribute their causes to specific allies and enemies, is the way that propaganda produces and directs orthopraxy through the propaganda of appearances.

Ellul, of course, believes propaganda denies our humanity; but from Machiavelli's perspective, we cannot escape from propaganda any more than we can escape from appearances. The only thing we can do is work within them. This is particularly the case in modern mass democracies. Zac Gershberg and Sean Illing call this the "paradox of democracy," or the fact that "democracies exist though an open communication environment, but this condition of freedom invites political actors to exploit novel media technologies and draw from demagogic rhetorical styles."[7] Yet theirs is not a counsel of despair. Instead, they stress the need for "an educational model that will help citizens guard against the onslaught of disinformation that awaits them in the public sphere."[8] They know this answer is not a panacea: "Educational reform won't come close to solving all our problems, but there's no path forward that doesn't involve rethinking how we prepare citizens to fulfill their democratic opportunities."[9] Therefore, despite recognizing the incredible challenge of fostering the type of sympathetic, resolute, and intelligent public opinion capable of meeting today's catastrophes, they choose not to condemn appearances but instead call for a renewed commitment to better interpreting and communicating them. The only way to avoid being ruined by the propaganda of appearances is to master it.

Machiavelli's very first assignment as second chancellor, in fact, was to study the propaganda of one of the genre's Renaissance masters. When he was in his twenties, he witnessed the dramatic ascent of one of the greatest prophetic voices of his age, the Dominican friar Girolamo Savonarola. Emerging fortuitously just as Italian politics would be upended by invasions by the European powers, Savonarola gave voice to the urgent fears and desperate hopes of the Florentine people at the moment when the golden age of Medici hegemony came to an end with the death of Lorenzo from illness in 1492. From that point forward, Florence seemed beset by a series of seemingly insurmountable catastrophes. The first came from the threat of foreign invasion. Soon, a massive French army was rampaging its way through the peninsula to conquer Naples. When Lorenzo's son Piero showed himself to be an incompetent leader by utterly capitulating to French demands, the people erupted in tumult, exiled the Medici, and sought a leader to restore the integrity of the republic. Savonarola stepped into the void. Claiming to speak for God, he helped save Florence from being sacked by meeting personally with the French king and flattering him into thinking that the French army was on a divine mission to purify Italy (a mission that did not include conquering Florence). After a brief nonviolent occupation, the French moved south, and Savonarola became a hero of the city.

Savonarola wasted no time exploiting his newfound authority. According to Machiavelli's friend and fellow political advisor Francesco Guicciardini, the "reverence, which Savonarola invoked, combined with the desire of many

Florentines, swept aside all opposition."[10] Deploying a populist rhetorical style through the propaganda of appearances, he embarked on an ambitious project to create a model Christian state. Savonarola inspired a religious revival in Florence that energized the previous disempowered classes of the popolo and used his newfound power to set up a grand council that was the most inclusive governing body since Ancient Greece. His justification was that Florence would be the saving Ark in the time of a second Flood that would purge all of Italy of corruption and sin. For he believed with all his heart that (in Savonarola's own words) that "the time is coming and is yet to be in which God will make known the things that lie hidden in hearts and in the shadows."[11] Savonarola spoke with a prophetic voice to communicate these realities to the Florentine people so they could prepare themselves for war, plague, and suffering, thereby saving not only themselves but also the entire Christian world.

Machiavelli enters documented history at this point. The first writing we possess in Machiavelli's hand is a report he prepared for the Chancellery after attending one of Savonarola's sermons in 1498. Composed as part of his duties as second chancellor of the new post-Medici republic, Machiavelli provides a dispassionate rhetorical criticism of Savonarola's persuasive strategies:

> [Savonarola] said that all mankind had had and continues to have an end, but that it differs: for Christians, this end is Christ; for others, past and present, their end has been and continues to be something else, depending upon their religious sects. Since we who are Christians tend toward this end which is Christ, we ought to preserve His honor with the utmost prudence and regard for the times; and whenever the times call upon us to imperil our lives for Him, to do so; and whenever it is time for a man to go into hiding, to do so, as we read about Christ and about St. Paul. And so he added we ought to do, and so we have done; therefore, when it came time to rise up against violence, we have done so, as we did on Ascension Day, because the honor of God and the times required it. Now when the honor of God demands that we give in to wrath, we have given in. After he had given this short address, he delineated two ranks: once which soldiered under God, that is, himself and his adherents; the other, under the Devil, that is, his adversaries.[12]

Machiavelli was unconcerned with whether Savonarola honestly saw visions or was even being sincere in his confessions. Machiavelli's only interest was in the lines of argument, patterns of metaphor, and their potential effects on an audience's thought and action. According to Machiavelli, Savonarola saw politics as the duty to follow the dictates of God in the assumption that triumph would follow. Exploiting his authority both as a friar and a would-be prophet of God, Savonarola articulated the end goal of Christ and demanded complete sacrifice and obedience to his own vision of purifying Florence. As Machiavelli notes in his letter, Savonarola contrasts the intrinsic "goodness" of his followers with the tyrannical natures of his enemies, specifically the Borgia pope, Alexander VI. This contrast thus divided the godly Florentines from the Devil in Rome. For Machiavelli, of course, all of this was just an exercise in weaponizing religion for political gain. With characteristic dryness, Machiavelli concluded that the friar was doing what any savvy political actor would do; he simply "acts in accordance with the times and colors his lies accordingly."[13] This was not necessarily an insult.

Savonarola, of course, did not believe he was lying. He saw himself as a divine messenger. He believed politics should be directed by prophetic vision, not by political persuasion. As a charismatic friar, he claimed to possess the prophetic light that could chase away the darkness and wake the slumbering masses; in his apologetic writings, he proclaimed that "the truth, once it is set forth, will quickly penetrate the minds of those who hear it, even when it is disputed."[14] A prophet, therefore, was one who spoke the truth. He continued, "Prophets, divinely given to the church, are like channels between God and the people. They are illuminated and directed by God so effectively, that they may to no extent be deceived regarding the things that they see and foretell in the Lord's name."[15] And he had, at first, good reason to believe he was correct. Guicciardini writes that "at the time when Italy enjoyed the greatest tranquility, he had often predicted the coming of foreign armies into Italy who would so terrify the people that neither walls nor armies would be able to resist them. And he had furthermore asserted that he was foretelling this and many other things which he was continually predicting, not by human reasoning or knowledge of the Scriptures, but simply by divine revelation."[16] Savonarola foretold the death of Lorenzo de' Medici and the king of France; they both died soon after. He spoke of a foreign army that would be the scourge of decadent Italy; soon the young French king Charles VIII was marching through the streets of Florence. And in 1494 the city was saved from destruction only by the soothing words of the Dominican friar. According to Martinez, "during the Savonarolan historical moment lasting from November 1494 to the spring or summer of 1497, no other man in Florence, or group of men, could begin to rival his stature," his enjoying "such popularity that the leading figures did not dare stand up to him in public."[17] Everything had come to pass. For Savonarola, the truth had triumphed over lies. He would be the divine instrument of the city's salvation.

Savonarola thus presents an ideal case study to understand the role of propaganda in Machiavellian politics. Savonarola's case is so illuminating because he was a practical master of propaganda who never ceased condemning propaganda. From his perspective, he merely spoke the truth and let God's word do its work. But from Machiavelli's perspective, Savonarola's rise (and eventual fall) clearly demonstrated how political power is founded upon appearances. Even the acquisition of arms, for Machiavelli, depends largely on the rhetorical manipulation of those appearances. Although realities exist and should not be ignored, any modern political order requiring the consent and mobilization of the people necessitates reaching them through what they can directly perceive and imaginatively experience. Therefore, even prophets like Savonarola who believe they have direct access to reality must account for the fact that, in politics, the effectual truth is the only measure that matters. In Machiavelli's famous formulation, "the common people will be convinced by appearances and by the end result. And the world is made up of common people, among whom the few dissenters who can see beyond appearances do not count when the majority can point to the prince's success."[18] For Machiavelli, there may be a few individuals close enough to the facts that they have a better grasp of reality; yet they will be ignored or silenced when their communication of that reality contradicts the appearances that the people have taken to be reality, especially when those appearances accompany tangible benefits. Whether Savonarola was a prophet or not (or even whether or not he believed himself to be so) had little relevance to understanding the nature of his political power. Savonarola rose on the tide of events and used the propaganda of appearances to propel him to prominence.

But not even the propaganda of appearances can ever fully dominate the necessity of fortune. Just four years later, on May 23, 1498, the remains of Savonarola's charred body hung from the center square of Florence before his corpse was pulled down, pulverized, and thrown into the Arno River. During those four years, events had turned against him. Pope Alexander VI had retaliated against Savonarola's attacks on the church by suspending him in 1495 on suspicion of heresy and then threatening excommunication of the entire city. The papal threat coincided with a period of grain shortages, famine, and plague. Savonarola also stubbornly insisted on supporting France (believing his own visions) despite the threat of a second French invasion that was setting all of Italy on edge. Soon "the city was openly divided: in the public councils one faction fought against the other, and as happens in divided cities, no man took thought of the common good, so intent was he upon smashing his adversary's reputation."[19] On the one side were the *piagnoni* ("snivelers" or "weepers") who supported Savonarola, often with great passionate displays, and on the other side were the *compagnacci* ("ugly companions"), a group of upper-class pleasure seekers who would roam the streets and engage in fights with the *piagnoni*; they were joined by the *arrabbiati* ("angry ones"), who represented a loose political grouping of all those opposed to Savonarola. In the end, the anti-Savonarola forces won. They fought their way into the Dominican convent at San Marco, extracted a confession from Savonarola under torture, and executed him and two other friars in the Piazza della Signoria. After the fire had burned away most of his flesh and the corpse began to shed legs and arms, boys took turns throwing stones at the remains; "their aim was to make the stumps fall, so that they would then be able to drag the blackened things, the charred flesh and bones, around the great piazza."[20] Such was the ignominious end of the prophet.

For Machiavelli, Savonarola's defeat was due to his failure to fully grasp the notion that political power is grounded not on realities but on appearances. Savonarola had ridden the wave of appearances but then had dismissed them in favor of a vision of reality only accessible to his own imagination. For Machiavelli, that refusal to attend to changing appearances was his downfall. Savonarola had initially capitalized on the power of appearances, but he interpreted these appearances as genuine signs of a divine will. And because he believed in a single vision of perfection and a fixed understanding of God, he was incapable of adapting his message when events turned against him. The populist rhetoric that had energized the Florentine people and identified them with the chosen people of the new Ark sounded hollow the moment the city was beset with suffering and fraught with conflict. As hostile forces consolidated power, Savonarola retreated behind the walls of San Marco, muttering the same pieties. Eventually, he found himself almost completely without protection except for his remaining loyal followers. But a few axes and crossbows wielded in the hands of a dozen friars can do little to resist an angry mob. The arms acquired through propaganda of appearances were thus lost as quickly as they had been acquired.

Responding to catastrophe through the propaganda of appearances is thus a double-edged sword. On the one hand, only through the propaganda of appearances can leaders orchestrate a mass, popular response to sudden catastrophic events. Propaganda, in fact, thrives in response to specific events, especially when even the designations of bare facts (like the approach of a French army) have the capacity to provoke panic, anger, and desperation on their own. And when panic strikes a population, neither republican deliberation nor authoritarian dictates are sufficient responses. These events call out for interpretation. Propaganda meets that public demand through the rhetorical manipulation of appearances. On the other hand, propaganda that responds this way to catastrophe often ends up consuming itself in the process. Not only does it create false expectations that are often immediately thwarted by subsequent events but its effort to create group identification often comes at the expense of widening preexisting social divisions even further. This consequence is due to the fact that propagandists, when seeking to exploit particular events, must paradoxically appeal to what Ellul calls those "fundamental currents" that already exist in society, which is to say its presuppositions, stereotypes, ideologies, reflexes, and myths. For Ellul, "propaganda can have solid *reality* and *power* over man only because of its rapport with fundamental currents, but it has seductive excitement and a capacity to move him only by its ties to the most volatile immediacy."[21] Yet this means that a propagandist must respond to a novel event by appealing to long-held biases and beliefs, some of them explaining away catastrophe by subsuming it under myth, others placing blame upon traditional scapegoats. Thus we have the spectacle of Savonarola meeting the challenge of the French invasion by rewriting the story of Noah's Ark while blaming Italy's suffering on simony and sodomy.

There is no easy answer to this problem. But we can begin to construct a Machiavellian way of understanding the nature of the challenge by distinguishing between three types of existences—*realities, appearances*, and *outcomes*. For Machiavelli, *appearances* are publicly accessible justifications, performances, representations, and events that influence the attitudes and beliefs of a people. For instance, when Machiavelli raises the question of when it is praiseworthy or blameworthy for a prince to keep his promises, he takes it for granted that a prince should also take great care that "to see him and hear him, he should appear all mercy, all faith, all honesty, all humanity, all religion."[22] But appearances are more than just the veneer of one's personal character. Appearances can represent any phenomenon that is understood as a sign or indication of something else. In this way, appearances are not *unrealities* but *slivers* of realities that point away from themselves, in time or space, to some more stable existence from which we assume they emanate or toward which they indicate. The colors, sounds, textures, smells, and tastes of appearances are very much realities, sometimes shockingly so. Yet what makes them exist to us as appearances is their promise of *more*. Appearances are dialectical, meaning they encompass a relationship between the immediate phenomena perceived and the imagined *more*, meaning the object, event, or quality to which they point as their origin. That is how the appearance of a French army became a sign of God's imminent judgment.

Whereas appearances are always open to inspection, *realities* are those frequently hidden or unknown aspects of the world that cause us to act in ways we might not otherwise wish. Realities come in two forms. *Private realities* are the relatively inaccessible private motives of individuals that drive the decisions of leaders. As Machiavelli explains, "men in general judge more by their eyes than by their hands, because seeing is given to everyone, touching to few. Everyone sees how you appear, few touch what you are."[23] Here, realities are those private motives that drive individuals that few can see outside of a person's close acquaintances. *Empirical realities*, by contrast, are the recalcitrant necessities that constrain action and threaten consequences. For instance, Machiavelli observes that the existence of realities makes it impossible to "observe all those things for which men are held good, since he is often under a necessity, to maintain his state, of acting against faith, against charity, against humanity, against religion."[24] In this case, being "under a necessity" points to the empirical realities that must be confronted in order to preserve the state, even if it means violating some notion of goodness. Empirical realities often have something of a law-like quality for Machiavelli, something that can be represented by a principle or communicated through a rule; it is akin to what he calls an "order of things," as when he remarks "the *order of things* is such that as soon as a powerful foreigner enters a province, all those in it who are less powerful adhere to him, moved by the envy they have against whoever has held power over them."[25] This reality exists nowhere in particular but nonetheless captures a regularity of behavior that governs, more or less, the behavior of agents when they find themselves in analogous situations.

Finally, *outcomes* are those "end results" that are the tangible effects experienced by the people that they connect in their mind to a particular action, judgment, or law. Outcomes thus have a relationship both to realities and to appearances. Outcomes are a direct result of the order of things that determines cause and effect in the empirical world; but as appearances, they may not be associated with the empirical cause but be attributed to either a benefactor or a scapegoat. For example, when Florence celebrated the peaceful departure of French troops, they celebrated this outcome as a result of Savonarola's influence on the French king. But a few years later, Savonarola was blamed for the outcomes of crop failures and disease. The perceived causal relationship between action and outcome might not be connected in empirical fact. What matters, politically speaking, is that they are connected in public opinion. Outcomes can be understood as appearances of a specific type, namely those qualities or occurrences that are connected in people's minds, rightly or wrongly, to the consequences of an event that directly impacts the people's lives. Outcomes are causal appearances that make a difference and are used to justify or condemn certain actions by oneself or others.

Machiavelli's terminology helps explain how, in the face of catastrophe, Savonarola could rise to power on the tide of a propaganda of appearances only to fall so quickly once the situation changed. During his ascent, Savonarola relied heavily on his creating an image of himself as a prophet capable of reading the signs of appearances to discern not only God's will but the fate of Italy. The death of Lorenzo followed by the appearance of French troops invading from the north had already made emotions run high. Savonarola exploited this opportunity to interpret these events in a way that called for the appearance of God's judgment, writing that "there is no one of sound mind who can now doubt that the scourge is at hand, when there is such manifest cause for divine vengeance."[26] For those who still doubted, Savonarola laid out his evidence by pointing to other appearances: "And so you should certainly have the utmost confidence that it will come to pass. There is a well-known proverb: 'the voice of the people is the voice of God.' As if we ourselves did not witness the beginning of great evils! Was not everything thrown into confusion at a precise moment, after the French king swept swiftly through Italy? Nation rose up against nation, people against people. And then pestilence and famine reached the gates. What else should we judge these things to be except the start of all the suffering? What more can one ask for? Or do you need signs and portents from heaven?"[27] In themselves, famines, pestilences, and wars are realities that can be investigated to determine their unique causes; but when cited as proof of a larger reality, they are appearances—in this case, the appearances that God is sending a scourge to cleanse and then redeem Italy. Savonarola believed these physical appearances were so convincing that one did not need even more dramatic portents from heaven that rip open the skies and send fire from the clouds. But it is also important to point out that Savonarola himself represents an appearance. Savonarola appeared to the people not just through his sermons and spectacles but through the publication of his writings. Notably, these writings were not reproduced by hand but by machine, for he exploited the "the striking development of the new printing press."[28] The appearances of Savonarola through the mass-reproduction of cheap print transformed the appearances of Italy's suffering into prophetic wisdom that became the foundation of his popular political power. Media themselves thus constitute a large part of the appearances of propaganda.

The fundamental current that most buoyed Savonarola during his rise was that of myth. But it is important to interpret myth in propagandistic and not cultural or religious terms. For Ellul, myth refers not just to a story with a particular content, such as a tale of gods and heroes. Myths include such stories, but they are not exclusive to them. What is significant is not myth's content but its function, which is to provide people "an explanation for all questions in an image of a future world in which all contradictions will be resolved."[29] Myths thus are general stories rooted in a specific culture that provide accounts of origins, promises of destiny, and justifications for holding loosely defined values and their concomitant hatreds. In sum, Ellul defines myth as "an all-encompassing, activating image: a sort of vision of desirable objectives that have lost their material, practical character, have become strongly colored, overwhelming, all-encompassing, and which displace from the conscious all that is not related to it. Such an image pushes man's action precisely because it includes all that he feels is good, just, and true."[30] But Ellul is also clear about the dangers of myth. Particularly in catastrophic rhetorical situations fraught with divisions, reliance on myth effectively eliminates the possibility of critical thought. Being all-encompassing, myth pushes out the possibility for detachment, attention to individual facts, and the weighing of alternatives and prediction of consequences. As Ellul writes, "through the myth it creates, propaganda imposes a complete range of intuitive knowledge, susceptible of only one interpretation, unique and one-sided, and precluding any divergence."[31] In the case of Savonarola, his myth brought together Christian apocalyptic thought with Florentine exceptionalism, resulting in a popular desire to make Florence great again. But this also meant that anyone who didn't conform to this stereotype was branded an outcast.

Unfortunately for Savonarola, the predicted utopia never arrived. As McQueen writes, during the period of his rise, "Savonarola's popularity soared and his sermons continued to whip the city into a state of heightened apocalyptic expectation. Now, the dominant theme was earthly renewal rather than worldly annihilation."[32] But soon this tendency was reversed. Negative outcomes connected with his leadership soon began to accumulate due to his inability to effectively deal with wider empirical realities. Guicciardini records that as diplomatic relationships between Florence and the Vatican grew ever more tense, especially in the midst of Florence's effort to regain control over Pisa, Savonarola's opponents also "reproved him because his foolhardiness might result in changing the Pope's mind, especially at a time when negotiations regarding the restitution of Pisa were being discussed with the Pope and the other allies, and when, therefore, it was wise to do everything possible to encourage papal support."[33] Furthermore, Guicciardini describes how "besides the long travails and serious expenses suffered by that city, there also occurred a very great famine that year as a result of which it might be presumed that the hungry people would desire a new order of things."[34] Thus the famines that Savonarola took to be signs of God's punishment were interpreted by many people to be outcomes of the poor leadership by his followers in the Florentine Republic. Just as a wave of appearances had ridden Savonarola into power, it would just as quickly pull him back with the receding tide.

One Machiavellian explanation for Savonarola's failure targeted the overall weakness of relying on the popular propaganda of appearances to justify bold and impetuous campaigns. For Machiavelli was well aware of the power of spectacle to arouse the passions and ambitions of free people in a republic. For when "gain is seen in the things that are put before the people . . . and when it appears spirited, even though there is the ruin of the republic concealed underneath, it will always be easy to persuade the multitude of it."[35] And here is the core problem of judging one's power by the short-term success of the propaganda of appearances: that realities have a way of undermining expectations and producing the opposite outcomes. The tragic irony of public enthusiasm is that "many times, deceived by a false image of good, the people desires its own ruin."[36] Virtuous leadership, of course, might prevent such outcomes, as when the public is made aware "what the good is, by someone in whom it has faith."[37] But this faith is hard to come by in a corrupted state. Thus, "when fate makes the people not have faith in someone, as happens at some time after it has been deceived in the past either by things or by men, it of necessity comes to ruin."[38] The people had lost faith in the Medici and had thrown their support to Savonarola, who had, in turn, built a constituency by persuading the Florentine people that they were inhabitants of a new Noah's Ark. But events had made this ark come to feel more like a prison. And then they lost faith a second time.

The other Machiavellian explanation for Savonarola's downfall was his inability to translate his early popular success into a committed source of arms that could withstand the inevitable attack of wolves. Once again, being "armed" in Machiavelli's writing does not simply mean possessing the physical instruments of war; being armed carries a distinctively political meaning. In fact, acquiring arms was often a rhetorical affair. Machiavelli believed strongly, writes Benner, that "there is greater profit in methods that strengthen one's 'own arms' through voluntary friendships and agreements than attempts to gain power through making subjects."[39] A leader thus acquires one's "own arms" neither by surrounding himself with weapons nor by paying mercenaries and assassins, but by persuading others to freely cooperate in forming a military force that fights not for pay but for honor. For this reason, Machiavelli argued against the policy of a new prince disarming the people and oppressing them through an occupying force. Instead, a new prince should provide them with weapons: "For when they are armed, these arms become yours; those whom you suspected become faithful, and those who were faithful remain so; and from subjects they are made into your partisans."[40] Machiavelli's lifelong ambition to create a Florentine civic militia in the model of today's volunteer military was the practical expression of this principle. For Machiavelli knew that power is not found solely in possession or availability of physical weapons, which are mere material agencies that remain useless without a collective will to make use of them for a common purpose. Coming to possess one's "own arms" is usually the *outcome* of a campaign of persuasion and political action, not the *starting* point of action. Leaders who spurn politics as mere empty words inevitably find themselves suffering in exile or hanging from the end of a rope.

For Machiavelli, the core lesson of Savonarola had nothing at all to do with his religious beliefs or his civic ideals; it had everything to do with the friar's failure to use the propaganda of appearances to properly arm himself in the long term to confront realities. Savonarola had faith that God's reality alone was sufficient to establish the new Heavenly City in Florence, so he refused to weaponize appearances and construct for himself a firm base of political and military power. Instead, retreating behind the walls of his convent, Savonarola allowed himself to be crushed by the arrabbiati. According to Machiavelli, there exist two types of prophet who seek to change the political order. One type of prophet relies solely on the means of virtue, the other combines virtue and force: "In the first case they will always come to ill and never accomplish anything; but when they depend on their own and are able to use force, then it is that they are rarely in peril. From this it arises that all the armed prophets conquered and the unarmed ones were ruined."[41] St. John the Baptist might be an example of an unarmed prophet; Moses was an example of one who came armed.[42] The reasoning behind this distinction is quite simple: "The nature of peoples is variable; and it is easy to persuade them of something, but difficult to keep them in that persuasion."[43] This failure to keep the people in persuasion through arms was Savonarola's problem: "He was ruined in his new orders as soon the multitude began not to believe in them, and he had no mode for holding firm those who had believed nor making unbelievers believe."[44] Savonarola was a victim of his own propaganda. He believed there was only one interpretation that could be drawn from the phenomena of the world; his faith in this stability ruined him. According to Machiavelli, Savonarola "did not know that one cannot wait for the time, goodness is not enough, fortune varies, and malignity does not find a gift that appeases it."[45] When making moves on the gameboard of political realism, one must always be responding to events through a continuously adapting propaganda of appearances. For one either defines the meaning of the times or is defined by them.

In the end, Savonarola was ruined in spectacular fashion by a dramatic appearance he could no longer control. This was a trial by fire. Realizing Savonarola was in a precarious position after violating the order to cease preaching, the archrivals of the Dominican order, the Franciscans, demonstrated their love of God by challenging Savonarola to prove his prophetic ethos. Guicciardini writes that eventually a disciple of Savonarola and a Franciscan friar "agreed upon a trial by fire in the presence of the entire populace, so that the Dominican either being spared or burned would make it clear to everybody whether Savonarola was a prophet or a fraud."[46] The ordeal was set for April 7 in the Piazza della Signoria. At considerable expense, the government had built a thirty-meter-long, two-meter-high platform on which was built a corridor of logs, pitch, straw, and gunpowder: "Death or miracle had to be the outcome, for as one and was set on fire, the Dominican and the Franciscan were to enter the inferno at the opposite end, which would then be immediately ignited."[47] The Piazza was soon packed. But then hours passed as the participants argued over details, until eventually the clouds opened and rain and hail poured down upon the frustrated crowds. Members of the arrabbiati then agitated for a tumult, and the next day a mob stormed San Marco and took Savonarola prisoner.

In the end, Savonarola's enemies proved more adept at manipulating appearances. Instead of leading the state, Savonarola found himself submitting to the *strappado*, the preferred method of extracting confession. With his wrists tied behind his back and hooked to a pulley, he was lifted up high before being dropped to a point just high enough from the floor that the sudden jerk would dislocate his shoulders. On his failing to satisfy his interrogators, his shoulders would be popped back into place and the procedure would be repeated. Through this method a written confession was produced and disseminated to the people in which Savonarola was said to have admitted that he never spoke to God, that he was only interested in fame and power, and that he had an ambition to be "the first man of the world."[48] Diarist and Savonarola supporter Lucca Landucci recorded his reaction to these new appearances:

> He whom we had held to be a prophet, confessed that he was no prophet and had not received from God the things which he preached, and he confessed many things that had occurred during the course of his preaching were contrary to what he had given us to understand. I was present when this protocol was read, and I marveled, feeling utterly dumbfounded with surprise. My heart was grieved to see such an edifice fall to the ground on account of having been founded on a lie. Florence had been expecting a new Jerusalem, from which would issue just laws and splendor and an example of righteous life and to see the renovation of the church, the conversion of unbelievers and the consolation of the righteous; and I felt that everything was exactly contrary, and had to resign myself with the thought: "Lord, in thy hands are all things."[49]

The appearances that might have thrown doubt on the validity of this confession, namely Savonarola's broken body in prison and his frequent recantations of his confessions after recovering from torture, were all hidden from Landucci. Similarly, the voice of the friar was silenced as he was taken to the scaffold, a metal nail likely pierced through his cheeks and tongue to prevent his speech. Landucci was given only the spectacle of a written confession, read out loud in the Piazza della Signoria, joined with the visual spectacle of the blackened and burned flesh of the man he once thought to be a prophet. These were signs not of redemption but of judgment.

Despite Savonarola's downfall, Machiavelli recognized and perhaps even grudgingly admired his rare accomplishments even as he blamed him for his errors. The friar showed that the propaganda of appearances, if deployed at the right moment, may constitute a powerful movement capable of reforming a civic order, challenging church authority, and giving hope and direction to the people. Savonarola showed, in short, that some degree of popular reform of a corrupt republic was, in fact, possible. Yet he also proved quite clearly that a movement based on a narrow religious ideology that puts its faith in prophecy rather than politics sacrifices the hope for long-term reform in the name of short-term ecstasy. By believing his own lies, Savonarola had entered the political fray both unarmed and unable to adapt to changing conditions. The fact that political power rests on the complex and changing relationships between appearances, outcomes, and realities provides the justification for what Skinner characterizes as Machiavelli's "central political belief: that the clue to successful statecraft lies in recognizing the force of circumstances, accepting what necessity dictates, and harmonizing one's behavior with the times."[50] But even here, Machiavelli's counsel seems hollow. If Savonarola had heeded this advice, he may not have fared any better. His very authority rested on his ethos as a prophet, so to alter his message would have been to betray the followers who had remained loyal to his cause.

In this way, Machiavelli's rather weak (but irresistibly quotable) argument concerning Savonarola's inability to properly arm himself overshadows his more significant insight into the limits of the populist rhetoric of catastrophe. Machiavelli had observed that the people are often most passionate about spectacular plans that bring eventual ruin while tending to shun prudent approaches that require immediate sacrifice. Thus, when interpreted in light of Machiavelli's own political theory, Savonarola's choice to meet the challenge of catastrophe by pursuing power through the propaganda of appearances had trapped the friar in a paradox. This paradox is that as catastrophes expand in scale and magnitude, the necessity to mobilize a great mass of people to meet these challenges requires a propaganda of appearances that flatters its audience and reduces complex problems to matters of myth. One must either arouse the people to action through distorted facts and false hopes or speak the difficult truths and be ignored. Should one choose propaganda, one ends up encouraging a path to action that sows the seeds of ruin even if it begins in success. As Machiavelli remarks, a republic would then face yet another recurrence of a situation Dante writes of in *On Monarchy*, namely, "that many times the people cries: 'Life!' to its death and 'Death!' to its life."[51] But even Machiavelli recognized that for a state to continue, it cannot persist in facing catastrophe after catastrophe by wallowing in myth, fostering division, and raising up new prophets only to send them to their doom. At some point, people must actually learn to start saying "Life!" to life.

Easier said than done. As catastrophes increase in scope and complexity, the temptation for escapism only grows. And always ready to meet this need will be a type of propaganda that offers simplistic solutions that flatter the virtues of its audience and explain material causes through the moral failings of popular scapegoats. This type of propaganda will never go away. It forms a relatively constant and impenetrable bulwark of ignorance virtually immune to any amount of facts or education. That is because pure denialism stands at its core. In our time, this might include the denial of history, the denial of evolution, the denial of genocide, the denial of global warming, the denial of vaccines, the denial of viruses, the denial of racism, and even the denial of a spherical earth. The list goes on. But these denials all have in common a shared desire to reject change. Denialism arises from the recognition that certain facts, should they be true, would demand a response that a population simply does not wish to give. The power of resistance to change should never be underestimated. During the COVID-19 pandemic, people who refused to wear masks would often go to great lengths to concoct complex conspiracy theories to justify their refusal. The fact that many of these people contracted the virus and died from it did nothing to weaken the bulwark of ignorance. The will to believe, when bolstered by propaganda, often becomes in practical terms a willingness to suffer and die.

But perhaps we should take solace in imagining Machiavelli's nonchalant response to this seemingly modern phenomenon. For if you showed Machiavelli the latest QAnon conspiracy influencer videos claiming that democratic governments are run by a cabal of pedophiles who drink the blood of babies, he would probably respond, with a shrug, that they are simply acting in accordance with the times and coloring their lies accordingly. If there is solace here, it is in the fact that we are dealing with a historical constant of human nature. While technologies and mediums certainly alter the pace, scale, and pattern of human communication in unique ways, the content of those messages remains surprisingly uniform. Propaganda must always respond to real necessities by manipulating appearances and defining outcomes to mobilize popular masses to belief and action. And a significant percentage of this propaganda will always target the basest motives of human beings who wish only to be reassured that the life they currently lead is the best of all possible lives. But not all propaganda. For every statement, there is a counterstatement. For every lie, there is a truth. To people concerned with the sorry state of public opinion, Machiavelli might advise getting over it and crafting better messages. There is no alternative to propaganda in an age of propaganda. One either engages in the fight or gives up the field to a rival. In meeting the catastrophes of our time, a propaganda campaign committed to intelligent reform must be engaging, informed, continuous, total, and inclusive. But this means it will also be expensive. The war of words cannot be won on the cheap. We must invest in a democratically formed and scientifically informed propaganda of appearances or lose the fight to an army of trolls, bots, and grifters. Without a rhetorical equivalent to acquiring one's "own arms," the prophetic voices who warn of our impending collapse will suffer a worse fate than that of Savonarola—they will actually *live* to see everything they love come to ruin.

CHAPTER 10

Why Catastrophe Demands Good Leaders but Often Empowers Bad Ones

C ATASTROPHE CALLS OUT FOR LEADERSHIP. AS THE DISASTROUS effects of climate change accumulate, so has the desperate call for political profiles in courage. Following the 2022 release of the Intergovernmental Panel on Climate Change report, Secretary-General of the United Nations António Guterres said that the report is "an atlas of human suffering and a damning indictment of failed climate leadership."[1] The report detailed, in Guterres's words, how "people and the planet are getting clobbered by climate change," how "nearly half of humanity is living in the danger zone," how "many ecosystems are at the point of no return," and how "unchecked carbon pollution is forcing the world's most vulnerable on a frog march to destruction."[2] Yet despite many global agreements and commitments, carbon emissions continue to grow and the effects multiply. And because the failure to act "spells catastrophe," the "abdication of leadership is criminal."[3] Months later, in August 2022, another report that projected possible worst-case climate scenarios led to this headline in the *Irish Mirror*: "Climate Endgame: Risk to Human Extinction or Total Societal Collapse 'Dangerously Underexplored' Say Scientists."[4] These types of headlines have led even conservative politicians, such as US senator Mitt Romney, to call for a leader who can stop being in denial about climate change, "who can rise above the din to unite us behind the truth," rise "above our grievances and resentments," and "grasp the mantle of leadership our country so badly needs."[5]

To approach Machiavelli's conception of leadership through the example of climate catastrophe is not far-fetched. Robert Clines, for instance, published a 2020 editorial in the *Washington Post* titled "What Machiavelli Would Do about Climate Change" (with the subtitle "One of History's Most Famous Thinkers Had a Solution for Natural Disasters").[6] For Clines, today's leaders have much to gain by returning to Machiavelli's famous dichotomy between fortuna and virtú. Recall that Machiavelli had used the metaphor of a natural disaster to explain their relationship. On the one side, he likened fortuna "to one of these violent rivers which, when they become enraged, flood the plains, ruin the trees and buildings, lift earth from this part, drop in another; each person flees before them, everyone yields to their impetus without being able to hinder them in any regard."[7] On the other side, virtú represented the vision and will to build "dikes and dams" during times of quiet, so that when the waters "rise later, either they go by a canal or their impetus is neither so wanton nor so damaging."[8] For Clines, this was the type of virtú needed to confront catastrophic times—the virtú not of force and cunning but of forethought and commitment. If Machiavelli were alive today, Clines writes, he would tell us that virtuous leadership calls "for immediate intervention as well as long-term solutions focused on the common good" and that the public "must continue to demand that our leaders address climate-related natural disasters rather than ignore them or use them as pretenses for self-aggrandizement."[9] All sound advice from the Florentine second chancellor.

On this more positive reading of Machiavelli, virtú should be associated less with the type of boldness and impetuousness of Cesare Borgia and more with the steadfastness and vision of Brutus. This version of virtú emphasizes the capacity of a leader to see far ahead and prepare for what is to come. It is this quality that Pocock emphasizes when he argues that "*virtú* is preeminently that by which the individual is rendered outstanding in the context of innovation and in the role of innovator."[10] Similarly, Benner writes that "*virtú* includes an aptitude for organization, industry, and far-sighted prudence. It further includes unclouded knowledge of one's limits, the wisdom and self-discipline not to overreach them, and the ingenuity to use whatever opportunities and resources one has, however scarce they might be."[11] This is the type of virtú Machiavelli emphasized when he wrote to his friend Vettori that "the duty of a prudent man is constantly to consider what may harm him and to foresee problems in the distance—to aid the good and to thwart the evil in plenty of time."[12] The art of politics, in other words, involves collaborative efforts to design those dikes and dams to meet the coming storms. In this sense, virtú is a benign and worthy virtue for which leaders should strive.

Yet Machiavelli realized that even a leader who possessed such virtú did not have an easy task ahead. When it comes to actually implementing far-sighted policies, the most prudent republican leader must still overcome the natural inertia of a public accustomed to enjoying the benefits of its traditional modes and orders. When catastrophe appears imminent, people as a whole generally resist making real sacrifices in the present for merely hypothetical benefits in the future. Just as they are often deceived by a false image of the good that conceals future dangers, so, too, "it may always be difficult to persuade it of these politics if either cowardice or loss might appear, even though safety and gain might be concealed underneath."[13] And should leaders push ahead despite public reluctance, telling themselves that dramatic changes in the existing order are necessary to confront catastrophe, they must then decide on how fast or slow to implement radical policies. There are two choices: "These orders have to be renewed either all at a stroke, when they are discovered to be no longer good, or little by little, before they are recognized by everyone."[14] But even here, Machiavelli emphasizes the tragic character of this choice, for "both of these two things are almost impossible."[15] In the first case, even implementing gradual changes is difficult when the danger is distant. In the second case, sudden change requires such forceful modes that good leaders shun them and bad leaders exploit them.

A closer look at these two bad alternatives reveals just how enormous is the challenge of leadership in the face of catastrophe. The obstacle to the gradualist option is fundamentally rhetorical. Machiavelli writes that even when that rare leader comes about who "sees this inconvenience from very far away and when it arises," that leader will "never be able to persuade anyone else of what he himself understands. For men used to living in one mode do not wish to vary it, and so much the more when they do not look the evil in its face but have to have it shown to them by conjecture."[16] In short, conjecture does little in times of peace and prosperity. The propaganda of appearances requires timely events that stimulate fear and provoke action. To paraphrase the maxim of Villani, people do not act until they hurt all over. But by that time, the ability to actually respond to the crisis has usually passed. Hence the desire to respect the people's customary habits, traditional beliefs, and immediate needs leads to a situation in which leaders are left without the required dikes and dams to meet the catastrophe when it arrives.

But one faces even greater and more sinister obstacles to implementing widespread change at a stroke. For the sheer force required to institute revolutionary reforms in a time of crisis requires abandoning ordinary modes and resorting to "the extraordinary, such as violence and arms."[17] And because employing these modes requires a leader who has learned how not to be good, rarely does one find both qualities of a commitment to "good" ends and an embrace of "evil" means in a single person. As Machiavelli explains, "because the reordering of a city for a political way of life presupposes a good man, and becoming prince of a republic by violence presupposes a bad man, one will find that it very rarely happens that someone good wishes to become prince by bad ways, even though his end be good, and that someone wicked, having become prince, wishes to work well, and that it will ever occur to his mind to use well the authority that he has acquired badly."[18] In other words, this option will be refused by those leaders actually concerned with preserving freedom and securing justice but will be embraced by one who enjoys doing evil. This option thus invites the temptation of fascist authoritarian solutions in which charismatic demagogues exploit catastrophe by promising a total rebirth and a purification of corrupt orders. But by relying on a propaganda of agitation to catapult themselves to power, such leaders inevitably end up catalyzing hatreds and divisions that in turn thwart any remaining intention they may have to intelligently implement prudent policies.

For Machiavelli, Savonarola's downfall demonstrated the practical and ethical paradoxes faced by any reformer. In order to have succeeded, Savonarola would have had to have pursued a complete and vigorous "regeneration of arms and a change in orders."[19] But to actually employ the modes necessary to accomplish this regeneration would have required Savonarola to learn a lesson that was anathema to his conscience. In Machiavelli's pithy phrase, Savonarola would have had to "learn to be able not to be good, and to use this and not use this according to necessity."[20] To learn to be able not to be good does not necessarily mean to learn how to be evil, although that may be an option on the table. It means that should one employ evil means, "it is necessary for him to be so prudent as to know how to avoid infamy of those vices that would take his state from him."[21] According to Viroli, to learn how not to be good is "to learn not to fear to be blamed for having qualities which are not considered to be good."[22] In sum, to learn "not to be good" requires (1) learning how not to let a guilty conscience get in the way of prudential political calculus, (2) learning the art of manipulating appearances so that even cruel or selfish actions are made to appear good to the people, and (3) learning to accept a reputation for not being good if that reputation is the price of surviving catastrophe. Savonarola failed in this respect because he was bound by his strict religious conscience. His insistence of being "good" thus allowed even worse men to destroy him.

The clear Machiavellian conclusion, therefore, is that catastrophe tends to attract the leadership of "bad men" for a strictly practical reason: only those types of leaders have sufficiently mastered the techniques of how not to be good. Machiavelli does not necessarily celebrate this fact. He understands and even appreciates that it would be desirable that every political leader should be faithful, humane, honest, agreeable, and generous. But for him, the constant threat of fortune's malignancy invites leaders like Cesare Borgia to the forefront by necessity. One must, as Machiavelli constantly stresses, adapt to the times. What is most required is the ability to apply the standards of effectual truth to evaluate courses of action quite irrespective of whether they are traditionally considered "good" or "bad." First, learning how not to be good means being able to willingly embrace those "vices without which it is difficult to save one's state."[23] Second, it means learning how to resist the compulsion to be good for its own sake, for "if one considers everything well, one will find something appears to be virtue, which if pursued would be one's ruin, and something else appears to be vice, which if pursued results in one's security and well-being."[24] Machiavelli gives examples. For instance, being generous to people brings short-term gratitude, but over time "you become either poor and contemptible or, to escape poverty, rapacious and hateful."[25] Being merciful to one's enemies seems humane, but when Florence was merciful "to escape a name for cruelty, [it] allowed Pistoia to be destroyed."[26] And even "Cesare Borgia was held to be cruel; nonetheless his cruelty restored the Romagna, united it, and reduced it to peace and to faith."[27] In each case, every action is judged by the standards of effectual truth alone. After such a prudential analysis, these arguably "bad" individuals are then prepared to use force and fraud as necessary to achieve justified results while also possessing mastery of the propaganda of appearances to cloak these actions in the trappings of honor and glory.

In contemporary political theory, Machiavelli's observation that leadership requires learning "how not to be good" has been called the problem of "dirty hands." As defined by Michael Walzer, to be confronted with a dirty hands dilemma is to be forced to consider a "particular act of government" that "may be exactly the right thing to do in utilitarian terms and yet leave the man who does it guilty of a moral wrong."[28] For example, Walzer imagines a situation in which a leader of a colonial power genuinely has "pledged to de-colonization and peace," and yet on arriving at the colonial capital this leader finds it in the grip of a terrorist attack.[29] Specifically, "he is asked to authorize the torture of a captured rebel leader who knows or probably knows the lo-cation of a number of bombs hiding in apartment buildings around the city, set to go off within the next twenty-four hours."[30] There are no good options. The leader must either be "good" and refrain from torture, thus condemn-ing innocent people to maiming and death, or be "bad" and commit torture to save lives, despite believing that "torture is wrong, indeed abominable, not just sometimes but always."[31] Walzer sees no way around these problems. A political leader must ultimately accept Machiavelli's counsel. But Walzer also stresses that these actions must be exceptions to the rule and that those who commit bad acts must "acknowledge their responsibility for the violation by accepting punishment or doing penance."[32] Consistent with what Walzer sees as the Catholic doctrine prevalent even in Machiavelli's time, dirty hands are inevitable but through penance can be cleaned.

Yet for Demetris Tillyris, the dirty hands problem is far more extensive and systematic in political life than even Walzer portrays. Tillyris calls the standard conception of the problem the *paradox of action*, in which in "certain inescapable and tragic circumstances an innocent course of action is unfea-sible."[33] But he also says that this form of the paradox of action fails to fully capture "Machiavelli's message and its terrifying implications."[34] The prob-lem with this framing is that it presents this paradox as an exception to the rule. It suggests that "the conflict between morality and politics involves a momentary and relatively rare paradox of action—a mere anomaly which disrupts the normality of past and future harmony."[35] The reality, however, is that learning "how not to be good" should be thought of "as a *practice* and a *way of life*" consistent with an enduring and dynamic political culture.[36] By limiting "not being good" only to tragic circumstances (like ticking time bomb or lifeboat scenarios), Walzer is able to reaffirm a moral order grounded in Catholic notions of confession and penance once the crisis has passed, in ef-fect restoring a conservative moral order. But what happens in an environ-ment, particularly one characterized by catastrophe, when this type of para-dox of action becomes the norm? Then learning "how not to be good" does not refer to this or that act but to an entire disposition of one's character. To survive in this context "is possible only if one irretrievably relinquishes his innocence by cultivating the necessary vices conducive to virtuous political practice."[37] To imitate the lessons of Cesare Borgia is not simply to adopt this or that mode of acting; it is to embody his virtú and internalize his attitudes and dispositions.

In order to explore how Machiavelli negotiated the dirty hands problem in Florentine history, we can turn to the tragic end of the Renaissance republic, which occurred during Machiavelli's lifetime. By doing so, we also discover a biographical reason why Machiavelli placed so much importance on learning "how not to be good." Machiavelli would always blame his long-time political patron and supporter, Piero Soderini, for having failed to make the tragic decisions necessary to save the republic. In the years following the fall of Savonarola in 1498, Machiavelli had thrived. The city had burned the friar at the stake, but it retained much of the republican structure Savonarola had instituted, including the ban on the Medici family and their allies. The decision to maintain a popular regime "had placated the middle strata of Florentine society but had alienated many patricians who believed that public affairs should be reserved for citizens of wealth, status, and experience."[38] In an effort to appease the patricians, in 1502 the republic elected Piero Soderini to the new position of permanent gonfaloniere of justice. Soderini promptly selected Machiavelli as the youngest chancellor ever to hold the office. The two would maintain a close relationship during the fourteen years they worked together, and Machiavelli would become a central figure in the state because of Soderini's steadfast support. Yet when Florence was beset by new enemies, Soderini chased chimeras rather than acting like the fox or the lion. Worse still, he allowed "goodness" to prevent him from eliminating his enemies inside the city, which Machiavelli believed would have secured the state. When the Medici were restored to power, Machiavelli endured torture for his republican sympathies. In prison, he undoubtedly had time to reflect on Soderini's failures.

Although arguably self-serving, Machiavelli would ultimately blame Soderini for the fall of the Second Republic for having failed to make the tragic choices necessary to preserve the freedom of his city. Part of the problem, as Machiavelli saw it, was that Soderini failed to comprehend his own tenuous hold on power. Soderini had been chosen to fill his position because he was the most prominent member of the Signoria and would presumably represent patrician interests against the middle class. But Soderini "refused to become a tool of the great families but instead sought to maintain a balance between the aristocratic and the popular factions."[39] This attempt to be fair and impartial (to be "good") galvanized the aristocratic factions behind the Medici exiles. But the greater problem was that he downplayed the Medici threat and then refused to arrest, exile, or execute their supporters in the city when he had the opportunity (because this would have been "not good"). Recalling the example of Brutus who executed his own sons to save the Roman Republic, Machiavelli concludes that Soderini failed to learn this lesson. The remaining Medici partisans were clearly analogous to the sons of Brutus, but it was "Soderini, who believed he would overcome with his patience and goodness the appetite that was in the sons of Brutus for returning to another government, and who deceived himself."[40] That self-deception would be his undoing the moment the Medici exiles saw the opportunity to strike.

A more detailed exploration of these events will show the complex nature of the paradoxes of action that confronted Soderini during perhaps the most catastrophic period in Florentine history. To understand the situation that led to Soderini's downfall, one must look at Florence in the context of European politics in the late fifteenth century. This was a time when the rising nations of Europe were beginning to exert ever-greater influence on the Italian peninsula, forcing Italian states to continually play the greater powers against one another in order to maintain some vestige of independence. Florence had traditionally allied itself with France, but this placed the city on a collision course with the ambitions of Pope Julius II, who had organized the so-called Holy League to expel France from its hold in the northern Italian peninsula. Florence had refused to join. But when French forces suddenly withdrew, leaving Florence without a strong defender, the Medici exiles found their opportunity to align themselves with the interests of the Holy League and return to power under the guise of restoring Italian independence and papal autonomy. Led by a viceroy who was also a Medici partisan, the army marched in 1512 toward Florence to force an ultimatum—either expel Gonfaloniere Soderini and allow the return of the Medici to Florence or be attacked. When Soderini refused these demands, the army of the Holy League, composed of forces from Spain, Venice, England, and the Papal Armies, decided on August 28, 1512, "to crush the Republican regime and restore the Medici."[41]

The sense of impending catastrophe in Florence was captured by Guicciardini in his history. The moment the Florentines heard of the coming of the Spaniards and the papal forces, "a terrible wave of terror spread throughout the city, for fear of the dissensions among the citizens and the fact that many of them more inclined toward a change of government."[42] The citizens suddenly realized that there were factions sympathetic with Medici interests and willing to betray the city if it meant reinstating their factions to power. Consequently, when the viceroy's "proposal was made known throughout the city, there were as many differences of opinion among the citizens as there are judgments, passions, and fears."[43] But Soderini remained committed to defending the independence of the city and the legitimacy of his rule; he would make the tragic decision to fight for their freedom against superior forces. With the help of Machiavelli, who was commander of the city militia, Florence under Soderini's leadership assembled two thousand foot soldiers and sent the men and artillery to Prato, ten miles from Florence, which was the city they believed the viceroy would besiege first. If they could hold out in Prato, it was believed, they could negotiate better terms on a treaty. Unfortunately, as Guicciardini remarked in light of what happened, "nothing flies away faster than opportunity, nothing more dangerous than to judge other people's intentions, nothing more harmful than immoderate suspicion."[44] Ruin would have its day.

Machiavelli recounted the tragic fate of Prato in a letter to a noblewoman on September 16, 1512. In August of that year, "the Spanish army had appeared before Prato and attacked it vigorously" but were "unable to take it by storm."[45] Meanwhile the viceroy sent envoys to Florence, declaring that the Holy League was not seeking a change in government, only the expulsion of Soderini because he was a "French supporter."[46] In his response to this request, Soderini gave voice to the highest republican sentiments, replying "that he had not come into the office through either force or fraud but that he had been put there by the people. Therefore, even if all the kings in the world keep together they should order him to relinquish it, he would never do so; but if the people of Florence wanted him to leave it, he would willingly."[47] With this reassertion of republican piety, he was unanimously supported in his position; inspired by his leadership, the Florentines would fight on. Meanwhile Prato continued to resist the siege, forcing representatives of Pope Julius II to negotiate with the Florentine ambassador for "a certain amount of money" and a vague assurance that the pope would continue to negotiate with Florence over the return of the Medici.[48] Soderini then began to feel as if he was playing a stronger hand: "When the ambassadors arrived with this proposal, reported on the weakened condition of the Spaniards, and asserted that they might die of hunger and that Prato was going to hold out, the gonfalonier and the scores of people with whom he was consulting were inspired with such great confidence that despite the advice from the wise for peace on that basis, the gonfalonier kept on postponing matters."[49] But then necessity shattered their confidence and their illusions. Machiavelli writes, "Two days later news of Prato's capture arrived and of how the Spaniards, having broken through some of the walls, began to force the defenders back and to terrify them. So that, after slight resistance, they all fled and the Spaniards took possession of the city, put it to sack, and massacred the city's population in a pitiable spectacle of calamity. In order to spare your ladyship cause for worry in your spirit, I shall not report on the details. I shall merely say that better than 4000 died; the remainder were captured and, through various means, were obliged to pay ransom. Nor did they spare the virgins cloistered in holy sites, which were all filled with acts of rape and pillage."[50]

Machiavelli describes Soderini as being far enough away from the pathetic cries of dying men, the raped women, and the enslaved children that he soldiered on: "This news caused the city great consternation; nevertheless, the gonfalonier, relying on some chimeras of his own, did not take fright."[51] Inspired by delusions of his own security, he was confident he could reach agreement with the Spaniards by lavishing money on them. But it was all fantasy. The Florentine resistance collapsed. In a final blow, the Medici partisans were released from prison. A few days later, a group of armed men forced the expulsion of Soderini from the city, followed a few weeks later by the armed occupation of the Palazzo della Signoria by Medici partisans who, to the Medici cry of "Palle, palle," installed Lorenzo's son Guiliano as ruler. Soon afterwards, Machiavelli was accused of conspiring against the new regime. For twenty-two days Machiavelli was imprisoned and tortured with the *strappado*. Only when another of Lorenzo's sons, Giovanni de Medici, became Pope Leo X, were prisoners given a general amnesty.

If Machiavelli was to locate a single cause for the city's ruin, it would have been Soderini's unshakeable belief in chimeras. Strictly speaking, a chimera is a beast from Greek mythology, a fire-breathing monster with a lion's head, a goat's body, and a serpent's tail. But chimeras also symbolize fantastic creations of the imagination that one might believe or wish to be real but which are illusory or impossible to achieve (as when Machiavelli, in private letters, makes fun of himself and his friends as being "petty, fickle, lascivious, and directed toward chimerical matters").[52] These chimerical matters were similar to those castles in the air he accused himself of sometimes constructing for his own amusement and self-gratification. Chimeras in Machiavelli's thought are thus the very opposite of effectual truths. Rather than emerging out of a careful analysis of a situation and its lines of force to aid us in making hard choices, chimeras simply fly down from the sky to amuse and flatter us.

By Machiavelli's account, Soderini hallucinated five different chimeras. The first chimera was his faith in the strong bonds of the people's love. At the early stages of the conflict, the people had showered him with gratitude for his leadership, and he had taken this to mean they would have his back to the end. Instead, they fled to the opposition. The second chimera was his vision of Florentine military strength. Emboldened by false reports of Prato's heroic resistance, Soderini believed he had a strong hand to play in a contest of force. The result was the brutal massacre of Prato's inhabitants. The third chimera was his trust that goodness and generosity could defeat great malignancy. In Machiavelli's words, Soderini thought "he could extinguish new humors with patience and goodness and wear away some of the enmity to himself with rewards."[53] Instead, the recipients of these rewards paid him back with ingratitude and betrayal. The fourth chimera was his confidence in the legitimacy of the established order. But in the name of preserving civil equality and law, Soderini allowed them both to be destroyed. And the final chimera was his belief in his own intrinsic goodness. Soderini saw himself as a virtuous and noble leader and believed it was below him to learn how not to be good. Instead of acting boldly to eliminate threats, he chose to "allow an evil to run loose out of respect for good, when that good could easily be crushed by that evil."[54] And so the Medici lay in wait under the cover of Soderini's goodness until they were able to strike when the opportunity presented itself to restore their tyranny. In short, "not knowing how to be like Brutus, he lost not only his fatherland but his state and his reputation."[55] Machiavelli in exile would never fully forgive this failure. And Soderini's failure to imitate the lesson of Brutus would haunt him.

But we should be cautious about being seduced by Machiavelli's realist style in this case. The notion that Soderini's regime could have survived this onslaught intact was fanciful. Florence faced only bad options. Such is the nature of tragic choices. Machiavelli faults the gonfalonier for his overreliance on goodness, which is to say his trust that all misfortunes can be worked out in the end when people recognize their common humanity and acknowledge their pride and misconceptions. Soderini's trust in others' virtue, in Machiavelli's analysis, clouded the clarity of his vision that would have made him realize "that if he wished to strike his opponents vigorously and to beat down his adversaries, he would have needed to take up extraordinary authority and break up civil equality together with the laws."[56] But Soderini had good reason not to pursue this option. Chimera or not, trying to uphold Florence as a republic of laws was the way he believed would rally the people to his side based on their love of country. Machiavelli blamed Soderini for this judgment, but he does not properly consider the alternative. Had Soderini eliminated his enemies in a bold stroke of cruelty, he would have only temporarily secured his rule at the cost of sacrificing all of his republican principles, creating hatred among his own citizens, and ensuring a violent sack of the city once it inevitably fell to the superior forces of the Holy League. Soderini chose the path he believed had the best chance of preserving the republic and saving the lives of its people. And although Florence fell, the city was occupied but not sacked and a veneer of republic order remained. Soderini had sacrificed his own leadership, honors, and power to protect the people he governed. In many ways, we can ask no more of our leaders than to put the common good before their own private interest.

In addition, there is evidence to show that Soderini was not as naive about the Medici threat as Machiavelli portrayed. In fact, the case seems quite the opposite. In Guicciardini's competing history, Soderini is cast in a very different light. When the Florentines were given the ultimatum by the viceroy, many of the city's leaders lacked confidence in Machiavelli's citizen militia and began convincing themselves that they should accept the terms of the deal. In their minds, sacrificing Soderini and allowing the Medici to return as private citizens would entail no great change in the city's freedoms and character. After all, the Medici had been the de facto rulers for decades, so their return would be more of a restoration. Soderini, however, rejected this optimism. He argued that the Medici who would take power would behave nothing like their predecessors. Guicciardini reconstructs Soderini's speech to the Grand Council this way:

> Be aware of the danger facing you, and do not let any expenses and difficulties seem too heavy to bear when it is a question of maintaining your freedom; how precious freedom is you will realize better, if fruitlessly (I dread to say it) you are deprived of it. Nor should anyone delude himself that government by the Medici would be the same as it was before they were exiled, because the form and basis of things have changed: at that time, raised amongst almost like private citizens, [possessing] the richest

means in view of their position, harmed by no one, they based their rule on the goodwill of the citizens, discussed public affairs with the outstanding men, and made every effort to cover themselves with the cloak of civic virtue as soon and their ambitions were revealed. But now, having dwelt so many years outside of Florence, brought up in foreign ways, and for this reason out of touch with civic matters, remembering their exile and the harsh manner in which they had been treated, very reduced in means and distrusted by so many families; aware that most, indeed, almost the entire city abhors tyranny, they would not share their councils with any citizen; and forced by poverty and suspicion, they would arrogate everything to themselves, depending primarily not on goodwill and love but force and arms . . . I wanted to say this to those who preach about the time and rule of Lorenzo the magnificent. For, although conditions were hard then and there was a tyranny (although milder than many others), by comparison with this, Lorenzo's rule would be an age of gold.[57]

This speech is one of the most eloquent orations in all of Guicciardini's history. Soderini shows himself to be a highly skilled political strategist who is keenly aware of the changed political landscape. Whereas the Medici hegemony of the mid-fifteenth century had created stability due to their need to constantly cover their ambitions with the cloak of civic virtue in order to maintain the guise of republicanism, a triumphant Medici restoration would rely on force and arms to suppress dissent and install the family as foreign-backed tyrants. Soderini thus embodied the republican style of politics, using the power of persuasion to convince his fellow citizens that it was in their best interests to maintain solidarity against the Medici and defend republican liberty.

Lastly, even Machiavelli's own analysis hints at the fact that his political patron may have been playing a longer game than the second chancellor. For Soderini did not refuse extraordinary authority out of a bad conscience; he did so as a result of projecting the effectual truth of such actions farther down the line. Soderini reasoned that the negative consequences of breaking up civil equality would not be confined to the short-term emergency; they would have long-term effects that would ultimately undermine the security and stability of the state. From Soderini's perspective, "even though afterward it would not be used tyrannically by him, this thing would have so terrified the collectivity that it would never after join together, after his death, to remake a gonfalonier for life—which order, he judged, it would be good to increase and maintain."[58] In other words, he feared that the experience with temporary dictatorship, no matter how justified, would delegitimize the state and make the people fearful of maintaining the position of lifetime gonfalonier that he believed was necessary for the stability of the republic. Machiavelli summarily dismissed this fear using the traditional "dirty hands" justification, noting that "since his works and his intention had to be judged by the end, he should have believed that if fortune and life had stayed with him, everyone would certify that what he had done was for the safety of the fatherland and not for his own ambition; and he could regulate things so that a successor of his would not be able to do for evil what he had done for good."[59] But by recognizing that Soderini would still have to make a public confession of his motives, Machiavelli admits that the danger Soderini feared was real.

That Machiavelli chose to rather flippantly dismiss this threat, in fact, might indicate more about the bad faith of his criticism than the prudence of his analysis in this case. After all, the reasons for Soderini's restraint were completely grounded on the premises of Machiavelli's own political realism. For it was entirely clear why suspending republican freedoms might create the very tyranny Soderini was fighting to prevent. Employing the propaganda of appearances, a "bad" leader would constitute a catastrophic rhetorical situation in a way that necessitated a tragic choice of concentrating power in rule by a single authoritarian ruler. Translating love of country into loyalty to sect and faction, this ruler would create a passionate identification through a cult of personality while polarizing divisions and creating opportunities for suppression and exploitation. Meanwhile, having mastered the art of not being good, this leader would frame cruel and violent actions as prudent and just policies, boasting of his strong will to perform necessary evils in the name of the common good. And by the time the catastrophe passed, there would be no return to "normalcy." Catastrophe would have created an opportunity to institute new modes and orders that enshrined oppression within the state and ensured minority rule over the people led by a charismatic leader. By the time the people realized they had shouted "Life!" to their death, it would have been too late. The republic would have been long dead. The only recourse left to the people would be tumult, cruelty, and revolution.

Machiavelli's realist style thus reveals the larger problem with the type of "dirty hands" analysis he pursues. Machiavelli here writes as if the complex nature of politics, with all its rhetorical complexity and situational contingency, could be reduced to predictable laws of motion on a flat plain. As Hariman comments, under Machiavelli's influence, "politics has been transformed into the strategic application of force, which is a material reality contrasted with verbal artistry and depicted topographically."[60] Consequently, the problem of "dirty hands" in this political realist worldview often reduces to a few simple cause and effect solutions that guarantee predictable outcomes of a different type than found in the messiness of discourse. Tillyris notes, for instance, how we are often seduced by pictures that "oversimplify our complex moral reality."[61] For instance, Walzer's torture example is not merely an example of the paradox of action; it is also a "sociological fantasy."[62] First, the ticking time bomb scenario assumes proficiency in the art of torture and a guarantee that torture is always effective, neither of which is reliably true. Second, it ignores the political consequences that come from the disclosure of such methods, which in the hypothetical example Walzer uses would utterly undermine the leader's legitimacy in the eyes of the colonized nation. And, lastly, it assumes that the act of torturing does not have lasting and often devastating impacts on the torturer, thus eroding any real commitment to peace. In a political realist worldview, all of these complexities are replaced with a simple, linear logic. In the case of Florence, for instance, the complexity of northern Italian politics at the time can be reduced to a single formula: had Soderini killed the Medici partisans, there would have been no insurgency, and the city would have survived. But this picture was clearly just Machiavelli's own treasured chimera, crafted in part to bolster his own reputation and scapegoat his old boss for military and political defeat.

Ironically, I believe that should one look for a model of "good" leadership in Machiavelli's history, one could do worse than hold up Soderini as an example. After all, with Machiavelli by his side, Soderini had successfully led the Florentine republic for over a decade "owing to his considerable political skills, sound fiscal management, success in foreign policy and 'concern to work within the law.'"[63] Machiavelli found these modes praiseworthy within a context of peace, but then he blamed Soderini for not killing the sons of Brutus when faced with imminent catastrophe. Zuckert notes, however, that Machiavelli's use of Brutus in this case is deceptive: "Machiavelli's comments on Soderini lets readers see that in praising Brutus, Machiavelli emphasizes his use of fraud and force, but does not mention that way he fought like a man, with laws."[64] Brutus, after all, had not killed his sons in violation of the law based on some state of exception. The executions were carried out precisely to defend the republican ideal that everyone is equal under the law. Similarly, when Soderini refused to imprison his remaining political opposition and summarily execute all of them regardless of their innocence, he was actually imitating Brutus. Like his republican predecessor, Soderini fought against his enemies in the way that even Machiavelli recognizes is the mode most proper to a human being—with reason and with law. And when confronted with wolves, he tried his best to act the lion by rallying his own arms.

None of this negates the very real moral and political contradictions that a political leader must navigate when confronted with a paradox of action. Particularly in the face of catastrophe, leaders often find the norms of goodness, the rule of law, and the structures of order to come under significant strain. Before the catastrophe, these things may have seemed enabling conditions that direct habits and thoughts into "good" channels; but during the crisis, they suddenly appear as constraints and obstructions, inhibiting the extraordinary modes that seem to leaders to be necessary to avoid ruin. But one of Machiavelli's constant themes is that an extraordinary action taken to meet an immediate need often erodes the foundations of long-term stability. Just as cruelty provokes hatred and violence creates enemies, so does fraud erode trust and manipulation undermine legitimacy. While it would be naive to deny that even good leaders often face situations in which they feel they must "learn not to be good," it is pure idealism to believe that the effect of "evil" modes can be limited to the immediate present or redeemed through the spectacle of public repentance. As Soderini understood, a single act can initiate a cascade of disastrous and unforeseen consequences, while exceptions to the rule tend to very quickly become the rule. Virtuous leaders are thus not blind to the paradoxes of action; they simply recognize that these paradoxes are recurrent aspects of the political environment. Catastrophes are no exception. To act virtuously in crisis is to meet necessities by adapting within the rule of law and the orders of justice, while at the same being prepared to advocate changes in those rules and orders when they no longer meet the changing needs of the time. One must confront the present with the future in mind. None of this is foreign to Machiavellian virtù. It is all contained within an expanded logic of effectual truth.

There is no shortage of calls for extraordinary actions, for good or ill, amid the current catastrophes. The fear of migration stimulates the building of walls, the imprisoning of children, and the organization of citizen militias. The risk of pandemic has enabled unprecedented lockdowns, the surveillance of individuals, and the mandate of vaccines. Diminishing water resources have led to the damming of rivers, the flooding of towns, and the militarization of aquifers. Anxiety about overpopulation has seen a resurgence in calls for restrictions of women's reproductive rights, forced sterilization, and birth control. Rising demand for food production has seen protected forests and oceans opened up to farming and fishing. At the same time, rising global temperatures have led to a call to protect and restore those same lands while also eliminating older forms of energy, innovating new sources of power while at the same time planning highly speculative geoengineering projects that seek to directly alter the planet's atmosphere. And all the while, the constant threat of war looms ever closer, as nations out of pure desperation seek to protect their own people in a global competition over diminishing resources. One can easily imagine a breaking point at which a major power decides to go it alone. The cascading impacts of this decision would create a human catastrophe on a scale never before witnessed in history.

At the same time, something must be done. That much is obvious. Today, climate catastrophes in particular threaten the very foundations of civic justice as we have come to define them. Much of what we believed were good laws and good arms from the prior century now appear outdated or impotent, while the pressures of global disruption offer the temptation for extraordinary actions done in the name of the common good but serving private gain. Jason Stanley warns, for instance, that "we will soon find ourselves confronted by movements of disadvantaged people across borders that dwarfed those of previous eras."[65] This makes a situation ripe for the rise of authoritarian leaders prepared to appeal to the worst elements of humanity to protect their small corner of the globe at the price of inflicting collective suffering. Stanley predicts the inevitable outcome of a politics of catastrophe: "Traumatized, impoverished, and in need of aid, refugees, including legal immigrants, will be recast to fit racist stereotypes by leaders and movements committed to maintaining hierarchical group privilege and using fascist politics."[66] The need for virtuous leadership capable of meeting the threats of climate change without succumbing to fascist-style solutions has never been greater. The more each nation closes itself within walls and struggles over diminishing resources, the more traumatized and impoverished populations will accumulate on their borders, leading to a feedback loop that results in starker divisions and increased suffering. The effectual truth of the matter is that unless we cooperate in meeting these necessities, we will all race headlong toward collective suicide.

The lesson I take away from this analysis is that catastrophes of scale simply cannot be met with simplistic and impetuous dirty hands tactics. Certainly, leaders must consider extraordinary actions when faced with immediate and localized threats of the type imagined in the ticking time bomb scenarios. But when a catastrophic threat is widespread and chronic, no amount of emergency actions can resist ruin for long. In fact, as Soderini warned, such violations of civil order can only increase the hatreds and the factional strife that ultimately lead people to embrace authoritarian solutions. The better strategy, as Clines has rightly pointed out, is to prepare for climate catastrophes by constructing those "dikes and dams" that can withstand the torrents of fortune. This constructive project is visionary, long-term, resource intensive, law governed, and collaborative, requiring widespread cooperation and investment to meet a shared crisis. Yet this arguably "republican" strategy returns us again to the same problem of public opinion. As long as people are unpersuaded by the magnitude of the threat and prefer quick fixes to expensive solutions, they will continue to empower bad leaders and shun good ones. And even Machiavelli acknowledges that a resort to force, in this context, is not an efficient option even for well-intentioned leaders. There is no alternative to force except for a sustained campaign of popular persuasion that lifts people's eyes toward the distant horizon where they can see and feel the storm approaching. Only when they viscerally can imagine their own impending ruin will the people embrace those policies that demand present sacrifice for a future happiness. The lingering question, of course, is whether that moment will come too late.

CHAPTER 11

An Exhortation to Resist the Coming Barbarism

T HE FINAL COLLAPSE OF MACHIAVELLI'S ITALIAN DREAM OF IN-
dependence occurred in the last years of his life. On May 6, 1527, a
starving, angry mob representing the combined Spanish and German forces
of the Holy Roman Emperor Charles V overwhelmed the meager defenses
of Rome and brutally sacked the city. The ancient seat of Christianity had
paid the price for the hapless Pope Clement VII having chosen the wrong
side in the battle for European supremacy. In a high stakes gamble, Clement had sided with the weakened king of France only to be left exposed when
the French retreated behind their borders. Cowering behind the walls of
the Castel Sant'Angelo, the pope could only watch helplessly as the undisci-
plined rabble of "Christian" soldiers, including both Spanish Catholics and
Lutheran Protestants, engaged in widespread rape, looting, torture, vandal-
ism, the death of over ten thousand innocent men, women, and children. The
sack of Rome saw Machiavelli's worst fears come true; the very center of Italian power, lacking leadership and without its own arms, had been crushed by
overwhelming imperial troops funded by gold pillaged by Spanish conquista-
dors wielding cannon and harquebus.

The end of the Florentine dream of liberty was soon to follow. In the
short term, what was Rome's loss appeared to be Florence's gain: "When
news of Rome's disaster and the pope's plight reached Florence, a group of
republicans organized a movement to overthrow the Medici state."[1] With
little violence, the Third Florentine Republic was established on May 16,
1527. For a few years, it enjoyed a tenuous freedom. But there would be no

long-term victory. At the behest of the emperor, the Medici pope Clement VII ordered his family's regime be returned to power. With the last of their virtú, the citizens of Florence fought for their freedom until the bitter end. Behind defenses designed by Michelangelo, Machiavelli-inspired citizen militias held off the onslaught of Spanish arms for ten months between October 1529 and August 1530. Then "hunger and famine weakened the city's will to resist" and "the regime capitulated and Spanish troops entered the starving city."[2] Guicciardini narrates the republic's pathetic end. Under a new breed of absolute Medici dukes, Florence lay "bereft of money as a result of so long and dreadful war, deprived of many of its inhabitants, both within and without the walls, its houses lost, its goods and property elsewhere destroyed, and more than ever divided against itself."[3]

Perhaps the only pity that fortune showed to Machiavelli was to let him die before the fall of the Third Republic. But even then, fortune retained her cruel sense of humor. On hearing the news that the Florentine republic had returned, Machiavelli sought a position in the new administration, believing his republican credentials were impeccable. Ironically, however, he was rebuffed by the new leaders precisely because of the books he had written for the Medici, namely *The Prince* and the *Florentine Histories*. Despite his tarnished reputation, however, he remained hopeful until the end. One of the last letters we have in Machiavelli's hand was written to his son, Guido, on April 2, 1527, just a few months before his death. In that letter, he gives this fatherly advice: "You must study and, since you no longer have illness as an excuse, take pains to learn letters and music, for you are aware how much distinction is given me for what little ability I possess. Thus, my son, if you want to please me and to bring profit and honor to yourself, study, do well, and learn, because everyone will help you if you help yourself."[4] Machiavelli's language here reflects the same counsel he gives to his "redeemer" in the final chapter of *The Prince*. Writing to his ideal prince, he says that although God may achieve extraordinary things, "the remainder you must do yourself. God does not want to do everything, so as to take free will from us and that part of the glory that falls to us."[5] In this way, one might say that Machiavelli spoke to his son in the same way he addressed a future prince. He believed that the virtues of his son could be developed with self-conscious effort and turned toward glory.

Despite the horrors he had witnessed in his own lifetime, Machiavelli still believed that human beings had the ability to craft, through mastery of politics, a better life. And even if they couldn't accomplish these things in reality, there was still a kind of virtue in hoping against all odds for redemption. In *The Mandrake*, for instance, Machiavelli wrote, "Nothing is ever so desperate that there is no grounds for hope. Even if the hope is vain and foolish, a man's will and desire to achieve what he wants will make it seem not to be."[6] This hope makes people open to manipulation, to be sure, but it also drives them to pursue higher ideals and greater ambitions. For Machiavelli, even when faced with great necessity, every individual preserves some small degree of free will by which their virtú might adapt to fortune and achieve glory. Only by believing in the power of his free will, Machiavelli tells his son, can he train his will to become free. Machiavelli would die at his villa two months later on June 21, 1527, still an exile from the city he loved more than his own soul.

To see Machiavelli as a father is to take many of the hard edges off of his writing. Like all parents, he did not want his children to live under a tyranny, to suffer arbitrary cruelty, or to constantly be under threat of losing life or property. Machiavelli hoped they would be able to fall in love and have a family, to acquire a profession and prosper economically, and perhaps even to gain honors through the state. All of these things, in Machiavelli's mind, required a stable order of justice. Given the course of actual history that would follow his writing of *The Prince*, therefore, we might better appreciate the human emotions that drove that work. Knowing the ruin that would soon descend upon Italy, the words of Petrarch Machiavelli uses to close his book take on new meaning: "Virtue will take up arms against fury, and make the battle short, because the ancient valor in Italian hearts is not yet dead."[7] Machiavelli quotes these verses knowing that a catastrophe loomed on the horizon that threatened suffering for all of Italy. No wonder, then, that he hoped for a triumphant rebirth of Roman virtue in Italian hearts that would make them unified, courageous, and powerful. His own children's fate depended on it.

But I cannot help thinking that the authoritarian solution he appeared to recommend was (and remains) no more real than Callimaco's cure for impotence. The entire appeal of authoritarianism is the promise of the charismatic virtú of a single head to constitute unity and power in a context of division and impotence. But by Machiavelli's own logic, the only means to attain this unity (especially when faced with the resistance of formerly free peoples) is through violence and cruelty rather than persuasion and law. Machiavelli cleverly covers over this problem with the suggestion that force can literally make people believe, but almost all of his principles undermine the faith of this idea in practice. Force might gain complicity through coercion, but ultimately it fosters hatred and rebellion. Meanwhile, the cost of imposing force upon a reluctant population forces economic hardship while making even the simplest reform labor intensive and slow. Finally, the fear, paranoia, divisions, and suffering that pervade a populace destroy any vestige of love of country, reducing a state to a cacophony of factions held together through the threat of steel. If such a state does not disintegrate from its own divisions, it creates its own inferno through its last gasp of foreign or civil war. Perhaps Machiavelli genuinely believed that such constraints could be overcome by sheer strength of virtú. But then he would no longer be a realist but an idealist.

I prefer the realist Machiavelli. For once we look at our own context through a Machiavellian political realist calculus, the only way to meet the immediate threat of catastrophe in a way that creates the foundation of lasting power is through the dynamic relationship between populist and republican rhetoric. As disruptive events accumulate, the propaganda of appearances can constitute these events as symptomatic of a catastrophic situation that calls a public into being. This public, in turn, puts pressure on political elites to respond, ultimately overcoming institutional recalcitrance by initiating tumults that disrupt the ordinary functioning of the state in order to force it to consider changes in law. Republican rhetoric then becomes the medium by which orders are reformed and renewed through law; for only through republican orders can multiple constituencies collaborate and come to consensus on developing a comprehensive solution to complex problems. Neither the simplifications of authoritarian rhetoric nor the spectacles of populist propaganda can ever reach the level of detail, foresight, and intelligence as those policies developed through republican political reasoning—at least when this reasoning is done out in the open. Whereas populist rhetoric is necessary to provide the energy and impetus for reform, a republican rhetoric informed by democratic principles must ultimately be the means by which modes and orders are adapted to catastrophic times.

Still, we should never underestimate the attraction of taking the easy way to Hell. Certainly, one can find such a way in Machiavelli's writings. For by his reasoning, even if an individual republic becomes well-ordered, "it is impossible for a republic to succeed in staying quiet and enjoying its freedom and little borders."[8] Machiavelli reasons that because it is in the nature of human beings to acquire, ambition never stays quiet when it has encountered an artificial limit; it immediately seeks to overreach it. And herein lies the tragic nature of republican freedom. Owing to the ambitions of its people, if a republic will not expand to conquer others, it will turn its ambitions upon itself. In Machiavelli's words, even if does not desire to "molest others, it will be molested, and from being molested will arise the wish and the necessity to acquire; and if it does not have an enemy outside, it will find one at home, as it appears necessarily happens to all great cities."[9] Mikael Hörnqvist interprets Machiavelli's counsel this way: "Instead of quenching natural drive to power, the task of the prudent statesman should be to direct it outward, towards the pursuit of empire, territorial growth, greatness, and glory."[10] And this, historically, is precisely the course that modernity charted, with the past two centuries showcasing arguably free and democratic societies agitating for freedoms and liberties at home while embarking on colonial or imperial conquests abroad. In other words, even if a republic does not succumb to authoritarian rhetoric domestically, it must implement it on the international stage. History, sadly, has borne this out.

As long as the nations of the world remain trapped within this sixteenth-century Machiavellian mindset, nothing else found in the writings of the second chancellor will prevent us from continuing along this self-destructive path. Just as the city-states of Renaissance Italy fought each other for scraps until being massacred by foreign arms, so the nations of the world today, each claiming sovereignty over their domain, will strip the planet of resources until it literally becomes an inferno. The only end of this zero-sum game is global catastrophe. To pursue such "realism" on a global stage today is to inhabit one of Machiavelli's castles in the air, for it is a realism based on the nationalistic fantasy of autonomy, or that which in the fascist ideal is called "autarky." But nations today are not autonomous. They exist in an interconnected world. The microcosm of Florentine history must therefore be expanded not simply to the nation-state but the global community of nations that constitute humanity. The only republic capable of confronting the catastrophe of climate change and its accompanying political crises is an international one. Cooperation, too, is an essential mode of political realism.

The enormity of the challenge today is captured by the title of Isabelle Stengers's book *In Catastrophic Times: Resisting the Coming Barbarism*. For Stengers, a catastrophic time represents that moment in which people realize that "the epoch has changed," meaning that the old modes and orders are no longer capable of meeting the scale of apocalyptic events.[11] Ideally, being confronted with this undeniable fact should be an opportunity to pay attention to the world around us, thereby "giving this observation the power to make us think, feel, imagine, and act."[12] But the reality is often quite different. The catastrophic times we face have empowered those prepared to exploit the present suffering to further accumulate financial and political power and put the future "under the sign of barbarism."[13] By this term, she means neither the Athenian nor the Florentine epithet for uncivilized people. She instead means a paternalistic rule by those who float utopian technocratic fixes funded by capital enterprise while their actual policies accelerate resource depletion and foster social inequality. Thus, for Stengers, "it is barbarism to which we are also condemned by the tales and reasoning that we are drowning in, which illustrate or take as a given the passivity of people, the demand for ready-made solutions, their tendency to follow the first demagogue to come along."[14] Instead of genuine leadership, the public is offered nonstop tours of castles in the air that serve not so much to convert us as to merely temporarily populate "the devastated desert of our imagination."[15]

We are approaching inferno. But instead of having Virgil as our guide, we have Machiavelli. If we listen to his counsel without thinking, we will most certainly run straight down the path to our own destruction. Heeding his exhortation at the close of *The Prince*, we will look upon fortuna as something to be battered and beaten down, believing that when we act with ferocity and impetuousness, we will be able to "command her with more audacity."[16] We will look out upon the state of suffering and chaos and then fall into despair that the world exists "without a head, without order, beaten, despoiled, torn, pillaged, and having endured ruin of every sort."[17] This carnage, we will tell ourselves, can be tolerated no more. We will seek for a redeemer to give vigor and life to the scattered limbs of so many nations. We will seek to subdue our enemies and exploit their resources, believing that with the right organization and technology we can bring the Earth itself under our complete domination. And those that resist will suffer the cruelty and violence they deserve, for they stand in the way of the regeneration of arms and changing orders required to make the planet great again.

But if we take the time to think and to listen, we may hear in Machiavelli a voice that counsels another path. This voice comes from the Machiavelli who fears and respects fortuna, who sees virtú not as an overwhelming power but as an extension of our collective free will, our ability to adapt to the overwhelming necessity. Stengers believes that the ancient term *Gaia* captures this more awesome conception of fortuna. In the past Gaia was honored as "the fearsome one, as she who was addressed by peasants, who knew that humans depend on something much greater than them, something that tolerates them, but with the tolerance that is not to be abused."[18] Once fortuna is viewed as an extension of Gaia, Machiavelli's counsel takes on a different character. No longer can a single individual dominate fortune through sheer strength of will. Our collective survival requires cooperation, intelligence, sympathy, sacrifice, and even humility. And most of all it requires communication, which was his motive for writing the *Discourses on Livy* in the first place. Speaking of himself, Machiavelli writes that "it is the duty of a good man to teach others the good that you could not work because of the malignity of the times in a fortune, so that when many are capable of it, some one of them more loved by heaven may be able to work it."[19] We all may play a small part in history, Machiavelli suggests, but we nonetheless have a responsibility to pass on the wisdom we have to others in the hope they might secure a better future.

For Machiavelli, the rhetoric of catastrophe can only successfully adapt to the necessity of fortune through the constitution of power. For it was only through the capacity for people to voluntarily act in concert that a state could overcome great obstacles and maintain unity in the face of necessity. And I think it is clear from his writings that the most stable and lasting form of power in Machiavelli's work was, at its best, always *republican* power. Although he argued that princes were sometimes necessary in times of disunity, they secured their legacies only by helping to found free republics in which the competing humors of the nobles and the people could resolve their tensions through the orders of the state. Today, this negotiation takes place by means of the communicative capabilities of digital networks to build lasting connections between communities and nations. Once we expand the circumference of the rhetorical situation to affect all of the states of the world, the effectual truth of Machiavelli can be translated into the pragmatics of democratic humanism in which we see politics as a way of cultivating human potentiality. If we are neither to live in denial nor chase the chimera of fascism, we must confront the consequences of our action and inaction and develop new modes and orders capable of constituting and channeling the democratic power necessary to face catastrophe.

I may very well be wrong about Machiavelli. There are good arguments that, in the final analysis, he really was a teacher of evil. To me, that conclusion does nothing to undermine his virtue as a guide. If Machiavelli taught evil well, then we had best learn his lesson well so as not to commit or fall victim to evil. That was the whole justification for his hiring the Devil as a preacher. Unfortunately, however, the utopian notion still exists that the only worthy guide speaks on the side of the Angels. I cannot imagine an education any duller. Having seen my share of representations of the Last Judgment in Italian Renaissance art, the last place I would want to spend eternity is standing in a straight line, arms folded in prayer, silent at the right hand of God. On this point, Machiavelli and I are in full agreement. According to legend, on June 21, 1527, Machiavelli in his last hours recounted a "dream" to the faithful friends waiting by his bedside. Viroli eloquently recounts the legend this way:

> In his dream, he had seen a band of poorly dressed men, ragged and miserable in appearance. He asked them who they were. They replied, "We are the saintly and the blessed; we are on our way to Heaven." Then he saw a crowd of solemnly attired men, noble and grave in appearance, speaking seriously of important political matters. In their midst he recognized the great philosophers and historians of antiquity who had written fundamental works on politics and the state, such as Plato, Plutarch, and Tacitus. Again, he asked them who they were and where they were going. "We are the damned of Hell" was their answer. After telling his friends of his dream, Machiavelli remarked that he would be far happier in Hell, where he could discuss politics with the great men of the ancient world, than in Heaven, where he would languish in boredom among the blessed and the saintly.[20]

This story may be apocryphal. But whether fictional or not, it so perfectly captures Machiavelli's attitude that it remains aesthetically true, even if not factually so. Machiavelli was a lover of ideas and arguments and tactics and reversals. He had no patience for pious platitudes and self-congratulatory sermons. His ideal conversation was a sparring match with his motley crew of friends about the political crises of his day; and in these competitions, the best allies were often those classical writers of the past in all their brilliance and ugliness. To shun such allies in the name of promoting "goodness" was simply to disarm oneself—in addition to making life that much more boring, not to mention the afterlife. For him, a perfect life was not a life worth living. We were born to strive and to suffer, to triumph and to fail, and to try to meet the exigencies of our times with cleverness and courage. Perfection is not something that can be attained; it is something to be imagined as a means of inspiring greatness and achieving glory.

In any case, we should admit to ourselves this uncomfortable Machiavellian truth—that catastrophe is exciting. Doomscrolling happens for a reason. Human beings are crisis junkies. That is also why we flock to theaters to see the latest version of apocalypse, namely in order to witness ordinary people doing extraordinary things. Identifying with some hero is not exclusive to children. All grown men and women have, however briefly, wondered what greatness they might achieve when placed in a similar circumstance. As much as nobody actually wants to live through catastrophe, we cannot help being attracted to it. Catastrophes break us out of our habits, render obsolete our laws, throw us back onto our own resources, and force us to exert every bit of energy to make tragic choices. Catastrophes thus make possible a unique kind of happiness that one experiences when virtú overcomes necessity. We might very well condemn Machiavelli's praise of Cesare Borgia as misguided and barbaric; but it would be foolish to deny our inherent admiration for those who triumph over great adversity. We just want role models that look and act more like us. That is all to the good. As Machiavelli says, one must adapt one's modes to the times. But he would also stress that by living in *catastrophic* times, our modes must often be extraordinary. Perhaps civilization really is on the brink of collapse. So be it. There is something ennobling in rising to the challenge. Let us at least learn to fight like hell.

Notes

CHAPTER 1

1. James B. Atkinson and David Sices, trans., *Machiavelli and His Friends: Their Personal Correspondence* (DeKalb: Northern Illinois University Press, 1996), 336.

2. Atkinson and Sices, *Machiavelli and His Friends*, 336.

3. Atkinson and Sices, 336.

4. Andrei Ionescu, "Humanity Should Brace for Catastrophic Climate Change," Earth (website), August 1, 2022.

5. Mark Z. Barabak, "'Quarantini.' 'Doomscrolling.' Here's How the Coronavirus Is Changing the Way We Talk," *Los Angeles Times*, April 11, 2020.

6. Ishaan Tharoor, "The World's Climate Catastrophe Worsens amid the Pandemic," *Washington Post*, June 29, 2020.

7. Tharoor, "Climate Catastrophe."

8. Tharoor.

9. See Amitav Ghosh, *The Great Derangement: Climate Change and the Unthinkable* (Chicago: University of Chicago Press, 2016); David Wallace-Wells, *The Uninhabitable Earth: A Story of the Future* (London: Allen Lane, 2019).

10. David Ignatius, "Donald Trump Is the American Machiavelli," *Washington Post*, November 10, 2016.

11. Matthew Slaboch, "Putin and Political Theory: A Machiavellian and Pan-Slav Mindset," *Europe Now*, February 24, 2022.

12. Scott Savitz, "Applying Machiavellian Discourses to the Wars in Afghanistan and Iraq," *TheRANDblog* (blog), August 9, 2021.

13. Sean Illing, "What Machiavelli Can Teach Us about Trump and the Decline of Liberal Democracy," Vox (website), November 16, 2018.

14. David Polansky, "Machiavelli's Lessons for America's Jan. 6 Tumult," *Foreign Policy*, January 8, 2022.

15. Alexander Lee, "What Machiavelli Knew about Pandemics," *New Statesman*, June 3, 2020.

16. Daniil Kotsyubinsky, "Why Putin Still Has a Lot to Learn from Machiavelli," *Open Democracy*, December 2, 2011.

17. Robert Clines, "What Machiavelli Would Do about Climate Change," *Washington Post*, February 23, 2020.

18. Josef Joffe, "Let's Dance the Machiavelli," *American Interest*, May 4, 2018.

19. Louis Althusser, *Machiavelli and Us*, trans. Gregory Elliott (New York: Verso, 1999), 7.

20. Patrick Boucheron, *Machiavelli: The Art of Teaching People What to Fear* (New York: Other Press, 2020), 31.

21. Jerrold E. Seigel, *Rhetoric and Philosophy in Renaissance Humanism: The Union of Eloquence and Wisdom, Petrarch to Valla* (Princeton, NJ: Princeton University Press, 1968), 65.

22. Atkinson and Sices, 264.

23. Atkinson and Sices, 225.

24. Leo Strauss, *Thoughts on Machiavelli* (Chicago: University of Chicago Press, 1958), 292.

25. Strauss, *Thoughts on Machiavelli*, 292.

26. Strauss, 292.

27. Strauss, 9.

28. Erica Benner, *Machiavelli's "Prince": A New Reading* (Oxford: Oxford University Press, 2013), 96.

29. Erica Benner, *Machiavelli's Ethics* (Princeton, NJ: Princeton University Press, 2009), 5.

30. Benner, *Machiavelli's "Prince"*, xxii.

31. Walt Whitman, "Song of Myself, 51," Poets (website), accessed November 20, 2023.

32. Nathan Crick, *Dewey for a New Age of Fascism: Teaching Democratic Habits* (State College: Pennsylvania State University Press, 2019), 8.

33. John Bew, *Realpolitik: A History* (Oxford: Oxford University Press, 2016), 2.

34. Robert Hariman, "Introduction," in Robert Hariman and Ralph Cintron, *Culture, Catastrophe, and Rhetoric: The Texture of Political Action* (New York: Berghahn, 2020), 12.

35. Hariman and Cintron, *Culture, Catastrophe, and Rhetoric*, 13.

36. Hariman and Cintron, 11.

37. Hariman, "Introduction," Hariman and Cintron, *Culture, Catastrophe, and Rhetoric*, 11.

38. Diana Goncalves, *9/11: Culture, Catastrophe and the Critique of Singularity* (Berlin: Walter de Gruyter, 2016), 30.

39. Goncalves, *9/11*, 37.

40. Murdoch Stephens, *Critical Environmental Communication: How Does Critique Respond to the Urgency of Climate Change?* (Lanham, MD: Lexington Books, 2018), 80.

41. Antonio Y. Vázquez-Arroyo, "How Not to Learn from Catastrophe: Habermas, Critical Theory and the 'Catastrophization' of Political Life," *Political Theory* 41, no. 5 (2013): 745.

42. Garnet Kindervater, "Catastrophe and Catastrophic Thoughts," in *Biopolitical Disaster*, ed. Jennifer L. Lawrence and Sarah Marie Wiebe (New York: Taylor and Francis, 2017), 102.

43. Alison McQueen, *Political Realism in Apocalyptic Times* (Cambridge, UK: Cambridge University Press, 2018), 11.

44. McQueen, *Political Realism*, 9.

45. McQueen, 56.

46. McQueen, 10.

47. McQueen, 9–10.

48. Robert Hariman, *Political Style: The Artistry of Power* (Chicago: Chicago University Press, 1995), 16–17.

49. Hariman, *Political Style*, 24.

50. Hariman, *Political Style*, 25.

51. David N. Levy, *Wily Elites and Spirited Peoples in Machiavelli's Republicanism* (Lanham, MD: Lexington Books, 2014), 106.

52. Rogier Creemers, "A Machiavellian Guide to Getting ahead in Academia," *Times Higher Education*, December 21, 2017.

53. Anna Maria Cabrini, "Machiavelli's Florentine Histories," in *The Cambridge Companion to Machiavelli*, ed. John M. Najemy (Cambridge, UK: Cambridge University Press, 2010), 132.

54. Cabrini, "Machiavelli's Florentine Histories," 133.

55. Werner Jaeger, *Paideia: The Ideals of Greek Culture*, vol. 3, *In Search of the Divine Centre*, trans. Gilbert Highet (Oxford: Oxford University Press, 1971), 392.

56. Kenneth Burke, *The Philosophy of Literary Form* (New York: Vintage, 1953), 253.

57. Burke, *Philosophy of Literary Form*, 256. Emphasis in original.

58. Burke, 262. Emphasis in original.

59. Burke, *Philosophy of Literary Form*, 262.

60. Ned O'Gorman, *Politics for Everybody: Reading Hannah Arendt in Uncertain Times* (Chicago: University of Chicago Press, 2020), 140.

61. Dante Alighieri, *The Divine Comedy*, trans. C. H. Sisson (Oxford: Oxford University Press, 1980), 26: 73–84

62. See Bruno Latour, *Down to Earth: Politics in the New Climatic Regime* (Cambridge, UK: Polity Press, 2018).

CHAPTER 2

1. Niccolò Machiavelli, *The Prince*, trans. Harvey C. Mansfield Jr. (Chicago: University of Chicago Press, 1998), 91.

2. Cornel West, *The American Evasion of Philosophy: A Genealogy of Pragmatism* (Madison: University of Wisconsin Press, 1989), 120.

3. Isaiah Berlin, *Four Essays on Liberty* (Oxford: Oxford University Press, 1969), 169.

4. Eva Horn, *The Future as Catastrophe: Imagining Disaster in the Modern Age* (New York: Columbia University Press, 2018), 121.

5. Horn, *Future as Catastrophe*, 120.

6. Horn, 121.

7. Horn, 112.

8. Friedrich Meinecke, *Machiavellism: The Doctrine of Raison d'État and Its Place in Modern History* (New Brunswick, NJ: Transaction Publishers, 1997), 36.

9. Machiavelli, *Prince*, 32–33.

10. *Prince*, 29.

11. *Prince*, 30.

12. David C. Hendrickson, "Machiavelli and Machiavellianism," in *Machiavelli's Legacy: "The Prince" after Five Hundred Years*, ed. Timothy Fuller, 105–26 (Philadelphia: University of Pennsylvania Press, 2016), 108.

13. Hendrickson, "Machiavelli and Machiavellianism," 108.

14. *Prince*, 101.

15. James B. Atkinson and David Sices, trans., *Machiavelli and His Friends: Their Personal Correspondence* (DeKalb: Northern Illinois University Press, 1996), 265.

16. Felix Gilbert, *Machiavelli and Guicciardini: Politics and History in Sixteenth-Century Florence* (Princeton, NJ: Princeton University Press. 1965), 179.

17. Gilbert, *Machiavelli and Guicciardini*, 179.

18. Guido Ruggiero, *Machiavelli in Love: Sex, Self, and Society in the Italian Renaissance* (Baltimore: Johns Hopkins University Press, 2007), 188.

19. Atkinson and Sices, *Machiavelli and His Friends*, 249.

20. Catherine H. Zuckert, *Machiavelli's Politics* (Chicago: University of Chicago Press, 2017), 100.

21. *Prince*, 98.

22. Atkinson and Sices, 135.

23. Ruggiero, *Machiavelli in Love*, 222.

24. *Prince*, 105.

25. *Prince*, 32.

26. *Prince*, 55.

27. Niccolò Machiavelli, *Discourses on Livy*, trans. Harvey C. Mansfield Jr. and Nathan Tarcov (Chicago: University of Chicago Press, 1996), 246.

28. Machiavelli, *Discourses on Livy*, 246.

29. *Discourses on Livy*, 254.

30. *Discourses on Livy*, 198.

31. Leo Strauss, *Thoughts on Machiavelli* (Chicago: University of Chicago Press, 1958), 81–82.

32. Stephen J. Harnett, "'Lock Her Up!' Fascism as a Political Style from Mussolini to Trump," in *The Rhetoric of Fascism*, ed. Nathan Crick (Tuscaloosa: University of Alabama Press, 2022), 38.

33. Harnett, "'Lock Her Up!'" 47.

34. Harnett, 47.

35. Antonio Y. Vázquez-Arroyo, "Antimonies of Violence and Catastrophe: Structures, Orders, and Agents," *New Political Science* 34, no. 2 (2012): 212.

36. Garnet Kindervater, "Catastrophe and Catastrophic Thoughts," in *Biopolitical*

Disaster, ed. Jennifer L. Lawrence and Sarah Marie Wiebe (New York: Taylor and Francis, 2017), 98.

37. Kindervater, "Catastrophe," 100.

38. Kindervater, 99.

39. Adi Ophir, "The Politics of Catastrophization: Emergency and Exception," in *States of Emergency: The Politics of Military and Humanitarian Interventions*, ed. Didier Fassin and Mariella Pandolfi (New York: Zone Books, 2008), 63.

40. Kindervater, 102.

41. Lloyd Bitzer, "The Rhetorical Situation," *Philosophy and Rhetoric* 1, no. 1 (1968): 3.

42. Bitzer, "Rhetorical Situation," 3.

43. Bitzer, 6.

44. Erica Benner, *Machiavelli's Ethics* (Princeton, NJ: Princeton University Press, 2009), 151.

45. Benner, *Machiavelli's Ethics*, 150.

46. Benner, 150.

47. Benner, 150.

48. Benner, 150.

49. Benner, 164.

50. Benner, 151.

51. Nathan Crick, "Rhetoric and Events," *Philosophy and Rhetoric* 47, no. 3 (2014): 267.

52. Crick, "Rhetoric and Events," 267.

53. Crick, 268.

54. Antonio Y. Vázquez-Arroyo, "How Not to Learn from Catastrophe: Habermas, Critical Theory and the 'Catastrophization' of Political Life," *Political Theory* 41, no. 5 (2013): 739.

55. Kindervater, 103.

56. Kindervater, 103.

57. Kindervater, 103.

58. Kindervater, 104.

59. Kindervater, 105.

60. *Prince*, 23.

61. *Discourses on Livy*, 45.

62. Raymond Angelo Belliotti, *Niccolò Machiavelli: The Laughing Lion and the Strutting Fox* (New York: Rowman and Littlefield, 2010), 113.

63. *Discourses on Livy*, 214.

64. Plutarch, *The Lives of the Noble Grecians and Romans*, vol. 2, trans. John Dryden, ed. Arthur Hugh Clough (New York: Modern Library, 1992), 572.

65. Virgil, *The Aeneid*, trans. Robert Fitzgerald (New York: Random House, 1983), 6.823–24.

66. *Discourses on Livy*, 214.

67. *Discourses on Livy*, 45.

68. Harvey Mansfield, *Machiavelli's Virtue* (Chicago: University of Chicago Press, 1998), 25.

69. *Discourses on Livy*, 30.

70. *Prince*, 61.

71. Filippo del Lucchese, *The Political Philosophy of Niccolò Machiavelli* (Edinburgh: Edinburgh University Press, 2015), 26.

72. Yves Winter, *Machiavelli and the Orders of Violence* (Cambridge, UK: Cambridge University Press, 2018), 64.

73. Isabelle Stengers, *In Catastrophic Times: Resisting the Coming Barbarism* (Paris: Open Humanities Press, 2015), 137.

74. Bruno Latour, *After Lockdown: A Metamorphosis*, trans. Julie Rose (Cambridge, UK: Polity Press, 2021), 39.

75. Kenneth Burke, *Permanence and Change: An Anatomy of Purpose* (Berkeley: University of California Press, 1954), xlvii.

76. J. G. A. Pocock, *The Machiavellian Moment: Florentine Political Thought and the Atlantic Republican Tradition* (Princeton, NJ: Princeton University Press, 1975), 269.

77. Burke, *Permanence and Change*, 272.

CHAPTER 3

1. Cicero, *On Duties*, trans. M. T. Griffin and E. M. Atkins (Cambridge, UK: Cambridge University Press, 1991), 1:41 (19).

2. Leo Strauss, *Thoughts on Machiavelli* (Chicago: University of Chicago Press, 1958), 78.

3. Strauss, *Thoughts on Machiavelli*, 78.

4. Niccolò Machiavelli, *The Prince*, trans. Harvey C. Mansfield Jr. (Chicago: University of Chicago Press, 1998), 69.

5. Timothy J. Lukes, "Lionizing Machiavelli," *American Political Science Review* 95, no. 3 (September 2001), 563.

6. Machiavelli, *Prince*, 69.

7. *Prince*, 69.

8. Erica Benner, *Machiavelli's Ethics* (Princeton, NJ: Princeton University Press, 2009), 197.

9. Benner, *Machiavelli's Ethics*, 197–98.

10. Yves Winter, *Machiavelli and the Orders of Violence* (Cambridge, UK: Cambridge University Press, 2018), 27.

11. Winter, *Machiavelli and the Orders*, 27.

12. Erica Benner, *Be Like the Fox: Machiavelli in His World* (New York: W. W. Norton, 2017), 151.

13. Benner, *Be Like the Fox*, 151.

14. Francis Bacon, *The Works of Lord Bacon: With an Introductory Essay, and a Portrait: In Two Vols* (London: Reeves and Turner, 1879), 265.

15. Stephen Levitsky and Daniel Ziblatt, *How Democracies Die* (New York: Penguin Random House, 2018), 21–22.

16. Levitsky and Ziblatt, *How Democracies Die*, 20.

17. Levitsky and Ziblatt, 102, 107.

18. Gene A. Brucker, *Renaissance Florence* (Berkeley: University of California Press, 1969), 32.

19. Brucker, *Renaissance Florence*, 32.

20. Niccolò Machiavelli, *Florentine Histories*, trans. Laura F. Banfield and Harvey C. Mansfield Jr. (Princeton, NJ: Princeton University Press, 1988), 57.

21. Machiavelli, *Florentine Histories*, 57.

22. *Florentine Histories*, 58.

23. *Florentine Histories*, 64.

24. *Florentine Histories*, 68.

25. Dino Compagni, *Dino Compagni's Chronicle of Florence*, trans. Daniel E. Bornstein (Philadelphia: University of Pennsylvania Press, 1986), 22.

26. Compagni, *Chronicle*, 22.

27. Compagni, 22.

28. Compagni, 23.

29. Compagni, 23.

30. Compagni, 34.

31. *Florentine Histories*, 68–69.

32. *Florentine Histories*, 69.

33. *Florentine Histories*, 69.

34. Compagni, 24.

35. *Florentine Histories*, 66.

36. *Florentine Histories*, 67.

37. *Florentine Histories*, 71.

38. *Florentine Histories*, 71.

39. Compagni, 33–34.

40. Compagni, 34.

41. Compagni, 37.

42. Compagni, 37.

43. Compagni, 38.

44. Compagni, 38.

45. Compagni, 39.

46. Compagni, 41.

47. Compagni, 41.

48. Compagni, 41.

49. Compagni, 42.

50. Compagni, 42.

51. Compagni, 43.

52. Compagni, 39.

53. Compagni, 39.

54. Compagni, 43.

55. Compagni, 43.

56. Compagni 43.

57. Compagni, 43–44.

58. Compagni, 43.

59. Compagni, 48.

60. Compagni, 51.

61. Compagni, 50.

62. Compagni, 49.

63. Compagni, 49.

64. Compagni, 48.

65. Compagni, 51.

66. *Florentine Histories*, 73.

67. *Florentine Histories*, 73.

68. *Florentine Histories*, 77.

69. *Florentine Histories*, 77.

70. Compagni, *Chronicle*, 84.

71. Niccolò Machiavelli, *Discourses on Livy*, trans. Harvey C. Mansfield Jr. and Nathan Tarcov (Chicago: University of Chicago Press, 1996), 115.

72. Levitsky and Ziblatt, 7.

73. Levitsky and Ziblatt, 112.

74. Levitsky and Ziblatt, 20.

75. *Discourses on Livy*, 301.

76. *Discourses on Livy*, 302.

77. Machiavelli, *Prince*, 57.

78. *Prince*, 48.

79. *Prince*, 48.

80. *Prince*, 48.

CHAPTER 4

1. Judith Nisse Shklar, *Ordinary Vices* (Cambridge, MA: Belknap Press, 1984), 44.

2. Shklar, *Ordinary Vices*, 8.

3. Shklar, 7.

4. Marina Levina, "Whiteness and the Joys of Cruelty," *Communication and Critical/Cultural Studies* 15, no. 1 (2018): 75.

5. Levina, "Whiteness," 75.

6. Adam Serwer, "The Cruelty Is the Point," *Atlantic*, October 3, 2018.

7. Serwer, "Cruelty Is the Point."

8. Shklar, 30.

9. Antonio Gramsci, *Selections from the Prison Notebooks*, trans. Quintin Hoare and Geoffrey Nowell Smith (New York: International Publishers, 1971), 172.

10. Niccolò Machiavelli, *The Prince*, trans. Harvey C. Mansfield Jr. (Chicago: University of Chicago Press, 1998), 34.

11. Machiavelli, *Prince*, 34.

12. *Prince*, 35.

13. *Prince*, 35.

14. *Prince*, 37.

15. *Prince*, 37.

16. *Prince*, 37–38.

17. *Prince*, 38.

18. *Prince*, 35.

19. *Prince*, 35.

20. Shklar, 11.

21. Yves Winter, *Machiavelli and the Orders of Violence* (Cambridge, UK: Cambridge University Press, 2018), 61.

22. *Prince*, 67.

23. Thomas Osborne, "Machiavelli and the Liberalism of Fear," *History of the Human Sciences* 30, no. 5 (2017): 68.

24. James B. Atkinson and David Sices, trans., *Machiavelli and His Friends: Their Personal Correspondence* (DeKalb: Northern Illinois University Press, 1996), 135.

25. Atkinson and Sices, *Machiavelli and His Friends*, 135.

26. Leo Strauss, *Thoughts on Machiavelli* (Chicago: University of Chicago Press, 1958) 241–42.

27. Winter, *Machiavelli and the Orders*, 24.

28. Winter, 28.

29. Winter, 28.

30. Winter, 23.

31. Winter, 110.

32. Winter, 98.

33. John P. McCormick, *Machiavellian Democracy* (Cambridge, UK: Cambridge University Press, 2011), 26.

34. Niccolò Machiavelli, *Discourses on Livy*, trans. Harvey C. Mansfield Jr. and Nathan Tarcov (Chicago: University of Chicago Press, 1996), 46.

35. Machiavelli, *Discourses on Livy*, 46.

36. *Discourses on Livy*, 46.

37. *Prince*, 56.

38. Niccolò Machiavelli, *Florentine Histories*, trans. Laura F. Banfield and Harvey C. Mansfield Jr. (Princeton, NJ: Princeton University Press, 1988), 86.

39. Machiavelli, *Florentine Histories*, 86.

40. Giovanni Villani, *The Final Book of Giovanni Villani's New Chronicle*, trans. Rala Diakité and Matthew Thomas Sneider (Kalamazoo: Western Michigan University Press, 2016), 30.

41. *Florentine Histories*, 89.

42. *Florentine Histories*, 89.

43. *Florentine Histories*, 90.

44. Leonardo Bruni, *History of the Florentine People*, vol. 3, ed. and trans. James Hankins (Cambridge, MA: Harvard University Press, 2007), 263.

45. Bruni, *History*, 269.

46. Rala Diakité and Matthew Thomas Sneider, "Introduction," in Villani, *Final Book*, 2.

47. Villani, *Final Book*, 5.

48. Villani, 39.

49. Diakité and Sneider, "Introduction," 14.

50. Diakité and Sneider, 14.

51. Villani, 26.

52. Villani, 26.

53. Villani, 26.

54. Villani, 27.

55. Villani, 27.

56. Villani, 28.

57. Gene A. Brucker, *Renaissance Florence* (Berkeley: University of California Press, 1969), 258.

58. Villani, 28.

59. Villani, 29.

60. Villani, 35.

61. Villani, 35.

62. Villani, 35.

63. Villani, 38.

64. Villani, 35.

65. Villani, 39.

66. Villani, 39.

67. Villani, 39.

68. Villani, 39.

69. Villani, 40.

70. *Florentine Histories*, 94.

71. *Florentine Histories*, 95.

72. *Florentine Histories*, 95.

73. *Florentine Histories*, 95.

74. *Florentine Histories*, 95.

75. Villani, 44.

76. *Florentine Histories*, 97.

77. *Florentine Histories*, 97.

78. Villani, 48.

79. Villani, 48.

80. Villani, 49.

81. Villani, 50.

82. Villani, 52.

83. Villani, 52.

84. Villani, 52.

85. Villani, 52.

86. Villani, 52–53.

87. *Florentine Histories*, 99.

88. Villani, 53.

89. *Florentine Histories*, 99.

90. Villani, 53.

91. *Florentine Histories*, 99.

92. *Prince*, 67.

CHAPTER 5

1. Michael Harvey, "Lost in the Wilderness: Love and Longing in L'Asino," in *The Comedy and Tragedy of Machiavelli: Essays on the Literary Works*, ed. Vickie B. Sullivan (New Haven, CT: Yale University Press, 2000), 35.

2. Harvey, "Love and Longing," 35.

3. Harvey, 35.

4. Harvey, 35.

5. James B. Atkinson and David Sices, trans., *Machiavelli and His Friends: Their Personal Correspondence* (DeKalb: Northern Illinois University Press, 1996), 416.

6. Maurizio Viroli, *Machiavelli* (Oxford: Oxford University Press, 1998), 161.

7. Viroli, *Machiavelli*, 161

8. Niccolò Machiavelli, *Florentine Histories*, trans. Laura F. Banfield and Harvey C. Mansfield Jr. (Princeton, NJ: Princeton University Press, 1988), 92.

9. Machiavelli, *Florentine Histories*, 92.

10. Niccolò Machiavelli, *The Prince*, trans. Harvey C. Mansfield Jr. (Chicago: University of Chicago Press, 1998), 66.

11. Stephen Holmes, "Loyalty in Adversity," in *Machiavelli on Liberty and Conflict*, ed. David Johnston, Nadia Urbinati, and Camila Vergara (Chicago: University of Chicago Press, 2017), 194.

12. Machiavelli, *Prince*, 66.

13. *Prince*, 67.

14. *Prince*, 66.

15. *Prince*, 65–66.

16. Yves Winter, *Machiavelli and the Orders of Violence* (Cambridge, UK: Cambridge University Press, 2018), 59.

17. Niccolò Machiavelli, *Discourses on Livy*, trans. Harvey C. Mansfield Jr. and Nathan Tarcov (Chicago: University of Chicago Press, 1996), 263.

18. Winter, *Machiavelli and the Orders*, 60.

19. Leo Strauss, *Thoughts on Machiavelli* (Chicago: University of Chicago Press, 1958), 281.

20. Strauss, *Thoughts on Machiavelli*, 281.

21. Strauss, 167.

22. Strauss, 171.

23. Erica Benner, *Machiavelli's "Prince": A New Reading* (Oxford, UK: Oxford University Press, 2013), 206.

24. *Prince*, 66.

25. *Prince*, 66.

26. *Prince*, 66.

27. *Prince*, 66.

28. *Prince*, 66.

29. *Prince*, 67.

30. Robert Kocis, *Machiavelli Redeemed: Retrieving His Humanist Perspectives on Equality, Power, and Glory* (Bethlehem, PA: Lehigh University Press, 1998), 98.

31. *Florentine Histories*, 91.

32. *Florentine Histories*, 91.

33. *Florentine Histories*, 91–92.

34. *Florentine Histories*, 92.

35. *Florentine Histories*, 92.

36. *Florentine Histories*, 93.

37. *Florentine Histories*, 91.

38. *Florentine Histories*, 92.

39. Raymond Angelo Belliotti, *Niccolò Machiavelli: The Laughing Lion and the Strutting Fox* (New York: Rowman and Littlefield, 2010), 7.

40. Winter, 133.

41. *Florentine Histories*, 92.

42. *Prince*, 21.

43. *Prince*, 21.

44. *Florentine Histories*, 92–93.

45. Winter, 134.

46. Winter, 134.

47. Marie Gaille, *Machiavelli on Freedom and Civil Conflict: An Historical and Medical Approach to Political Thinking* (Leiden, Netherlands: Brill, 2018), 20.

48. Winter, 136.

49. Kenneth Burke, *On Symbols and Society*, ed. Joseph R. Gusfield (Chicago: University of Chicago Press, 1989), 181. Emphasis in original.

50. Burke, *On Symbols and Society*, 181. Emphasis in original.

51. Burke, *On Symbols and Society*, 180. Emphasis in original.

52. Kenneth Burke, *Permanence and Change: An Anatomy of Purpose* (Berkeley: University of California Press, 1954), 71.

53. Burke, *Permanence and Change*, 71.

54. Burke, *Permanence and Change*, 71.

55. Burke, *Permanence and Change*, 74. Emphasis in original.

56. Burke, *Permanence and Change*, 72.

57. Nathan Crick, *Rhetoric and Power: The Drama of Classical Greece* (Columbia: University of South Carolina Press, 2015), 6.

58. Coluccio Salutati, *Political Writings*, trans. Rolf Bagemihl (Cambridge, MA: Harvard University Press, 2014), 391–93.

59. Crick, *Rhetoric and Power*, 6.

60. Robert Hariman, *Political Style: The Artistry of Power* (Chicago: Chicago University Press, 1995), 102.

61. Viroli, 149.

62. *Florentine Histories*, 98.

63. Burke, *On Symbols and Society*, 181. Emphasis in original.

64. Pope Francis, *Laudato si': On Care for Our Common Home* (Vatican City: Libreria Editrice Vaticana, 2015).

CHAPTER 6

1. Niccolò Machiavelli, *The Prince*, trans. Harvey C. Mansfield Jr. (Chicago: University of Chicago Press, 1998), 91.

2. Erica Benner, *Machiavelli's Ethics* (Princeton, NJ: Princeton University Press, 2009), 291.

3. Benner, *Machiavelli's Ethics*, 297.

4. Catherine H. Zuckert, *Machiavelli's Politics* (Chicago: University of Chicago Press, 2017), 476.

5. Robert Hariman, *Political Style: The Artistry of Power* (Chicago: Chicago University Press, 1995), 122.

6. Hariman, *Political Style*, 123.

7. Jennet Kirkpatrick, *Uncivil Disobedience: Studies in Violence and Democratic Politics* (Princeton, NJ: Princeton University Press, 2008), 9.

8. Kirkpatrick, *Uncivil Disobedience*, 4.

9. Kirkpatrick, 4.

10. Kirkpatrick, 4.

11. David Polansky, "Machiavelli's Lessons for America's Jan. 6 Tumult," *Foreign Policy*, January 8, 2022.

12. Polansky, "Machiavelli's Lessons."

13. Polansky.

14. *This Is Not a Drill: An Extinction Rebellion Handbook* (New York: Penguin Books, 2019).

15. Harvey Mansfield, *Machiavelli's New Modes and Orders: A Study of the "Discourses on Livy"* (Chicago: University of Chicago Press, 2001), 50.

16. Niccolò Machiavelli, *Discourses on Livy*, trans. Harvey C. Mansfield Jr. and Nathan Tarcov (Chicago: University of Chicago Press, 1996), 17.

17. Machiavelli, *Discourses on Livy*, 17.

18. Quentin Skinner, *The Foundations of Modern Political Thought*, vol. 1, *The Renaissance* (Cambridge, UK: Cambridge University Press, 1998), 182.

19. Gabriele Pedullà, *Machiavelli in Tumult: The Discourses on Livy and the Origins of Political Conflictualism* (Cambridge, UK: Cambridge University Press, 2018), 8.

20. Filippo del Lucchese, *Conflict, Power, and Multitude in Machiavelli and Spinoza: Tumult and Indignation* (London: A&C Black, 2011), 145.

21. Niccolò Machiavelli, *Florentine Histories*, trans. Laura F. Banfield and Harvey C. Mansfield Jr. (Princeton, NJ: Princeton University Press, 1988), 23.

22. Machiavelli, *Florentine Histories*, 97.

23. *Discourses on Livy*, 16.

24. *Discourses on Livy*, 16.

25. *Discourses on Livy*, 16.

26. *Discourses on Livy*, 17.

27. *Discourses on Livy*, 15.

28. *Discourses on Livy*, 15.

29. *Discourses on Livy*, 15.

30. John P. McCormick, *Machiavellian Democracy* (Cambridge, UK: Cambridge University Press, 2011), 7.

31. *Discourses on Livy*, 17.

32. *Discourses on Livy*, 48.

33. Yves Winter, "Plebeian Politics: Machiavelli and the Ciompi Uprising," *Political Theory* 40, no. 6 (2012): 736–37.

34. Norman Cantor, *In the Wake of the Plague: The Black Death and the World It Made* (New York: Perennial, 2001), 141.

35. Cantor, *In the Wake of the Plague*, 91.

36. Winter, 740.

37. Winter, 740.

38. Winter, 742.

39. *Florentine Histories*, 121.

40. John P. McCormick, *Reading Machiavelli: Scandalous Books, Suspect Engagements, and the Virtue of Populist Politics* (Princeton, NJ: Princeton University Press, 2018), 86.

41. *Florentine Histories*, 116.

42. *Discourses on Livy*, 18.

43. Robert Kocis, *Machiavelli Redeemed: Retrieving His Humanist Perspectives on Equality, Power, and Glory* (Bethlehem, PA: Lehigh University Press, 1998), 191.

44. Leo Strauss, *Thoughts on Machiavelli* (Chicago: University of Chicago Press, 1958), 256.

45. Maurizio Viroli, *Machiavelli* (Oxford, UK: Oxford University Press, 1998), 123.

46. Viroli, *Machiavelli*, 122.

47. *Florentine Histories*, 116–17.

48. *Florentine Histories*, 117.

49. *Florentine Histories*, 117.

50. *Florentine Histories*, 117.

51. *Discourses on Livy*, 23.

52. *Discourses on Livy*, 23–24.

53. *Discourses on Livy*, 27.

54. *Discourses on Livy*, 27.

55. *Discourses on Livy*, 27.

56. *Discourses on Livy*, 15.

57. *Discourses on Livy*, 15.

58. *Discourses on Livy*, 15.

59. Anti-Defamation League (website), "The January 6 Effect: An Evolution of Hate and Extremism," accessed February 14, 2023.

CHAPTER 7

1. Robert Hariman and Ralph Cintron, *Culture, Catastrophe, and Rhetoric: The Texture of Political Action* (New York: Berghahn, 2020), 11.

2. Hariman and Cintron, *Culture, Catastrophe, and Rhetoric*, 11.

3. Hariman and Cintron, 11.

4. Hariman and Cintron, 12.

5. Hannah Arendt, *On Revolution* (New York: Penguin Classics, 1977), 18.

6. Hannah Arendt, *Between Past and Future: Eight Exercises in Political Thought* (New York: Penguin, 1968), 136.

7. Arendt, *Between Past and Future*, 138.

8. Arendt, *On Revolution*, 26.

9. Niccolò Machiavelli, *Discourses on Livy*, trans. Harvey C. Mansfield Jr. and Nathan Tarcov (Chicago: University of Chicago Press, 1996), 5.

10. Arendt, *On Revolution*, 26.

11. Machiavelli, *Discourses on Livy*, 61.

12. *Discourses on Livy*, 61–62.

13. Theda Skocpol, *States and Social Revolutions: A Comparative Analysis of France, Russia and China* (New York: Cambridge University Press, 1979), 4.

14. Anthony Giddens, *Sociology* (Cambridge, UK: Polity Press, 1989), 604–5.

15. Arendt, *On Revolution*, 102.

16. Simone Weil, *Selected Essays, 1934–1943*, ed. and trans. Richard Rees (Eugene, OR: Wipf and Stock, 2015), 56.

17. Anna Maria Cabrini, "Machiavelli's Florentine Histories," in *The Cambridge Companion to Machiavelli*, ed. John M. Najemy (Cambridge, UK: Cambridge University Press, 2010), 136.

18. Yves Winter, "Plebeian Politics: Machiavelli and the Ciompi Uprising," *Political Theory* 40, no. 6 (2012): 736.

19. Antonio Gramsci, *Selections from the Prison Notebooks*, trans. Quintin Hoare and Geoffrey Nowell Smith (New York: International Publishers, 1971), 126.

20. Louis Althusser, *Machiavelli and Us*, trans. Gregory Elliott (New York: Verso, 1999), 25.

21. Althusser, *Machiavelli and Us*, 25.

22. Antonio Negri, *Insurgencies: Constituent Power and the Modern State*, trans. Maurizia Boscagli (Minneapolis: University of Minnesota Press, 1999), 68.

23. Niccolò Machiavelli, *Florentine Histories*, trans. Laura F. Banfield and Harvey C. Mansfield Jr. (Princeton, NJ: Princeton University Press, 1988), 114.

24. Machiavelli, *Florentine Histories*, 121.

25. *Florentine Histories*, 126–27.

26. *Florentine Histories*, 134.

27. *Florentine Histories*, 105.

28. *Florentine Histories*, 105.

29. *Florentine Histories*, 105.

30. *Florentine Histories*, 105.

31. *Florentine Histories*, 105.

32. *Florentine Histories*, 105.

33. *Florentine Histories*, 105–6.

34. Arendt, *On Revolution*, 25.

35. Winter, "Plebeian Politics," 742.

36. *Florentine Histories*, 126.

37. *Florentine Histories*, 126.

38. *Florentine Histories*, 126.

39. *Florentine Histories*, 108.

40. *Florentine Histories*, 108.

41. *Florentine Histories*, 118.

42. *Florentine Histories*, 119.

43. Leonardo Bruni, *History of the Florentine People*, vol. 3, ed. and trans. James Hankins (Cambridge, MA: Harvard University Press, 2007), 9.

44. *Florentine Histories*, 119.

45. *Florentine Histories*, 119.

46. *Florentine Histories*, 120.

47. *Florentine Histories*, 120.

48. *Florentine Histories*, 120.

49. *Florentine Histories*, 121.

50. Bruni, *History*, 9.

51. *Florentine Histories*, 121.

52. *Florentine Histories*, 122.

53. *Florentine Histories*, 122.

54. *Florentine Histories*, 122.

55. Yves Winter, *Machiavelli and the Orders of Violence* (Cambridge, UK: Cambridge University Press, 2018), 176.

56. Winter, *Machiavelli and the Orders*, 177.

57. Bruni, 9.

58. *Florentine Histories*, 122.

59. *Florentine Histories*, 122.

60. *Florentine Histories*, 122.

61. *Florentine Histories*, 122.

62. *Florentine Histories*, 123.

63. *Florentine Histories*, 123.

64. *Florentine Histories*, 123.

65. *Florentine Histories*, 122.

66. *Florentine Histories*, 122.

67. *Florentine Histories*, 123.

68. *Florentine Histories*, 123.

69. Harvey Mansfield, "Machiavelli on Necessity," in *Machiavelli on Liberty and Conflict*, ed. David Johnston, Nadia Urbinati, and Camila Vergara, 39–57 (Chicago: University of Chicago Press, 2017), 52.

70. *Florentine Histories*, 123.

71. *Florentine Histories*, 123.

72. *Florentine Histories*, 123.

73. Kenneth Burke, *Permanence and Change: An Anatomy of Purpose* (Berkeley: University of California Press, 1954),172. Emphasis in original.

74. Burke, *Permanence and Change*, 179.

75. Burke, 173.

76. *Florentine Histories*, 122.

77. Arendt, *On Revolution*, 19.

78. *Florentine Histories*, 122.

79. *Florentine Histories*, 123.

80. *Florentine Histories*, 123.

81. *Florentine Histories*, 124.

82. *Florentine Histories*, 124.

83. *Florentine Histories*, 125.

84. *Florentine Histories*, 125.

85. *Florentine Histories*, 127.

86. *Florentine Histories*, 128.

87. *Florentine Histories*, 128.

88. *Florentine Histories*, 128.

89. *Florentine Histories*, 128.

90. *Florentine Histories*, 129.

91. *Florentine Histories*, 129.

92. *Florentine Histories*, 129.

93. Winter, "Plebeian Politics," 742.

94. *Florentine Histories*, 130.

95. Steve Mirsky, "Tom Friedman's New Book—Hot, Flat, and Crowded," *Scientific American*, September 9, 2008.

96. Mirsky, "Tom Friedman's New Book."

97. Peter Staudenmaier, "Fascist Ecology: The 'Green Wing' of the Nazi Party and Its Historical Antecedents," in *Ecofascism: Lessons from the German Experience*, ed. Janet Biehl and Peter Staudenmaier (Porsgrunn, Norway: New Compass Press, 2011), 26.

98. Naomi Klein cited in Wen Stephenson, "Against Climate Barbarism: A Conversation with Naomi Klein," *Los Angeles Review of Books*, September 30, 2019.

99. Stephenson, "Against Climate Barbarism."

CHAPTER 8

1. Niccolò Machiavelli, "Rules for an Elegant Social Circle," in *The Essential Writings of Machiavelli*, ed. and trans. Peter Constantine (New York: Modern Library 2007), 382–83.

2. James B. Atkinson, "An Essay on Machiavelli and Comedy," in Niccolò Machiavelli, *The Comedies of Machiavelli*, ed. and trans. David Sices and James B. Atkinson (Indianapolis: Hackett, 1985), 14.

3. Atkinson, "Machiavelli and Comedy," 14.

4. Atkinson, 23.

5. Vickie B. Sullivan, "Introduction," in *The Comedy and Tragedy of Machiavelli: Essays on the Literary Works*, ed. Vickie B. Sullivan (New Haven, CT: Yale University Press, 2000), x.

6. Leo Strauss, *Thoughts on Machiavelli* (Chicago: University of Chicago Press, 1958), 286.

7. Thomas B. Farrell, *Norms of Rhetorical Culture* (New Haven, CT: Yale University Press, 1993), 245.

8. Machiavelli, *Comedies*, 283.

9. Kenneth Burke, *Attitudes toward History* (Berkeley: University of California Press, 1937), 41.

10. Burke, *Attitudes toward History*, 171.

11. Farrell, *Norms of Rhetorical Culture*, 245.

12. *Comedies*, 165.

13. *Comedies*, 191.

14. *Comedies*, 197.

15. *Comedies*, 205.

16. *Comedies*, 269.

17. *Comedies*, 275.

18. *Comedies*, 155.

19. Catherine H. Zuckert, *Machiavelli's Politics* (Chicago: University of Chicago Press, 2017), 296.

20. Zuckert, *Machiavelli's Politics*, 296.

21. Zuckert, 293.

22. *Comedies*, 219.

23. *Comedies*, 225.

24. Michael Hardt and Antonio Negri, *Empire* (Cambridge, MA: Harvard University Press, 2001), 162.

25. Hardt and Negri, *Empire*, 162.

26. Hardt and Negri, 163.

27. Antonio Negri, *Insurgencies: Constituent Power and the Modern State*, trans. Maurizia Boscagli (Minneapolis: University of Minnesota Press, 1999), 9.

28. Filippo del Lucchese, "Machiavelli and Constituent Power: The Revolutionary Foundation of Modern Political Thought," *European Journal of Political Theory* 16, no. 1 (2017): 19.

29. Zuckert, 477.

30. Christopher Hibbert, *The House of Medici: Its Rise and Fall* (New York: Harper Collins, 2012), 30.

31. Hibbert, *House of Medici*, 31.

32. Gene A. Brucker, *Renaissance Florence* (Berkeley: University of California Press, 1969), 121.

33. Niccolò Machiavelli, *Florentine Histories*, trans. Laura F. Banfield and Harvey C. Mansfield Jr. (Princeton, NJ: Princeton University Press, 1988), 161.

34. Hibbert, 34.

35. Hibbert, 35–36.

36. Lauro Martines, *April Blood: Florence and the Plot against the Medici* (Oxford: Oxford University Press, 2003), 38.

37. Paul D. McLean, *The Art of the Network: Strategic Interaction and Patronage in Renaissance Florence* (Durham, NC: Duke University Press, 2007), 8.

38. *Florentine Histories*, 161.

39. *Florentine Histories*, 147.

40. *Florentine Histories*, 161.

41. *Florentine Histories*, 126.

42. *Florentine Histories*, 126.

43. *Florentine History*, 146.

44. *Florentine History*, 146.

45. *Florentine Histories*, 147.

46. *Florentine Histories*, 149.

47. *Florentine Histories*, 152.

48. *Florentine Histories*, 154.

49. *Florentine Histories*, 154.

50. *Florentine Histories*, 155.

51. *Florentine Histories*, 155.

52. *Florentine Histories*, 155.

53. *Florentine Histories*, 281.

54. Hendrik Thijs van Veen, *Cosimo I de' Medici and the Self-Representation in Florentine Art and Culture* (Cambridge, UK: Cambridge University Press, 2006), 10.

55. *Florentine Histories*, 281.

56. *Florentine Histories*, 282.

57. Brucker, *Renaissance Florence*, 256.

58. *Florentine Histories*, 362.

59. *Florentine Histories*, 361.

60. *Florentine Histories*, 361.

61. *Florentine Histories*, 362.

62. *Florentine Histories*, 319.

63. Burke, *Attitudes toward History*, 54–55.

64. *Florentine Histories*, 308.

65. *Florentine Histories*, 309.

66. *Florentine Histories*, 309.

67. *Florentine Histories*, 317.

68. *Florentine Histories*, 326.

69. *Florentine Histories*, 340.

70. Robert Hariman, *Political Style: The Artistry of Power* (Chicago: Chicago University Press, 1995), 96.

71. Hariman, *Political Style*, 110.

72. Hariman, 110.

73. Kenneth Burke, *On Symbols and Society*, ed. Joseph R. Gusfield (Chicago: University of Chicago Press, 1989), 256.

74. Niccolò Machiavelli, *Discourses on Livy*, trans. Harvey C. Mansfield Jr. and Nathan Tarcov (Chicago: University of Chicago Press, 1996), 15.

CHAPTER 9

1. Martha C. Nussbaum, *The Fragility of Goodness: Luck and Ethics in Greek Tragedy and Philosophy* (Cambridge, UK: Cambridge University Press, 2001), 245.

2. Hannah Arendt, *Life of the Mind* (New York: Harcourt, 1978), 1:19.

3. Thomas B. Farrell, *Norms of Rhetorical Culture* (New Haven, CT: Yale University Press, 1993), 27.

4. Farrell, *Norms of Rhetorical Culture*, 283.

5. Jacques Ellul, *Propaganda: The Formation of Men's Attitudes* (New York: Vintage Books, 1965), 27.

6. Edward Bernays, *Propaganda* (New York: IG Publishing, 1928), 52.

7. Zac Gershberg and Sean Illing, *The Paradox of Democracy: Free Speech, Open Media, and Perilous Persuasion* (Chicago: University of Chicago Press, 2022), 1.

8. Gershberg and Illing, *Paradox of Democracy*, 254.

9. Gershberg and Illing, 254.

10. Francesco Guicciardini, *The History of Italy*, ed. and trans. Sidney Alexander (Princeton, NJ: Princeton University Press, 1969), 83.

11. Girolamo Savonarola, *Apologetic Writings*, ed. and trans. M. Michèle Mulchahey (Cambridge, MA: Harvard University Press, 2015), 313.

12. James B. Atkinson and David Sices, trans., *Machiavelli and His Friends: Their Personal Correspondence* (DeKalb: Northern Illinois University Press, 1996), 9.

13. Atkinson and Sices, *Machiavelli and His Friends*, 10.

14. Savonarola, *Apologetic Writings*, 295.

15. Savonarola, 147–49.

16. Guicciardini, *History of Italy*, 83.

17. Lauro Martines, *Fire in the City: Savonarola and the Struggle for the Soul of Renaissance Florence* (Oxford: Oxford University Press, 2007), 141.

18. Niccolò Machiavelli, *The Prince*, in *The Essential Writings of Machiavelli*, ed. and trans. Peter Constantine (New York: Random House, 2007), 70.

19. Guicciardini, 122.

20. Martines, *Fire in the City*, 276.

21. Ellul, *Propaganda*, emphasis in original.

22. Niccolò Machiavelli, *The Prince*, trans. Harvey C. Mansfield Jr. (Chicago: University of Chicago Press, 1998), 70.

23. *Prince*, 71.

24. *Prince*, 70.

25. *Prince*, 11 (emphasis added).

26. Savonarola, 287.

27. Savonarola, 287.

28. Martines, 115.

29. Ellul, 117.

30. Ellul, 21.

31. Ellul, 11.

32. Alison McQueen, *Political Realism in Apocalyptic Times* (Cambridge, UK: Cambridge University Press, 2018), 69.

33. Guicciardini, 128.

34. Guicciardini, 122.

35. Niccolò Machiavelli, *Discourses on Livy*, trans. Harvey C. Mansfield Jr. and Nathan Tarcov (Chicago: University of Chicago Press, 1996), 106.

36. Machiavelli, *Discourses on Livy*, 106.

37. *Discourses on Livy*, 106.

38. *Discourses on Livy*, 106.

39. Erica Benner, *Machiavelli's Ethics* (Princeton, NJ: Princeton University Press, 2009), 223.

40. *Prince*, 83.

41. *Prince*, 24.

42. Machiavelli would exclude, of course, Jesus Christ from consideration, as Christ was not a prophet in the Christian tradition but the Son of Go and hence not bound by the same necessities.

43. *Prince*, 24.

44. *Prince*, 24.

45. *Discourses on Livy*, 280.

46. Guicciardini, 128.

47. Martines, 225.

48. Donald Weinstein, *Savonarola: The Rise and Fall of a Renaissance Prophet* (New Haven, CT: Yale University Press, 2011), 286.

49. Cited in Gene A. Brucker, *Renaissance Florence* (Berkeley: University of California Press, 1969), 270–71.

50. Quintin Skinner, *Machiavelli: A Very Short Introduction* (Oxford: Oxford University Press, 1981), 43.

51. *Discourses on Livy*, 106.

CHAPTER 10

1. António Guterres, "Secretary-General's Video Message to the Press Conference Launch of IPCC Report," United Nations (website), accessed February 16, 2023.

2. Guterres, "Secretary-General's Video Message."

3. Guterres.

4. Shauna Corr, "Climate Endgame: Risk to Human Extinction or Total Societal Collapse 'Dangerously Underexplored' Say Scientists," *Irish Mirror*, August 4, 2022.

5. Mitt Romney, "America Is in Denial," *Atlantic*, July 4, 2022.

6. Robert Clines, "What Machiavelli Would Do about Climate Change," *Washington Post*, February 23, 2020.

7. Niccolò Machiavelli, *The Prince*, trans. Harvey C. Mansfield Jr. (Chicago: University of Chicago Press, 1998), 98.

8. Machiavelli, *Prince*, 98.

9. Clines, "What Machiavelli."

10. J. G. A. Pocock, *The Machiavellian Moment: Florentine Political Thought and the Atlantic Republican Tradition* (Princeton, NJ: Princeton University Press, 1975), 166–67.

11. Erica Benner, *Be Like the Fox: Machiavelli in His World* (New York: W. W. Norton, 2017), 180.

12. James B. Atkinson and David Sices, trans., *Machiavelli and His Friends: Their Personal Correspondence* (DeKalb: Northern Illinois University Press, 1996), 237.

13. Niccolò Machiavelli, *Discourses on Livy*, trans. Harvey C. Mansfield Jr. and Nathan Tarcov (Chicago: University of Chicago Press, 1996), 106.

14. Machiavelli, *Discourses on Livy*, 51.

15. *Discourses on Livy*, 51.

16. *Discourses on Livy*, 51.

17. *Discourses on Livy*, 51.

18. *Discourses on Livy*, 51.

19. *Prince*, 105.

20. *Prince*, 61.

21. *Prince*, 62.

22. Maurizio Viroli, *Machiavelli* (Oxford: Oxford University Press, 1998), 95.

23. *Prince*, 62.

24. *Prince*, 62.

25. *Prince*, 65.

26. *Prince*, 65.

27. *Prince*, 65.

28. Michael Walzer, "Political Action: The Problem of Dirty Hands," *Philosophy and Public Affairs* 2, no. 2 (1973): 161.

29. Walzer, "Political Action," 167.

30. Walzer, 167.

31. Walzer, 167.

32. Walzer, 178.

33. Demetris Tillyris, "'Learning How Not to Be Good': Machiavelli and the Standard Dirty Hands Thesis," *Ethical Theory and Moral Practice* 18, no. 1 (2015): 61.

34. Tillyris, "Learning How," 61

35. Tillyris, 64.

36. Tillyris, 64. Emphasis in original.

37. Tillyris, 73.

38. Gene A. Brucker, *Renaissance Florence* (Berkeley: University of California Press, 1969), 273.

39. Brucker, *Renaissance Florence*, 273

40. *Discourses on Livy*, 214.

41. Brucker, 273.

42. Francesco Guicciardini, *The History of Italy*, ed. and trans. Sidney Alexander (Princeton, NJ: Princeton University Press, 1969), 257.

43. Guicciardini, *History of Italy*, 258.

44. Guicciardini, 261.

45. Atkinson and Sices, *Machiavelli and His Friends*, 215.

46. Atkinson and Sices, 215.

47. Atkinson and Sices, 215.

48. Atkinson and Sices, 215.

49. Atkinson and Sices, 215.

50. Atkinson and Sices, 215–16.

51. Atkinson and Sices, 216.

52. Atkinson and Sices, letter 247 (page 312).

53. *Discourses on Livy*, 214–15.

54. *Discourses on Livy*, 215.

55. *Discourses on Livy*, 215.

56. *Discourses on Livy*, 215.

57. Guicciardini, 260.

58. *Discourses on Livy*, 215.

59. *Discourses on Livy*, 215.

60. Robert Hariman, *Political Style: The Artistry of Power* (Chicago: Chicago University Press, 1995), 37.

61. Tillyris, 65.

62. Tillyris, 65.

63. John M. Najemy, *A History of Florence, 1200–1575* (Malden, MA: Blackwell, 2006), 409.

64. Catherine H. Zuckert, *Machiavelli's Politics* (Chicago: University of Chicago Press, 2017), 214.

65. Jason Stanley, *How Fascism Works: The Politics of Us and Them* (New York: Random House, 2020), 192.

66. Stanley, *How Fascism Works*, 192.

CHAPTER 11

1. Gene A. Brucker, *Renaissance Florence* (Berkeley: University of California Press, 1969 277.

2. Brucker, *Renaissance Florence*, 277.

3. Francesco Guicciardini, *The History of Italy*, ed. and trans. Sidney Alexander (Princeton, NJ: Princeton University Press, 1969) 432.

4. James B. Atkinson and David Sices, trans., *Machiavelli and His Friends: Their Personal Correspondence* (DeKalb: Northern Illinois University Press, 1996), 413.

5. Niccolò Machiavelli, *The Prince*, trans. Harvey C. Mansfield Jr. (Chicago: University of Chicago Press, 1998), 103.

6. Niccolò Machiavelli, *The Comedies of Machiavelli*, trans. James B. Atkinson and David Sices (Indianapolis: Hackett, 1985), 167.

7. Machiavelli, *Prince*, 105.

8. Niccolò Machiavelli, *Discourses on Livy*, trans. Harvey C. Mansfield Jr. and Nathan Tarcov (Chicago: University of Chicago Press, 1996), 173.

9. Machiavelli, *Discourses on Livy*, 173.

10. Mikael Hörnqvist, *Machiavelli and Empire* (Cambridge, UK: Cambridge University Press, 2004), 74.

11. Isabelle Stengers, *In Catastrophic Times: Resisting the Coming Barbarism* (Paris: Open Humanities Press, 2015), 27.

12. Stengers, *In Catastrophic Times*, 27.

13. Stengers, 22.

14. Stengers, 132.

15. Stengers, 132.

16. *Prince*, 101.

17. *Prince*, 102.

18. Stengers, 45.

19. *Discourses on Livy*, 125.

20. Maurizio Viroli, *Niccolò's Smile: A Biography of Machiavelli* (New York: Farrar, Straus and Giroux, 2002), 3.

Works Cited

Alighieri, Dante. *The Divine Comedy*. Translated by C. H. Sisson. Oxford: Oxford University Press, 1980.

Althusser, Louis. *Machiavelli and Us*. Translated by Gregory Elliott. New York: Verso, 1999.

Anti-Defamation League (website). "The January 6 Effect: An Evolution of Hate and Extremism." Accessed February 14, 2023.

Arendt, Hannah. *Between Past and Future: Eight Exercises in Political Thought*. New York: Penguin, 1968.

———. *Life of the Mind*. New York: Harcourt, 1978.

———. *On Revolution*. New York: Penguin Classics, 1977.

Atkinson, James B. "An Essay on Machiavelli and Comedy." In *The Comedies of Machiavelli*, edited and translated by David Sices and James B. Atkinson, 1–34. Indianapolis: Hackett, 1985.

Atkinson, James B., and David Sices, trans. *Machiavelli and His Friends: Their Personal Correspondence*. DeKalb: Northern Illinois University Press, 1996.

Bacon, Francis. *The Works of Lord Bacon: With an Introductory Essay, and a Portrait: In Two Vols*. London: Reeves and Turner, 1879.

Barabak, Mark Z. "'Quarantini.' 'Doomscrolling.' Here's How the Coronavirus Is Changing the Way We Talk." *Los Angeles Times*, April 11, 2020.

Belliotti, Raymond Angelo. *Niccolò Machiavelli: The Laughing Lion and the Strutting Fox*. New York: Rowman and Littlefield, 2010.

Benner, Erica. *Be Like the Fox: Machiavelli in His World*. New York: W. W. Norton, 2017.

———. *Machiavelli's Ethics*. Princeton, NJ: Princeton University Press, 2009.

———. *Machiavelli's "Prince": A New Reading*. Oxford: Oxford University Press, 2013.

Berlin, Isaiah. *Four Essays on Liberty*. Oxford: Oxford University Press, 1969.

Bernays, Edward. *Propaganda*. New York: IG Publishing, 1928.

Bew, John. *Realpolitik: A History*. Oxford: Oxford University Press, 2016.

Bitzer, Lloyd. "The Rhetorical Situation." *Philosophy and Rhetoric* 1, no. 1 (1968): 1–14.

Boucheron, Patrick. *Machiavelli: The Art of Teaching People What to Fear*. New York: Other Press, 2020.

Brucker, Gene A. *Renaissance Florence*. Berkeley: University of California Press, 1969.

Bruni, Leonardo. *History of the Florentine People*. Vol. 3. Edited by and translated by James Hankins. Cambridge, MA: Harvard University Press, 2007.

Burke, Kenneth. *Attitudes toward History*. Berkeley: University of California Press, 1937.

———. *Permanence and Change: An Anatomy of Purpose*. Berkeley: University of California Press, 1954.

———. *The Philosophy of Literary Form*. New York: Vintage, 1953.

———. *On Symbols and Society*. Edited by Joseph R. Gusfield. Chicago: University of Chicago Press, 1989.

Cabrini, Anna Maria. "Machiavelli's Florentine Histories." In *The Cambridge Companion to Machiavelli*, edited by John M. Najemy, 128–43. Cambridge, UK: Cambridge University Press, 2010.

Cantor, Norman. *In the Wake of the Plague: The Black Death and the World It Made*. New York: Perennial, 2001.

Cicero. *On Duties*. Translated by M. T. Griffin and E. M. Atkins. Cambridge, UK: Cambridge University Press, 1991.

Clines, Robert. "What Machiavelli Would Do about Climate Change." *Washington Post*, February 23, 2020.

Compagni, Dino. *Dino Compagni's Chronicle of Florence*. Translated by Daniel E. Bornstein. Philadelphia: University of Pennsylvania Press, 1986.

Constantine, Peter, ed. and trans. *The Essential Writings of Machiavelli*. New York: Modern Library 2007.

Corr, Shauna. "Climate Endgame: Risk to Human Extinction or Total Societal Collapse 'Dangerously Underexplored' Say Scientists." *Irish Mirror*, August 4, 2022.

Creemers, Rogier. "A Machiavellian Guide to Getting Ahead in Academia." *Times Higher Education*, December 21, 2017.

Crick, Nathan. *Dewey for a New Age of Fascism: Teaching Democratic Habits*. State College: Pennsylvania State University Press, 2019.

———. "Rhetoric and Events." *Philosophy and Rhetoric* 47, no. 3 (2014): 251–72.

———. *Rhetoric and Power: The Drama of Classical Greece*. Columbia: University of South Carolina Press, 2015.

Diakité, Rala, and Matthew Thomas Sneider. "Introduction." In Villani, *Final Book*, 1–34.

Ellul, Jacques. *Propaganda: The Formation of Men's Attitudes*. New York: Vintage Books, 1965.

Farrell, Thomas B. *Norms of Rhetorical Culture*. New Haven, CT: Yale University Press, 1993.

Francis (Pope). *Laudato si': On Care for Our Common Home*. Vatican City: Libreria Editrice Vaticana, 2015.

Gaille, Marie. *Machiavelli on Freedom and Civil Conflict: An Historical and Medical Approach to Political Thinking*. Leiden, Netherlands: Brill, 2018.

Gershberg, Zac, and Sean Illing. *The Paradox of Democracy: Free Speech, Open Media, and Perilous Persuasion.* Chicago: University of Chicago Press, 2022.

Ghosh, Amitav. *The Great Derangement: Climate Change and the Unthinkable.* Chicago: University of Chicago Press, 2016.

Giddens, Anthony. *Sociology.* Cambridge, UK: Polity Press, 1989.

Gilbert, Felix. *Machiavelli and Guicciardini: Politics and History in Sixteenth-Century Florence.* Princeton, NJ: Princeton University Press. 1965.

Goncalves, Diana. *9/11: Culture, Catastrophe and the Critique of Singularity.* Berlin: Walter de Gruyter, 2016.

Gramsci, Antonio. *Selections from the Prison Notebooks.* Translated by Quintin Hoare and Geoffrey Nowell Smith. New York: International Publishers, 1971.

Guicciardini, Francesco. *The History of Italy.* Edited and translated by Sidney Alexander. Princeton, NJ: Princeton University Press, 1969.

Guterres, António. "Secretary-General's Video Message to the Press Conference Launch of IPCC Report." United Nations (website), February 2022.

Hardt, Michael, and Antonio Negri. *Empire.* Cambridge, MA: Harvard University Press, 2001.

Hariman, Robert. "Introduction." In Hariman and Cintron, *Culture, Catastrophe, and Rhetoric,* 1–24.

———. *Political Style: The Artistry of Power.* Chicago: Chicago University Press, 1995.

Hariman, Robert, and Ralph Cintron. *Culture, Catastrophe, and Rhetoric: The Texture of Political Action.* New York: Berghahn, 2020.

Harnett, Stephen J. "'Lock Her Up!' Fascism as a Political Style from Mussolini to Trump." In *The Rhetoric of Fascism,* edited by Nathan Crick, 34–56. Tuscaloosa: University of Alabama Press, 2022.

Harvey, Michael. "Lost in the Wilderness: Love and Longing in L'Asino." In Sullivan, *Comedy and Tragedy of Machiavelli,* 120–37.

Hendrickson, David C. "Machiavelli and Machiavellianism." In *Machiavelli's Legacy: "The Prince" after Five Hundred Years,* edited by Timothy Fuller, 105–26. Philadelphia: University of Pennsylvania Press, 2016.

Hibbert, Christopher. *The House of Medici: Its Rise and Fall.* New York: Harper Collins, 2012.

Holmes, Stephen. "Loyalty in Adversity." In Johnston, Urbinati, and Vergara, *Machiavelli on Liberty and Conflict,* 186–205.

Horn, Eva. *The Future as Catastrophe: Imagining Disaster in the Modern Age.* New York: Columbia University Press, 2018.

Hörnqvist, Mikael. *Machiavelli and Empire.* Cambridge, UK: Cambridge University Press, 2004.

Ignatius, David. "Donald Trump Is the American Machiavelli." *Washington Post,* November 10, 2016.

Illing, Sean. "What Machiavelli Can Teach Us about Trump and the Decline of Liberal Democracy." Vox (website), November 16, 2018.

Ionescu, Andrei. "Humanity Should Brace for Catastrophic Climate Change." Earth (website), August 1, 2022.

Jaeger, Werner. *Paideia: The Ideals of Greek Culture.* Vol. 3, *In Search of the Divine Centre.* Translated by Gilbert Highet. Oxford: Oxford University Press, 1971.

Joffe, Josef. "Let's Dance the Machiavelli." *American Interest,* May 4, 2018.

Johnston, David, Nadia Urbinati, and Camila Vergara, eds. *Machiavelli on Liberty and Conflict.* Chicago: University of Chicago Press, 2017.

Kindervater, Garnet. "Catastrophe and Catastrophic Thoughts." In *Biopolitical Disaster,* edited by Jennifer L. Lawrence and Sarah Marie Wiebe, 97–112. New York: Taylor and Francis, 2017.

Kirkpatrick, Jennet. *Uncivil Disobedience: Studies in Violence and Democratic Politics.* Princeton, NJ: Princeton University Press, 2008.

Kocis, Robert. *Machiavelli Redeemed: Retrieving His Humanist Perspectives on Equality, Power, and Glory.* Bethlehem, PA: Lehigh University Press, 1998.

Kotsyubinsky, Daniil. "Why Putin Still Has a Lot to Learn from Machiavelli." *Open Democracy,* December 2, 2011.

Latour, Bruno. *After Lockdown: A Metamorphosis.* Translated by Julie Rose. Cambridge, UK: Polity Press, 2021.

———. *Down to Earth: Politics in the New Climatic Regime.* Cambridge, UK: Polity Press, 2018.

Lee, Alexander. "What Machiavelli Knew about Pandemics." *New Statesman,* June 3, 2020.

Levina, Marina. "Whiteness and the Joys of Cruelty." *Communication and Critical/Cultural Studies* 15, no. 1 (2018): 73–78.

Levitsky, Stephen, and Daniel Ziblatt. *How Democracies Die.* New York: Penguin Random House, 2018.

Levy, David N. *Wily Elites and Spirited Peoples in Machiavelli's Republicanism.* Lanham, MD: Lexington Books, 2014.

Lucchese, Filippo del. *Conflict, Power, and Multitude in Machiavelli and Spinoza: Tumult and Indignation.* London: A&C Black, 2011.

———. "Machiavelli and Constituent Power: The Revolutionary Foundation of Modern Political Thought." *European Journal of Political Theory* 16, no. 1 (2017): 3–23.

———. *The Political Philosophy of Niccolò Machiavelli.* Edinburgh: Edinburgh University Press, 2015.

Lukes, Timothy J. "Lionizing Machiavelli." *American Political Science Review* 95, no. 3 (September 2001): 561–75.

Machiavelli, Niccolò. *The Comedies of Machiavelli.* Translated by James B. Atkinson and David Sices. Indianapolis: Hackett, 1985.

———. *Discourses on Livy.* Translated by Harvey C. Mansfield Jr. and Nathan Tarcov. Chicago: University of Chicago Press, 1996.

———. *Florentine Histories.* Translated by Laura F. Banfield and Harvey C. Mansfield Jr. Princeton, NJ: Princeton University Press, 1988.

———. *The Prince.* Translated by Harvey C. Mansfield Jr. Chicago: University of Chicago Press, 1998.

———. *The Prince.* In Constantine, *Essential Writings of Machiavelli,* 3–100.

———. "Rules for an Elegant Social Circle." In Constantine, *Essential Writings of Machiavelli,* 381–86.

Mansfield, Harvey. "Machiavelli on Necessity." In Johnston, Urbinati, and Vergara, *Machiavelli on Liberty and Conflict*, 39–57.

———. *Machiavelli's New Modes and Orders: A Study of the "Discourses on Livy"*. Chicago: University of Chicago Press, 2001.

———. *Machiavelli's Virtue*. Chicago: University of Chicago Press, 1998.

Martines, Lauro. *April Blood: Florence and the Plot against the Medici*. Oxford: Oxford University Press, 2003.

———. *Fire in the City: Savonarola and the Struggle for the Soul of Renaissance Florence*. Oxford: Oxford University Press, 2007.

McCormick, John P. *Machiavellian Democracy*. Cambridge, UK: Cambridge University Press, 2011.

———. *Reading Machiavelli: Scandalous Books, Suspect Engagements, and the Virtue of Populist Politics*. Princeton, NJ: Princeton University Press, 2018.

McLean, Paul D. *The Art of the Network: Strategic Interaction and Patronage in Renaissance Florence*. Durham, NC: Duke University Press, 2007.

McQueen, Alison. *Political Realism in Apocalyptic Times*. Cambridge, UK: Cambridge University Press, 2018.

Meinecke, Friedrich. *Machiavellism: The Doctrine of Raison d'État and Its Place in Modern History*. New Brunswick, NJ: Transaction Publishers, 1997.

Mirsky, Steve. "Tom Friedman's New Book—Hot, Flat, and Crowded." *Scientific American*, September 9, 2008.

Najemy, John M. *A History of Florence, 1200–1575*. Malden, MA: Blackwell, 2006.

Negri, Antonio. *Insurgencies: Constituent Power and the Modern State*. Translated by Maurizia Boscagli. Minneapolis: University of Minnesota Press, 1999.

Nussbaum, Martha C. *The Fragility of Goodness: Luck and Ethics in Greek Tragedy and Philosophy*. Cambridge, UK: Cambridge University Press, 2001.

O'Gorman, Ned. *Politics for Everybody: Reading Hannah Arendt in Uncertain Times*. Chicago: University of Chicago Press, 2020.

Ophir, Adi. "The Politics of Catastrophization: Emergency and Exception." In *States of Emergency: The Politics of Military and Humanitarian Interventions*, edited by Didier Fassin and Mariella Pandolfi, 59–88. New York: Zone Books, 2008.

Osborne, Thomas. "Machiavelli and the Liberalism of Fear." *History of the Human Sciences* 30, no. 5 (2017): 68–85.

Pedullà, Gabriele. *Machiavelli in Tumult: The Discourses on Livy and the Origins of Political Conflictualism*. Cambridge, MA: Cambridge University Press, 2018.

Plutarch. *The Lives of the Noble Grecians and Romans*. Vol. 2. Translated by John Dryden. Edited by Arthur Hugh Clough. New York: Modern Library, 1992.

Pocock, J. G. A. *The Machiavellian Moment: Florentine Political Thought and the Atlantic Republican Tradition*. Princeton, NJ: Princeton University Press, 1975.

Polansky, David. "Machiavelli's Lessons for America's Jan. 6 Tumult." *Foreign Policy*, January 8, 2022.

Romney, Mitt. "America Is in Denial." *Atlantic*, July 4, 2022.

Ruggiero, Guido. *Machiavelli in Love: Sex, Self, and Society in the Italian Renaissance*. Baltimore: Johns Hopkins University Press, 2007.

Salutati, Coluccio. *Political Writings*. Edited by Stefano Ugo Baldassarri. Translated by Rolf Bagemihl. Cambridge, MA: Harvard University Press, 2014.

Savitz, Scott. "Applying Machiavellian Discourses to the Wars in Afghanistan and Iraq." *TheRANDblog* (blog), August 9, 2021.

Savonarola, Girolamo. *Apologetic Writings*. Edited and translated by M. Michèle Mulchahey. Cambridge, MA: Harvard University Press, 2015.

Seigel, Jerrold E. *Rhetoric and Philosophy in Renaissance Humanism: The Union of Eloquence and Wisdom, Petrarch to Valla*. Princeton, NJ: Princeton University Press, 1968.

Serwer, Adam. "The Cruelty Is the Point." *Atlantic*, October 3, 2018.

Shklar, Judith Nisse. *Ordinary Vices*. Cambridge, MA: Belknap Press, 1984.

Skinner, Quentin. *The Foundations of Modern Political Thought*. Vol. 1, *The Renaissance*. Cambridge, UK: Cambridge University Press, 1998.

———. *Machiavelli: A Very Short Introduction*. Oxford: Oxford University Press, 1981.

Skocpol, Theda. *States and Social Revolutions: A Comparative Analysis of France, Russia and China*. New York: Cambridge University Press, 1979.

Slaboch, Matthew. "Putin and Political Theory: A Machiavellian and Pan-Slav Mindset." *Europe Now*, February 24, 2022.

Stanley, Jason. *How Fascism Works: The Politics of Us and Them*. New York: Random House, 2020.

Staudenmaier, Peter. "Fascist Ecology: The 'Green Wing' of the Nazi Party and Its Historical Antecedents." In *Ecofascism: Lessons from the German Experience*, edited by Janet Biehl and Peter Staudenmaier, 3–28. Porsgrunn, Norway: New Compass Press, 2011.

Stengers, Isabelle. *In Catastrophic Times: Resisting the Coming Barbarism*. Paris: Open Humanities Press, 2015

Stephens, Murdoch. *Critical Environmental Communication: How Does Critique Respond to the Urgency of Climate Change?* Lanham, MD: Lexington Books, 2018.

Stephenson, Wen. "Against Climate Barbarism: A Conversation with Naomi Klein." *Los Angeles Review of Books*, September 30, 2019.

Strauss, Leo. *Thoughts on Machiavelli*. Chicago: University of Chicago Press, 1958.

Sullivan, Vickie B. "Introduction." In Sullivan, *Comedy and Tragedy of Machiavelli*, ix–xxi.

Sullivan, Vickie B., ed. *The Comedy and Tragedy of Machiavelli: Essays on the Literary Works*. New Haven, CT: Yale University Press, 2000.

Tharoor, Ishaan. "The World's Climate Catastrophe Worsens amid the Pandemic." *Washington Post*, June 29, 2020.

This Is Not A Drill: An Extinction Rebellion Handbook. New York: Penguin Books, 2019.

Tillyris, Demetris. "'Learning How Not to Be Good': Machiavelli and the Standard Dirty Hands Thesis." *Ethical Theory and Moral Practice* 18, no. 1 (2015): 61–74.

van Veen, Hendrik Thijs. *Cosimo I de' Medici and the Self-Representation in Florentine Art and Culture*. Cambridge, UK: Cambridge University Press, 2006.

Vázquez-Arroyo, Antonio Y. "Antinomies of Violence and Catastrophe: Structures, Orders, and Agents." *New Political Science* 34, no. 2 (2012): 211–21.

———. "How Not to Learn from Catastrophe: Habermas, Critical Theory and the 'Catastrophization' of Political Life." *Political Theory* 41, no. 5 (2013): 738–65.

Villani, Giovanni. *The Final Book of Giovanni Villani's New Chronicle*. Translated by Rala Diakité and Matthew Thomas Sneider. Kalamazoo: Western Michigan University Press, 2016.

Virgil. *The Aeneid*. Translated by Robert Fitzgerald. New York: Random House, 1983.

Viroli, Maurizio. *Machiavelli*. Oxford: Oxford University Press, 1998.

———. *Niccolò's Smile: A Biography of Machiavelli*. New York: Farrar, Straus and Giroux, 2002.

Wallace-Wells, David. *The Uninhabitable Earth: A Story of the Future*. London: Allen Lane, 2019.

Walzer, Michael. "Political Action: The Problem of Dirty Hands." *Philosophy and Public Affairs* 2, no. 2 (1973): 160–80.

Weil, Simone. *Selected Essays, 1934–1943*. Edited and translated by Richard Rees. Eugene, OR: Wipf and Stock, 2015.

Weinstein, Donald. *Savonarola: The Rise and Fall of a Renaissance Prophet*. New Haven, CT: Yale University Press, 2011.

West, Cornel. *The American Evasion of Philosophy: A Genealogy of Pragmatism*. Madison: University of Wisconsin Press, 1989.

Winter, Yves. *Machiavelli and the Orders of Violence*. Cambridge, UK: Cambridge University Press, 2018.

———. "Plebeian Politics: Machiavelli and the Ciompi Uprising." *Political Theory* 40, no. 6 (2012): 736–66.

Zuckert, Catherine H. *Machiavelli's Politics*. Chicago: University of Chicago Press, 2017.

Index

Kirkpatrick, Jennet, 106–7
Kocis, Robert, 93, 116

Lando, Michele Di, 141–42
Landucci, Lucca, 180–81
last generations, 18, 38
Last Judgment, 53, 64, 209
Latour, Bruno, 38
law, 5–8, 18, 26, 32, 35–36, 41–42, 47,
  51, 53–55, 58, 60, 62–63, 68, 80–89,
  92–93, 106–12, 114–17, 119–29,
  122–23, 127, 130–33, 137, 143, 151,
  156, 175, 180, 194–95, 198–201,
  204–5, 210
leadership, 3, 16, 21, 26–27, 33–34, 36,
  44–45, 50, 54–55, 57, 59, 59, 61–62,
  66, 69, 75–77, 80, 82, 92–93, 100,
  103, 107, 120–21, 126–28, 133–34,
  138, 140, 143, 149, 153–54, 159,
  165, 168, 173–74, 177–78, 184–89,
  192, 194–95, 197–203, 207
Levina, Marina, 64–65
Levitsky, Stephen, 43–45, 59–60, 62
Levy, David N., x, 12
liberty, 27, 38, 60, 62, 74, 78, 81, 83, 89,
  96–97, 100–101, 109, 118, 121, 123,
  153, 196, 202
lies, 2, 43, 48, 55, 58, 121, 123, 165,
  170–71, 181, 183
Lukes, Timothy J., 41

Machiavelli, Niccoló, 9, 19, 27–29,
  33–44, 58–62, 66–75, 80–84, 90–94,
  97–100, 104–13, 115–19, 125–35,
  152–54, 165–82, 184–88; *The Art of
  War*, 146; character, 3–8, 12, 16–17,
  24, 40–41, 146–47, 193, 205, 209;
  Clizia, 147–48; *Discourses on Livy*,
  13, 17, 28, 36, 60, 72, 91, 109, 125,
  129, 208; *Florentine Histories*, 13–17,
  23, 56, 73, 94, 104, 126, 127, 133,
  135, 142, 149, 154, 203; life, 1–2,
  5–6, 13, 20–21, 24–26, 89, 146–47,
  168–69, 190–91, 193–95, 202–4; *The
  Mandrake*, 147, 150–52, 158, 204;

political realism, 7–9, 11, 16, 20–22,
  37, 54, 65, 69–70, 85, 88–89, 93,
  98–99, 102, 122, 149, 151, 166, 179,
  197, 205–6; *The Prince*, 3–5, 7, 10–
  11, 13–14, 16–17, 21, 23–27, 30–31,
  33, 66, 96, 105, 128, 203–4, 207; relevance, 3–5, 13, 15–18, 22, 29, 39,
  65, 84–86, 101–3, 120–23, 143–45,
  162–64, 182–83, 198–201, 205–10;
  Rules for an Elegant Social Circle, 146;
  style, 11–12, 14, 20, 23–24, 65, 194,
  197–98
machismo, 23–26, 28
malcontents, 128, 158, 161
malice, 54–55, 58, 63, 89, 149
Mansfield, Harvey, x, 36, 108, 137
Martines, Lauro, 155
masses, 55, 128, 170, 183
Mccormick, John, 72, 112, 115, 144
Mclean, Paul D., 155
McQueen, Alison, 11
Media, 29, 44, 85–86, 120–21, 168, 176
Medici, 5, 11, 13, 24, 27, 31, 77, 115,
  128, 135, 140, 147, 149–60, 153–63,
  168–70, 178, 190–96, 198, 202–3;
  Cosimo, 154, 158–60; Giovanni, 77;
  Giovanni di Bicci, 154–61; Giovanni
  di Lorenzo (Pope Leo X), 147, 193;
  Guilio (Pope Clement VII), 13, 202–
  3; Lorenzo di Piero, 24–25; Lorenzo,
  13, 24, 105, 154, 160–63, 168, 170,
  175, 193, 196; Piero, 154, 160; Piero
  di Lorenzo, 24, 168; Salvestro, 115,
  117–18, 120, 132, 140–41, 154
Meinecke, Friedrich, 20
mercenary, 22, 27, 61–62, 72, 157, 178
mercy, 36, 56, 67, 135, 173
militias, 22, 47, 50, 106, 121, 178, 192,
  195, 199, 203
misogyny, 24, 28, 86
mnemopoiesis, 97
modes, 5, 14–18, 20–21, 27–29, 33, 36,
  42–45, 50–55, 58–64, 67–69, 71–72,
  75–81, 84–85, 88, 92–97, 100, 103–
  6, 108–9, 111–12, 115–16, 118–19,

Pocock, J. G. A., 38, 185
Podestá, 47
Polanksy, David, 107, 120
political inferno, 18, 20, 71
political memoir, 96
politics, x, 4, 6, 9–17, 20–22, 27, 31,
    33–35, 42–46, 49, 54, 59, 65–66,
    68, 71, 85, 88–89, 94, 98, 100, 102,
    104–10, 115, 120, 128, 130, 136,
    143–47, 149–54, 169–62, 166, 168,
    170–71, 178, 181, 185–86, 189,
    196–98, 200, 204, 208–9
Popolo, 46–47, 50, 55, 57, 73, 76, 78,
    81, 83, 116, 141, 154, 169; grasso,
    46, 55, 74, 76–77, 113–15, 128,
    131, 140, 142, 154; mezzani, 76;
    minuto, 46, 76–79, 113–14, 128,
    154; popolani, 55, 74, 76–77, 79,
    115, 118, 128–29, 133, 135, 154,
    157
Power, x, 3–8, 10, 12, 14, 17–18, 22,
    26–278, 31, 33, 38, 42, 44–47, 54–
    56, 58–61, 63, 65, 75, 78, 80–81,
    85, 89, 94, 97, 99–108, 114–17,
    125, 127, 130–32, 138–39, 145, 147,
    149–50, 152–56, 159, 162, 164–65,
    171–82, 197, 200, 205, 208
pragmatism, 7, 9, 26, 27, 31–32, 37,
    122, 208
Prato, 77, 192–94
pride, 28, 51, 86, 89, 93, 95–96, 100,
    103, 112, 143, 194
princely animalism, 42, 45
promises, 43, 60, 97, 109, 128, 132, 151,
    161, 174
propaganda, 48, 85–86, 105, 123, 145,
    159, 165–88, 197, 205
prophets, 12, 33, 89, 138–39, 165–66,
    168–72, 175–76, 179–83
Protagoras, 166
Proverbs, 15, 54, 77, 80, 95, 102, 175
prudence, 1, 3, 7, 19, 26, 31, 35–36, 58,
    68–70, 84, 92, 102, 113, 122, 137,
    141–42, 155, 157–59, 163–64, 169,
    181, 185–88, 197, 206

punishment, 40, 68, 79, 84, 90, 92–93,
    96, 137, 140, 177, 189
public, 37, 57, 60, 65, 86, 99, 102, 114,
    117–19, 132, 140, 149, 151, 154,
    158–62, 171–73, 177–78, 185–86,
    190, 196, 201, 205, 207
public confessions, 77, 197, 199
public discourse, 100
public disturbances, 107
public freedom, 116
public memory, 96–98
public office, 47, 106, 159
public opinion, 121, 175, 183
public spectacle, 71, 76
public sphere, 29, 168
public trials, 119
Putin, Vladimir, 3–4

QAnon, 120, 182

realities, 137, 165, 169, 171–76, 179,
    181
reason, 18, 18, 25, 42, 45, 52–53, 57–
    59, 61–62, 100, 106, 112, 167, 178,
    199
republics, 1, 4, 17, 26, 28, 34–35, 40,
    43, 46–47, 50–52, 54, 58, 60, 62,
    66, 73, 74–76, 78, 81, 84, 88–89,
    93–94, 96–97, 99–101, 103–4,
    106–7, 109–21, 125, 128, 130, 132,
    135, 140, 142, 150, 153–54, 156,
    159–60, 162, 168–69, 177, 181–82,
    187, 190–91, 195, 197–98, 202–3,
    205–6
resistance, 43, 55, 60–61, 81, 85, 94,
    99, 105, 110, 122, 142, 182, 193–94
revolution, 7, 9–10, 34, 109, 123–31,
    133, 137, 139, 140, 142–45, 197
rhetoric, 4, 11, 12, 14–15, 17, 31, 71,
    98, 99, 147–48, 152, 165–67; au-
    thoritarian, 50, 52, 59, 76, 83, 88,
    101, 104, 109, 120, 153, 205–6;
    of catastrophe, 10, 17, 27, 30–
    34, 36, 104, 107, 124, 181, 208;
    comic, 149, 162; populist, 50, 55,